A NEW LIFE PLAN

A NEW LIFE PLAN:

A Guide for
the Divorced Woman

Louise Montague

DOLPHIN BOOKS
Doubleday & Company, Inc.
GARDEN CITY, NEW YORK
1978

ISBN: 0-385-13156-9
Library of Congress Catalog Card Number 77–76283

Contents

A NEW LIFE PLAN

Introduction

This year is the tenth anniversary of *The Divorcée's Handbook.* When Doubleday first published the book in 1967, divorce was anything but a household word. Today it is not only a household word, but the way of life for over 4 million American women. As the President of the National Association for Divorced Women, I can assure you that you are not alone.

This book, *A New Life Plan,* is just that, a guide to help you put together the life you want. As you read, keep in mind that every suggestion, every hint, every admonition is motivated by one criterion: what is best for you. That is *all* that concerns me at this moment, and it's all that should concern you, ever.

What of your children? It is my feeling that what is best for you is going to benefit them. I can't imagine something being bad for you and *good* for them. A well-motivated woman, content in her job, planning a sound future, living a full life is going to be a good mother. When her children are grown, she continues her development as a natural unfolding. She feels no overwhelming sense of loss, rather she feels the beginning of yet another exciting chapter in her life.

In writing this book I reread *The Divorcée's Handbook.* We've all come a long way, baby! Good, positive things have happened. We've gotten rid of a goodly share of job discrimination. Not all, by any means, but employers are hiring more women and, equally important, promoting more women. One of my closest women friends is the vice-president of an oil company. I know women in banking, in the stock market, and in petroleum engineering. Women lawyers and doctors are no longer a phenomenon.

Fashion, too, has taken a swing for the better. We dress now the way we want to, not the way the designers dictate. Casual is the password. Mothers and daughters share blouses and slacks as the age barriers are dropped.

Mothers and daughters share more than clothes. I feel there is a new honesty brought on by daughters who are not restricted by inherited stereotypes. We can be mentally and emotionally closer to our daughters (and our sons) than we could be to our mothers (and fathers).

The high divorce rate could be said to indicate that we are unwilling to settle for less. We want *more* of all that life has to offer. I'm certainly not recommending divorce as the answer to fulfilled living. What I will say, and recommend, is that as a divorced woman you have a unique opportunity to start again, and to do it differently this time.

I hope you will read the entire book and not just pick out the chapters which you feel apply to you and your particular problems. I find there is an overlap of ideas, a blending, a merging. One solution *does* affect another. Give yourself the benefit of all the many hours of experience that are represented here. Experience, after all, is the only teacher. There are no absolutes in divorce.

I have probably touched as many lives as anyone attempting to give advice on this subject. I have raised four children, whom I consider the stars in my crown. I look at them as firmly launched: I know I did the best I could.

The most profound truth I have learned is that the best person in the world to depend upon is *you*. You have within yourself *everything* you need to live exactly the type of life you choose. This is fact. I know you can do anything you put your head and your heart to, and I know you can do it to perfection. I don't feel it; I know it. When *you* know it, you're on your way.

1

Status

and the Divorced Woman

"Status" has two dictionary meanings. The first is your condition or position with regard to the law. You know how to answer that question: you are divorced. Legally you are a single woman who was formerly married. When filling out forms, the reason they have the category "divorced" instead of just "single," is primarily for the purpose of record-keeping. Without this, we would never know such figures as how many women over sixteen were married; how many divorced women head households, etc. The Bureau of Statistics in Washington can give you an answer to just about any question you can pose.

Divorced means that you legally ended a valid marriage. The law looks upon divorce as a *remedy*, not a punishment. Society says that since your marriage didn't work, you are allowed to dissolve it and start over. It's *never* that simple, though. Putting legal definitions and dispositions onto personal problems is not a satisfactory solution. But it is the only one we have!

Divorce leaves you in a tumultuous state at best. You are tired, uncertain, bitter, worried, and depressed—the list of bad feelings and distressing emotions is endless. However, my dear, you are also free! Anyone who says the fight for freedom isn't the toughest battle in the world has never tried to test it.

The second dictionary definition of "status" is your position, rank, and standing in regard to your job, family and community. Don't try to answer that now. We'll cover all those points later in the book. First, I want to give you my definition of *my* use of the word "status" and why I feel it is where you *must* begin in your monumental task of building a *new life*.

Status, to me, means how you think about yourself. Your opinion of yourself is, right now, the only opinion in the world that matters. Divorce has a way of leaving you with a low opinion of yourself. You wonder if what you did *was* right. You try to remember where the marriage began its descent and if in fact you could have saved it. You speculate on the choices, the missed opportunities, the forks in the road. You worry fretfully about your children and hope you've caused them no permanent damage. Most of all you fear the future because you don't know how you can possibly manage. In other words, you don't think too highly of yourself. Status: a mess.

Your divorce was a *choice* and now you are living the aftermath of that choice which I call the Divorce Dilemma. You are not alone. One look at the statistics should tell you that divorce is the new national pastime. The whole country seems to be in a divorce dilemma.[1]

That news, I realize, doesn't help you very much. The mere numbers do not make it any easier for you. The reason I mention the statistics at all, is to erase any notion that you may have of "standing out" because you have been through a divorce. That is one fear you can immediately cross off the list. You have enough real dilemmas to face without giving house room to the imagined ones.

Now for the good news. Divorce gives you one big, marvelous gift called Awareness. I realize that must seem strange—a gift from divorce—but that is precisely what awareness is. Divorce marks the absolute end in living by rote, reacting by the numbers, playing the role. You can't use those old reflex reactions any more. It's all new. Everything is. When you think about it, that's exciting! See how your mind has just jumped from nega-

[1] Four million divorced women in the U.S., with an additional one million added each year. (U. S. Bureau of Statistics)

tive thinking to grasping an uplifting idea? That's the power of Good News.

Awareness is exciting, but it is also frightening. The traditional role of woman has been passive. We have been reactors, always responding to what was going on around us. We have been prisoners of fate, buffeted about by outside forces, seldom if ur own lives. Now, suddenly, div constructed cocoon and we are world—a world filled with pre loopholes, disappointments, and about that? Well, for one thir yours. Lastly it's the beginnin ou lead is going to be *you*- cen to be—your life. I promise you, vouldn't want it any other way

THE FIVE DEMONS OF DIVORCE

To gain control of your life you must have a battle with five demons. Merely naming them and getting them out in the open wins the first round for you. That's the gift of "awareness" I've just talked about. You are going to put it to use to *get yourself ready for the fray*.

FIRST DEMON: DIVORCITIS

No one ever said that divorce was easy. Or fun. What it is is a second chance, a new beginning, a rebirth. For some (most) women, it's the *first* chance they have ever had to be alone to work out their own destiny. What divorce *isn't* is something to center your life upon. Let me explain what I mean.

All during the time of the *divorce* you were the center of attention. Your family was solicitous. Your children tiptoed past your bedroom door. Your friends called. Your lawyer patted your hand. You had a tale to tell and the curious listened. You found solace in being on center stage. It's all over now, so take your bow, Eloise, and exit. It's time to take off the grease paint, fold up your costume, and learn new lines.

The best way to stop talking about your "situation" is to replace the word "divorced" with the word "released." When someone asks, "When were you divorced?" your answer is, "I was released three months ago." Make this substitution, especially to yourself, when you start on a "divorce" thought. It's a healthy attitude to feel that all the problems, all the anxieties, all the hurts are no longer a part of you. *You* are released.

Dwelling on your divorce (or Divorcitis) deepens the old wounds. Give the scar tissue a chance to heal. You will cut yourself off from friends and family if you continue to use your divorce to solicit pity, approbation, or attention. You will also be less attractive to new people who come into your life. When you start dating again (how's *that* for an old-fashioned word) you will alienate men very quickly if you launch into a monologue on your divorce history. That life is *closed,* so put it on the shelf.

SECOND DEMON: FINDING FAULT

I have yet to talk to a divorced person (and I have probably talked to as many as anyone in the world) who has told me that her (or his) divorce was fair and equitable. Wasn't your divorce unfair in *some* way? Of course it was. In no other legal dealings or area of human emotions will you find such a world of inequities. So stop searching for justice. There isn't any. Most particularly, stop discussing your unfair treatment. Trust me. No one, and I mean *no one,* wants to hear your tale of woe. No matter how many times you tell it, you'll never know exactly whose fault it was. And, really, who cares now?

With this desire to find fault comes a not-so-quiet anger. What this anger represents is *your* reaction to how things *should* have been—but weren't. *He* didn't live up to your expectations; your life together didn't work the way it should have. You know the type of anger I mean. Disappointment. Disappointment in *externals*. If *all that* had been different, you wouldn't be where you are now.

Placing blame isn't an answer to anything. You can't relive yesterday no matter how you try. To rummage in your mind to see where it all got off the track is a dead-end street. The lesson here, and it's so important, is that from now on you're not going to *expect* anything from anyone, so you won't be disappointed. When marvelous events occur, deeds are done, promises kept—be happily surprised. The rest of the time the only adult whose actions should concern you—is you.

DEMON THREE: REGRET

Watch out for this demon because he slips in at your lowest ebb. You're washing dinner dishes and the sink clogs up. That seems to be the final straw to a day that began with a dead battery in your car. This was followed by a stern lecture from your boss on the attributes of punctuality. The school called at four to say your son was injured during football practice, so you had to leave work early (another lecture) to take him to the hospital for an X ray.

When you arrive home you found the second notice from the phone company about your bill and a dog puddle in the middle of the living room rug. By the time the sink decides that it absolutely isn't going to drain, you are a wilting rose. Tears run down your cheeks. You slump down at the kitchen table. At that moment you would give just about anything you possess in the world to have *him* back. If you just hadn't gotten the divorce he would be here to share all of this—and make it better.

No. Tilt. Wrong way. Right turn only. Stop! He wouldn't make it better. (Come on, he'd probably yell at you and make it worse.) However, that, my dear, is totally irrelevant. At this moment you are slipping into the morass of regret and you are only going to worsen your situation. You handled your day and you handled it well. What you are now feeling is pity mixed with anger that you were *forced* to have such a day. We *all* have such days. I know *that* doesn't make it any easier, does it?

This is bad news, but you will in all probability have many more such days. Now, when they happen you have two ways to go. You can sit at that kitchen table and look back at your missed opportunities, senseless mistakes, and anguished regrets —or you can remember your unheralded sacrifices, your unselfish labor and the truth you have lived. You can languish in remorse or bask in accomplishment.

Your mood machine is like a faucet, you can turn it to good or bad. One is constructive; the other destructive. When you begin to look back, to regret, turn that faucet to "off" and say to yourself that you are feeling regret because you are unsure *what* to do next. We look back when we can't look forward.

DEMON FOUR: FOOLISH ACTIONS

Perhaps "foolish" is an old-fashioned word, but it doesn't carry the guilt of a word like "destructive" or "self-defeating" or "demoralizing." Foolish actions can best be described as behavior which works *against* your best interest. Foolish actions are not permanently damaging or destructive unless you *continue* to act foolishly.

What constitutes foolish behavior? Here is a sample list: overeating; overdrinking; careless spending; wasting or killing time; sleeping too much; indiscriminate TV watching. Whatever you do that is a non-productive action is foolish. Divorce allows you to fib to yourself and say such things as: I'll quit sleeping so much when I get my strength back, or, If I didn't have my martinis to look forward to I couldn't make it to the end of the day.

Foolish behavior is a reaction to the confusion of divorce. When you were married your life had routine. A divorce robs you of the stability of set patterns and leaves you with pockets of free or unprogrammed time. Drinking to fill the hours between dinner and bed is one answer. It certainly is not a good answer. It may blot out the loneliness, but it also blots out time that could be spent in a creative pursuit with long-range potential. It also adds pounds, ruins your complexion, and makes holes in your budget.

The surest way out of this confusion is to develop a ruling intelligence. You do this by listening to yourself and trusting yourself. After all, who above all people in the world *should* you trust? Yourself. Exactly. And whom do you love above all others? Yourself, of course. So quit hurting yourself, going against your judgment, and letting foolish behavior into your life. *You* are in charge of your life now, so *you-center* all your activities.

DEMON FIVE: FEAR

Fear is the most destructive of all the demons. Since the time of Christ the admonition to mankind has been: Fear not. Why? Because fear is debilitating and immobilizing. Fear physically affects your thinking, breathing, and acting. Fear reverses forward action. Fear robs you of the necessary faith in yourself to meet your challenges.

What is fear? Basically, it is the feeling which comes over you when you can't handle the present moment. How can I find a job? I don't know how to do anything. How am I going to pay this bill? I can't make that phone call, I don't know what to say. You know these fears; they are the ones that stop you in your tracks.

There are also long-range fears. These fears make the future an unknown demon set to overpower you. I'll never make enough money to get out of debt. I can't go back to school, I'll never have the time. I can forget going anywhere until I'm seventy. Fear, as you can well see, is the archenemy of progress.

How do we overcome our fears? With knowledge. Fear is caused by the worry over an unsolved problem. So you start with the worry. Let's say you're living in a small house in the suburbs. You are responsible, under the divorce decree, for making the mortgage payments and paying the taxes. Toward this you receive child-support payments and alimony (which is limited to three years).[2] You're worried. Terribly worried. Should you sell the house and rent an apartment? A condominium? Should you leave the suburbs and move to town? What will happen in three years when the alimony ends? What will happen if the roof leaks? It goes on and on and on. Can you sit at the breakfast table over the second cup of coffee and solve this problem? Of course you can't.

So now what? You go after the knowledge to treat the problem. The best way is to start with a pencil and paper. List the mortgage payment, the taxes, utilities and a minimum upkeep figure (keep it the minimum with no remodeling or repainting for now). Next, list your income from child support, alimony and your job. This will tell you the percentage of your income that goes to the house.

Next, go look at what is available in apartments in your area. Talk to other renters and see what their costs are. Do the same with condominiums. Don't *ever* take salespeople at their word. Ask *renters* and *owners*. Then go into town and find out what apartments are renting for there. Write down *all* your figures. A message will emerge. It may turn out that staying in your house makes the most sense financially. The figures may indicate, however, that you'll be strapped in three years when the alimony stops.

You've treated one problem—where to live. You will stay in your home. But what about three years from now? Your knowledge tells you that you will have to think of a way to get enough money to offset the ending of your alimony. It's time for another list. What can you do in three years to increase your income? You can go to night school to acquire additional training. You can work toward a promotion. You can open

---

[2] Some states now use the term spousal support instead of alimony. They are the same. However the current tendency of our courts is to limit support payments to a specified period of time.

your own business. You can look for another job. (No, looking for another husband does *not* count on this list.) Start investigating all the possibilities the way you did the housing situation. Knowledge, knowledge, knowledge. No problem can last very long under an onslaught of information.

FIGHTING THE DEMONS

We've discussed ways to counteract each of the demons. We fight Divorcitis by keeping our mouths closed on that subject and thinking about something else. We fight the tendency to Find Fault by realizing *that* isn't going to do us any good. We dispel Regrets by remembering accomplishments. We stop our Foolish Actions by deciding to do only those things which work to our advantage. We curb our Fears by applying knowledge to our problems.

In addition to these measures, there are steps to be taken that work on all five demons at the same time.

1. *Learning to Make Decisions.* If you sincerely want to do the right thing, it is difficult to make a disastrous decision. Some decisions are better than others, of course, but don't add the fear of making decisions to your list. If you follow a pattern, the odds for a productive decision are in your favor. As we said, all decision making begins with fact finding. This should be an intensive search, not a couple of phone calls.

Begin your search in all the usual channels. Then see what unusual sources you can find. For example, go back to your problem of where to live. After you have looked at apartments and condominiums, think of how else people in your community live. What about mobile homes? Cabins at the lake outside town? Flats over stores? With this kind of thinking each idea brings another idea.

People are always excellent leads. Each time you talk to an apartment house owner or a real estate salesperson, ask him or her to suggest someone else. Keep lists and get intimately involved in your facts. Go through your lists many times. Give your brain time to absorb the information.

Set a time limit on your fact finding. You don't want to make it your life's work. You can overresearch a project. When you have spent a desired time, say six Saturdays, out looking, assemble your facts and start eliminating the obvious non-choices. If your decision has come down to either selling your home and renting an apartment or keeping your home, go over your facts in a very critical way. Do not make a decision conform to what you would *like*. Your decision has to be based on what's smart. This, after all, is the way to progress.

If the facts indicate that the financially sound thing to do is stay in your home, then *make* the decision, and that's it. Put away all the charts, lists and ads. Don't go back to that darling apartment for one last look. Forget it. The decision is made. All future plans will *include* this decision. You have acted!

There is a marvelous afterglow that comes from having made a decision. New vistas that have heretofore been clogged by fear will open. Making decisions will go from a fearful, hated task to an exciting adventure. You will get better at it. And better and better. Your trust in yourself will skyrocket.

2. *Beating Depression.* Depression can be caused by any number of emotions. If I had to pick one universal cause for depression among divorced women, I would say it is loneliness. Loneliness is the absence of everyone. In marriage there is that accessible other person, a *security-someone*. You can be lonely in marriage, but it is nothing to compare with the loneliness of divorce.

How do you cure loneliness? You don't. Loneliness has to be *filled*. As your new life settles into a pattern, watch to see when the loneliness, the self-pity, and the depression creep in. One of the most common times is just at the end of the day. This is the time *he* used to come home. Perhaps you shared a couple of glasses of wine while you fixed dinner and he read the paper. Maybe the two of you sat down with the children and talked. Whatever it was that you did, it was a time when you were not alone.

Since you know this time is coming up, be prepared for it. If you have children, plan to turn this into time devoted entirely to them. Take a walk with them before dinner, play a game of cards or just listen to the happenings in their day. But *listen*. Don't go through the motions while you secretly wish you felt better. That's self-pity again, creeping around the corner. Think how lucky you are to have children.

If your children are grown (or if you don't have children) devote this time to some hedonistic pleasure. You've worked hard all day. Put on your favorite records, draw a hot tub and read the evening paper in the bath. I have a friend who has an hour-and-a-half bus ride after work. When she gets home she draws a hot bath and lies in her tub doing needlepoint. She rests her head on a rubber cushion attached to her tub by suction cups. She keeps her needlepoint yarn and scissors on a plastic tray which fits across the tub. She says she loves this hour so dearly that she can hardly wait to get home. Even though she lives alone, she is not lonely.

Another bad time can be Saturday night. You used to do something, even if it was just to go to the movies. Don't let your Saturday nights go unplanned. Make a list of *all* the people you enjoy seeing. Then put together outrageous combinations of these people and plan Saturday night dinners for eight. You don't have to spend a lot of money. Plan a theme dinner and divide up the work.

Your first party could be A Night with a Pasha. Push your living room furniture back and put a bed sheet down on the floor. Tell all your guests to wear something "flowing" as they will be sitting on the floor and eating with their hands. Divide the work accordingly: You make the oven-baked chicken (cut up) for eight; Guest No. 1 will bring a salad; No. 2, flat bread; No. 3, a dessert (baklava?); Nos. 4 and 5, the wine; No. 6, a large pan of rice with almonds and raisins; No. 7, an album of belly dance music.

It's no secret that your funds are limited. That doesn't mean your *fun* has to be. What most people lack is imagination and initiative. When you supply that, the rest is easy. Give two or three of these parties and you will be the most popular hostess in town. What was that about being lonely Saturday night?

You can't always predict when a sudden attack of loneliness will send you diving into a deep depression. When this happens, move. I mean get up and physically move about. If it's a lazy Sunday afternoon and your anguish is excruciating, grab a bicycle and peddle. It doesn't matter where you go. Ride over to the park; down to the ice cream store; or over to a neighbor's house. Go far enough to feel physically tired.

When your body is engaged in strenuous exercise, it dispels a great deal of the depression. I don't know what happens. Perhaps it has to do with stimulating your circulation by sending more air into your lungs. Whatever it is, it works. If you stay still and let a depression sink in, it will affect your motor ability. Depressed people slump. Their facial muscles sag. Their feet drag. This reinforces their depression and telegraphs it to the world.

3. *Spread the Good News.* I have a daughter who walks as if she owned the world. Head high, shoulders back, eyes flashing, she takes long confident strides at a brisk pace. Her mouth is set in a half-smile. As she sails down the street I have seen more than one man stop, turn, and look after her. She is beautiful, but that's not the arresting quality. She looks as though she knows where she's going and it's going to be great when she gets there.

When I mentioned this to her, she laughed and said she walks like that because I used to look at her as a teen-ager and say that if *I* had legs like hers, I'd rule the world! In other words, she *knows* something good about herself and when she starts out she remembers it.

We can *all* smile when we're out. That's spreading good news. Did you ever smile at anyone who didn't smile back? To-morrow on your way to work try it out. You can't begin to know how much better a smile feels than a scowl. Compliments have the same effect. Each time you have occasion to talk with someone tomorrow, begin by mentioning something nice about the clothes they're wearing: It's a good-looking jacket; or an interesting belt; or, I like the way you tie your scarf.

I send messages of good news to myself. I tape inspiring passages onto my desk. One could be a paragraph clipped from a letter from someone who enjoyed reading a book of mine. You can't imagine the number of days when *that* helps. I copy down inspiring sentences from books I'm reading and thumbtack them on a door. I even tape fortune cookie messages to my datebook. It's reassuring to know "You will live to a ripe old age; happy in the love and respect of many children." When I'm dieting I tape my daily loss or gain on the refrigerator door. *That* has a sobering effect! Another friend of mine cut out a picture of a pantsuit she wanted, modeled by a slim woman, and taped it on her refrigerator with the notice: "Attention! Thin is in!"

This may all sound a little precious, but so what. We should all *do* in this life what works for us. If you have to read something over and over again to have it sink in, then write it out and tape it on the dashboard of your car. When you read an article with some advice you find particularly helpful, cut it out. Don't let it go by. When you try to remember it two or three days later, it's gone forever.

In addition to spreading the Good News, you should get rid of the bad news. We all carry around with us grudges, guilts, grievances, and any number of bad or unproductive thoughts. I have found one way to get some of them out of my system forever. It's called *Write Your Complaint!* After a particularly hairy day, take a magazine and a pencil to bed with you. Turn out the light, then sit up in bed, and in the dark starting writing in the magazine. Begin with your ex-husband and how mean he is not to have sent the support payment on time. Take on your job and all your grievances of the day. Tell what depressed you. Tell what frightened or frustrated you. If you have engaged in foolish behavior, write that down. Write until your arm is tired, then drop the magazine on the floor and go to sleep.

The next morning take the magazine and throw it away. Do

not look in it or attempt to read what you've written. You got *rid* of all that junk. Don't let it back in. If your curiosity gets the better of you and you peek at what you've written, you won't be able to figure it out. You wrote over printing and pictures and advertisements. *That's* the secret behind using a magazine!

ENJOYING YOUR STATUS

Many divorced women feel that the best use of their time is looking for a new husband. Once the decree is final, they begin a frantic ferreting out that would do credit to a trained bloodhound. Every waking hour is filled with plans and schemes designed to bring them to the altar. They display a singlemindedness of purpose that is frightening to behold.

My advice is to forget marriage. Forget your former marriage—forget your future marriage. By forgetting your former marriage you help fight those five demons. Why limit yourself by bringing *his* notion of how things should be done into your life? When you forget your marriage you don't carry around a false sense of guilt. You cease to be manipulated by an absent power. You belong to *you*.

If you dwell on remarriage, that becomes the first priority in your life. You fail to concentrate on your career. You assume that remarriage will solve your problems. This causes you to increase your foolish behavior. When you are concentrating on meeting men you care more about your wardrobe than you do about your job. You run the risk of spending countless hours with faceless men trying to find one who is marriage-ready. You sacrifice a chance at great happiness for an expedient match. You may get married, but then what?

Your greatest chance at a successful and lasting second marriage is to forget about it for now and concentrate on you. You are coming out of a debilitating experience. You need time to decide just what you *do* want out of life. Oh yes, it *is* up to you.

Every minute of your future can be *you-directed*. It begins by realizing that men do not have an exclusive franchise on what happens to you. You can work, achieve, become, go out, have fun, laugh, enjoy, love—without a man.

YOUR OWN NAME

Why don't you start your marvelous, new, exciting *you-directed* life with your own name! I mean your very own name which was bestowed upon you at birth. A great many women are using and keeping their own names even in marriage. Your name is *your* identification. Let's say your name has a distinct ethnic origin; Irish or Italian or Lebanese. That's your background, your link with family and with history. Every time you write that name on a job application or a check you are reaffirming your identity and your heritage.

Those who argue against the use of the maiden name say that they want to have the same name as their children. You know that is temporary. Your girls will marry and perhaps change their names. You yourself may remarry and want to take your new husband's name. These are all unresolved and unimportant arguments. Let your children decide when the time comes. It's their right, too.

If you take your own name back there will be no confusion when your ex-husband remarries. The first Mrs. Smith; the second Mrs. Smith; even the third Mrs. Smith—you don't want to be in that line-up. This will also save any number of problems with department stores and credit cards.

Your name is your name right now. You don't have to go to court to change it.[3] All you have to do is *decide* that you are going to use your maiden name and start doing it. You must, however, be absolutely consistent. The day I decided that I wanted my very own name back, I did it all in one day. After breakfast I went to the Department of Motor Vehicles and

[3] Check with your lawyer to be certain. I'm speaking of California.

filled out a name change form and turned it in. Next I went to the bank and had my name changed on my account and ordered new checks. Then off I went to the photographer's for new pictures for a new passport. At the passport office I was questioned—briefly. I think the man helping me recognized the fire in my eyes. He said something about my having to use my name for a year. I said that I had used it for twenty and not to give me any trouble. He didn't.

That was it. I am self-employed so I didn't have to change employment records. If you are employed, have the office change their records. You should not receive paychecks in two names. You don't *have* to give a reason.

Other places to change your name are:

1. Car registration. If you own a car, change the registration when you change your driver's license.
2. Voting. Go to the Registrar of Voters and ask to have your name changed.
3. Deeds to property. See your lawyer.
4. Insurance. See your insurance dealer.

It just isn't all that difficult. I can't tell you what a grown-up feeling it is to have your very own name. Do you know why I decided to take the plunge? I was in a library in a strange city and I decided to look myself up in the card file to see if they had any of my books. (*All* authors do this sometimes.) I started to look up the cookbook I'd written and I couldn't remember *whom* I was married to when I wrote it! I didn't know which name to check. I absolutely panicked. I ran out of the library and headed down the street. I had gone about four blocks before I realized I didn't know where I was. This compounded my panic and tears rolled down my cheeks. How stupid, how utterly, utterly stupid to be lost—*and* not know who you are.

I love my maiden name, *my* name. I think it's one of the most beautiful names in the world. When I decided to reclaim it, it was such a joyous decision that I wondered why I'd never thought of it before. It was a turning point in my career. I discovered a new momentum, a new faith in myself. I had a separate identity that didn't depend upon anyone else. My successes —or failures—were mine.

DOING YOUR THING

I think "doing your own thing" is one of the best expressions to come out of the new slang. It rings of a self-fulfillment that is self-satisfying. It suggests that you know who you are and what your "thing" is. A divorce frees you to do your own thing. It also frees—*you*.

When you were married, your husband took care of that part of you which society—and the law—required of him. He housed you, fed you, and clothed you. He paid doctors, dentists, and insurance people. The *rest* of you, that secret, private you, that being deep down, did he take care of her? Did he know her or administer to her needs? Did he have any idea what she thought about life? Her ambitions? Her dreams? Her joys?

The answer is no, isn't it? No, no, no. He didn't know *you* at all. He didn't know you because he couldn't (or wouldn't) take the time, the effort, the care to *bring* you out. You remember all those times when you felt like shouting, "You have no idea what I'm suffering inside." It was always easier—or more expedient—to suppress this other us. How many times were you told that you exaggerated problems and made mountains out of molehills?

That's all over now. You don't ever again have to be anyone but who you are. You don't have to perform to his specifications. You don't have to perform at all. You won't be able to turn off the *surface-you* all at once. It will take time to develop that secret you. After all, she's been beaten down for a long time. You shouldn't turn off the surface-you altogether until you are reasonably certain the real you is in control.

You don't want to burst out as if you were a chicken in a shell. We all know divorced women who have done crazy, zany things as the New Me! You don't want that to happen to you. I remember when the hippies were all the rage. More than one divorced woman, some with children, took off to live in communes, thumb their way across the country, and generally turn their back on organized society. Many of these women had a very hard time living. It was not an idyllic paradise. In some cases it was pure hell.

What you want is to slowly unravel. You want to dip your toe in freedom. I suggest you set aside an hour or two to indulge in a bit of fun. Play the "Who Would I Like To Be?" game. When I was in my pre-teens I was your basically unattractive kid. I used to imagine what I would look like if I could choose parts from different people. I had a perfect body figured out down to the toenails. The only part I can remember was Evelyn Keyes's nose.

This may sound like a ridiculous game, but it gave me goals at which to aim. It spurred me on to lose weight, care about my hair, and pay attention to my clothes. Sometimes it helps to think about others in order to learn how to think about yourself. Take a piece of paper and outline an ideal life. Start with where you would like to live. Then create an ideal job or profession. It helps to think in terms of achievements. How do you want to be remembered?

You can even refine the game to include an ideal home. Design it and choose the furniture. Pick out a bathroom wallpaper. Sketch the view out of the dining room window. Open your closet. What clothes do you find hanging there? Do you see an opera gown, jodhpurs, satin pajamas? What books are those on the library shelves? Is that a French Impressionist painting hanging over the mantel?

An enormously successful businessman once told me that what was wrong with most *other* businessmen was not that they didn't think big, but that they didn't think big enough! Why are we always so quick to say what we can't do? Why don't we say what we can do, hope to do, would like to do? You're not indulging in wishful thinking, you're exploring positive action. Once you decide to *have* some of what's on your list, you have started discovering the secret-you.

You see, I'm sure, what status is all about. It's what you want out of life for yourself. You are closer to it than you think. Why? Because you're beginning to think about it, aren't you? You're thinking that maybe you'll start that list. Maybe you'll start by picking out new wallpaper for your bathroom. Why wait? While you're at it, hang a fern over the bathtub. What's-his-name can't complain. He's gone, remember. How about two ferns?

Get with it! Never before in the history of women have women had such opportunity to achieve. It's a great time in which to *be* a woman. What's more, you're in charge. Have faith in yourself. I have faith in you. Great faith. Remember what St. Paul said:

"God hath not given us the spirit of fear, but of power, and of love, and of a sound mind."[4]

What more could you possibly need?

4 II Timothy 1:7.

2

Time

and the Divorced Woman

The moment you have right now is the *only* one you will ever have. Yesterday, as you well know, is gone, gone, gone. Unless you do something about today your tomorrow will be just like yesterday. That could be a frightening thought if yesterday was a dull day, unrewarding, a boring day in a long line of boring days. Or a sad day, full of self-pity. Or a frightening day full of menacing challenge. Or a frustrating day full of unfinished tasks.

How, then, do you take hold of today and make it count? You organize and plan it. Was that a deep moan I heard? If it was, then let me put it another way. What you face is Hobson's Choice. Remember the story of old Thomas Hobson, the British stablemaster? He used to rent out horses. One day he decided that his clients were taking entirely too long to ponder their choices. They were, he felt, seriously delaying his business by walking through the stables, looking first at this gray, then at that chestnut. So he lined up his horses and posted a sign:

YOU WILL TAKE THE NEXT HORSE IN LINE OR NO HORSE AT ALL

What you face is deciding on a course of action—or nothing at all. Moments simply do *not* become yours unless you harness them. I realize that the idea of planning your day, organizing your life, and budgeting your time can remind you of one of those decisions like telling yourself that you are going to lose five pounds. The mind is willing but the body is weak. Okay, but *this* time you are going to involve everyone under your roof. This time you are going to get organized!

Why am I such an advocate of organization? Because it is *the* secret to successful achievement, whether it's making a list before you go to the market or preparing plans for a twelve-story office building. The secret to successful living is mastering the use of your time. Your time is your life. To let it slip by in unaccountable moments is to waste that most precious gift.

A divorce has a way of absolutely upsetting our life schedule. We suddenly don't *do* anything the same way or at the same time. This is not necessarily a bad happening, but it does make you less efficient. That is why you should begin *today* to relegate your life to pencil and paper. Writing down schedules, jobs, goals and aims is absolutely the *only* way I know to make certain they will happen. There is an excitement and sense of accomplishment that comes from seeing your life in print.

To begin you need to make friends with yourself in the area of *will power*. Will power is a very sensitive mechanism. A certain way *not* to develop it is to push too hard. You will be beaten before you start. My first suggestion is to read all the way through this chapter before you begin making your charts. This will give you an overview of what to expect. It will also suggest to you areas of your life you never even *considered* needed organizing. You can pick your own trouble spot to begin.

Try not to limit yourself by making statements like, "I've never done that before, it won't work." How do you know it won't work if you've never done it before? Trust me. I have done *everything* in this chapter, and not with a little success, but with a huge bang of success. I was the prize basket case of the century. I stayed in bed for the better part of every day for nearly six months after my divorce. When I crawled out from under the covers with my final resolve to get it together, for heaven's sake, it was no easy task. Most days it was three steps forward and two back.

You can't resolve to *try* something new. You *do* it. You may do it with varying degrees of success, but you *do* it. You may

only do it for ten minutes a day, but you *do* it. The next time
you follow your plan for an hour, a half day, an entire week. If
you miscalculate on your time schedule, so what? You're doing
it. A mistake is simply a learning process in which each mistake
brings you closer to success. You have a *free will.* You know
what that means? You are free to do it *your* way!

Breaking Tradition. Every marriage develops a pattern. You
get up at a certain time, fix meals at certain times, wash on Tuesday, shop on Thursday, go to the movies Friday night. All these
behavior patterns belong to your marriage, so leave them there!
It is a mistake to try to carry on in the same old way. It's your
show now! When you start making your time chart, remember
that it is yours. The reason you are going to organize your life is
to make time for the activities and pursuits that are important
to you!

To give you an example of what I mean, take the three-meal-
a-day tradition. If I ate the prescribed three meals a day I
would not be able to get through the kitchen door. Most
women feel this way and most weight-conscious married women
get by on leftover oatmeal and crusts off the peanut butter and
jelly sandwiches because they know they have to eat dinner
when *he* comes home. Well, he ain't comin' home no more. So if
you want to have a cheese omelet and a croissant for breakfast,
an avocado and beansprout sandwich for lunch and no dinner
—that's *your* choice. A big evening meal was his tradition, but
it doesn't have to be yours. When my children were younger I
read to them during dinner, enabling me to share their company without sharing their meal.

You can change eating habits that you have developed on
your own like the way you spend your lunch hour at work.
When I was a copywriter for a large advertising agency, I took
my lunch hour in a small conference room and worked on my
second book (a cookbook). I wrote my first book, *The Divorcée's Handbook*, between customers in my showroom at the
California Apparel Mart when I was in the sportswear business.
I also work on manuscripts during long plane rides, in hotel
rooms, before work and after. I am not offering a thesis on my
work habits. I simply suggest to you that the three-meal-a-day

tradition is one area you can question and one place you can find precious moments to turn to *your* advantage.

Housework is another traditional area to attack. Maybe you don't want to do your housework the first thing in the morning. Maybe you want to work on a project of your own before you go off to work and face the house when you come home. How about marketing? Maybe you've always gone to the store Saturday morning. Why not do it Wednesday night and save Saturday for doing something with the children? Many stores are open a couple of nights a week and I find them far less crowded than on Saturdays. Besides, it's good to go out after dinner instead of being glued to the TV set.

Television. Before we go on, let me say a word about TV.

I don't own one. When ours went out of order we simply didn't repair it. When we moved we left it where it was. For the moon walk we went to a cozy bar in Carmel; for the political conventions we called friends and offered to bring dinner if we could watch with them. I suppose we miss some good shows, even great ones, but more important, we miss all the junk. We are never trapped by an old movie or a game show or infuriated by commercials or bored by boring newscasters. I guarantee you that it is a *tremendous* freedom.

Being without TV leaves marvelous pockets of time to do any number of challenging, rewarding activities. Your children will scream and cry that they are underprivileged and threaten to run away. If you can weather this storm, you will find that one day they will discover that they don't miss it either. I found that regulating their hours of watching just didn't do it. The kids would break the rules when I wasn't there or beg with such earnestness when I was that I would give in. There is a finality of just not having a TV that eliminates all discussion.

Before you get rid of the TV, lead up to it by encouraging each child to start a hobby: collecting stamps; raising tropical fish, making a piece-quilt; working on a motor; learning to cook; anything. The library has shelves of hobby books. Then turn off the TV for hobby time. One day put it in a closet, the attic or basement. Cover it with an old sheet and forget it. When the very important specials happen—the kind science or history teachers assign for homework—let the kids choose a friend to call in order to look at it at the friend's house. You'd be surprised how well this works.

Breaking behavior patterns is always hard. You know where you are if you keep the patterns, but you *don't* know what change will bring. Because you've "always done it that way" is *no reason* to continue. You're not wedded to any action or system unless you *choose* to be.

SO LET US BEGIN

List Your Categories. Every divorced woman has several roles to play: mother, career woman, desirable companion, daughter, student, volunteer—the list seems endless. The first task you face is to make a list of the categories in your life. To illustrate, I am going to diagram divorcée Janet, age thirty-eight.

Mother Janet—Three youngsters aged fifteen, thirteen, nine

Homemaker Janet—Three-bedroom house in North Hollywood

Career Woman Janet—Legal secretary

Companion Janet—Dates with men; outings with women friends; hostess

Daughter Janet—Visits with her family in Arizona three times a year. Letters; phone calls

Volunteer Janet—Teaches Sunday school

Sportswoman Janet—Bowls one night a week

This is the way Janet's life "categorizes."

The next step is to see what her week looks like.

Daily schedule

Monday: Breakfast
              Pack lunches
              Pick up house
              Drive to office
              Work until 5 P.M. (or later)
              Drive home

Market
Fix dinner—dishes/housework/or ironing
watch TV

Tuesday: Same schedule, but without stop at market because this is bowling night

Wednesday: Same schedule, but do a mid-week washing

Thursday: Same schedule, with occasional date to go to
dinner, movies, etc.

Friday: Same schedule, but without market stop. Usually takes kids for pizza unless has "grown-
up" social engagement

Saturday: Sleep late
Market
Errands
Shopping
Kids' doctor appointments
Dentist
Car lube, etc.
Clean house
Do laundry
Little League
Birthday parties
Date or dinner party

Sunday: Church
Sunday school
Work in garden
Relax

Naturally there are numerous interruptions to this very loose
schedule. Since the lives of the four people in this family are
conducted on the "cause and effect" system, little is accomplished. It's a day-to-day existence that gets the job done, but
that's *all* it is. Janet complains that the house is never *really*
clean; the meals aren't that good; and the money situation is
going slowly downhill as their cost of living goes up. Yes, she
receives child support from her ex-husband, but it certainly
doesn't cover all their needs. What is the main missing ingredient in Janet's life? A goal. A striving. She needs something in

her life that will add *immeasurably* to her existence, an activity or an undertaking that will make her feel that she is not the drudge, the maid, the chauffeur, the breadwinner.

When confronted with the question: What would *she* like to do? Janet said she would like to make more money. She loves working in a law office but she knows she has gone as far as she can as a secretary. She would like to be a court reporter, a research assistant, or—her secret dream—a lawyer!

Janet, however, has never thought seriously along these lines. She has had only two years of college and she has the kids to raise. She has a house to run. She doesn't have time. That has always been her answer to everything that looked like an undertaking. No time. Just do what you absolutely *have* to do, and don't create *more* work. Some days are better than others and she has a little time for herself. In the summer the kids stay a month with their father and two weeks with her family in Arizona. That helps. But that's all it does. It offers temporary relief to an ongoing problem. Janet's life, whether she knows it or not is slipping away from her—a day, an hour, a minute at a time.

Remaking the Daily Schedule. Janet (like all of us) has to start taking a firm grip on those hours and minutes. How? By organizing (no groans please). Start by making *your* list of categories. On another sheet of paper write out your daily time schedule. We are now going to revamp your program—but slowly. Nothing drastic. That's up to you when you see how far you can get by following my suggestions.

Mealtime. We must eat. That means marketing, cooking, and cleaning up. So it is to mealtime that we make our first concerted effort—the twenty-eight-day chart. Those of you who read *The Divorcée's Handbook* will remember this. It worked then, has continued to work, and will *always* work if you just give it a chance. It is the greatest boon to single parenthood that I can give you.

Breakfast. Take a piece of paper and section it with lines forming boxes representing the seven days of the week. At the top of each square write a day—MONDAY, TUESDAY, etc. Now choose a breakfast menu and fill in each square. Keep in mind which morning you get up early to drive the car pool and if you take a Saturday sleep-in. You know what your children will eat and what they won't, so don't choose any items that will be rejected. You are trying to *un*-complicate your life.

Lunch. Next, do the same thing for lunches. I am assuming that your children are brown-baggers. When you make the chart, fit the breakfast and lunch menus together. The day you have scrambled eggs for breakfast you would not plan deviled egg sandwiches for lunch.

For the weekend you can be more casual. When you look at the sample chart at the end of this chapter, you will see that I put the same entree for Saturday and Sunday. This again is to simplify your life. If I make up a batch of banana pancake batter, I make enough for *two* days. You don't have to vary the menu *every* day. As for weekend lunch, make it something *very* simple because it should be the least important event of the weekend.

Now you have a week of breakfasts and a week of lunches. Use them over and over. There truly *aren't* more than seven breakfasts anyway unless you get into eggs benedict or crepes. You haven't time for this, so just be happy with your seven choices. Why do you do this? So you can absolutely eliminate decision making in this area.

Dinner. The next chart is going to take more time and require you to put your nose in a cookbook for an hour or so. Take your pencil and paper and section a page for twenty-eight days (like a write-in calendar) with the four weeks one on top of the other. Write in the days of the week across the top. In each square put in a dinner menu. No, it isn't a lot of work. It's actually quite simple. Here are the *real* tricks:

1. Begin with Sundays and plan something that will last for a couple of days such as turkey, ham, beef stew, minestrone, etc.
2. Pick something for Saturday night that a baby sitter or the kids themselves can fix. Then if you have a date you are free to spend that extra time in a hot tub.
3. Simply specify vegetables and salads. When you make your market list pick what is currently in season: corn on the cob, zucchini, romaine, etc.

4. Leave out desserts. When my children were young, dessert was a freezer full of popsicles and ice cream bars (no baking; no dishes). When they grew older, one of my daughters took over dessert as her special contribution. She made her own market list, planned her baking time, and nearly ruined us all. We're now back to ice cream or, preferably, fresh fruit and a piece of cheese. If you absolutely *must* plan dessert, add Jello, chocolate pudding, pie, etc.

How It Works. What you have created is a perpetual calendar! You know every meal every day from now on! When you get to the end of the twenty-eight days, start over. No, it's not a dull, boring way to live. You'll discover when you start your chart that you are not serving even *half* that many choices right now. We all get bogged down with our favorites, our old standbys. This way you are offering a very acceptable selection.

Of course you will vary the chart. If you find a dinner that the kids don't like, strike it out and substitute their choice. You will vary it, too, from hot weather to cold weather. In fact, if you live where you have hot, hot summers and cold, cold winters you may want two charts. I've been doing this for so many years that I had four charts: Winter/Spring/Summer/Fall. In fact, I have a looseleaf binder full of charts. They became very specific because I now know practically to the day what is in season.

As your children grow you can begin to substitute more sophisticated fare. You will also find your daughter requesting that you cut out casseroles in order to help her lose weight. Or your son will decide he wants to have Friday night dinner at his girl friend's house. Your chart will change and grow, but it will give you *hours* of new time and *freedom* from the dumb worry: What the hell shall I fix for dinner?

How to Carry It Out. One of the great time-wasters of the world is daily marketing, or even tri-weekly marketing. Under the new menu-chart plan you should have to market only once a week! Choose the time best suited to you and stick to it. Let's say you've decided on Saturday morning. Pour yourself a second cup of coffee and get out your charts. Since you know every mouthful that your family will consume for breakfast, lunch, and dinner, you can make a market list for a week down to the last piece of bread.

Keep paper and a pencil in a handy spot in your kitchen and when you run low on staples—flour, salt, pancake syrup, laundry soap—write them down. On Saturday add them to your list. If your weeks menu features a casserole-type dish, go over *all* the ingredients in the recipe. Check your supply of garlic salt, tomato paste, canned corn, or other staple ingredients. Plan the lettuce salads and fresh vegetables for the first couple of meals after your shopping day and the frozen vegetables and molded salads for the last. Do the same with the meat, poultry and fish. Eat something just before you leave the house so you won't be the least bit hungry. Then remember these tips:

1. Don't buy packaged convenience foods. They're too expensive.
2. Forego packaged baked goods. They're too expensive and not that healthful.
3. Don't buy fancy frozen vegetables. You know, the ones cooked in butter with mushrooms or almonds. You can do that yourself.
4. Forget sugar-coated breakfast cereal. Buy granola or "health cereal."
5. Never succumb to frozen TV dinners.
6. Beware of impulse items. Stick *absolutely* to your list.
7. Watch out for expensive cleaning supplies such as blue toilet dyes. Liquid furniture polish is fine, so forget the aerosol cans. Just because it sprays doesn't mean it's better.
8. Avoid junk food which is mostly packaged air.
9. Pick out a good, big all-purpose supermarket and buy everything there. Don't drive all over town to try to save a few pennies on a can of tuna.
10. Buy large economy sizes and the house brand if possible.

I'm certain you've read all these tips in your favorite women's magazine. I repeat them simply because I know they work and work well, as does the perpetual food calendar.

Another timesaving device is to do things ahead of time. Wash the lettuce, chop the onions, grate the cheese. Pack the

PERPETUAL CALENDAR
Breakfast Menus

MONDAY	TUESDAY	WEDNESDAY	THURSDAY	FRIDAY	SATURDAY	SUNDAY
Orange juice	Orange juice	Orange juice	Orange juice	Orange juice	Pancakes or	French Toast
Hot cereal	Scrambled	Cold cereal	Poached egg	Hot or cold	waffles or	Syrup
Bacon	eggs	Fruit	on toast	cereal	omelets	Sausages
	Toast and	English		Hot biscuits		
	Jam	muffin				

1. MARKET ONCE A WEEK
2. SUBSTITUTE FRESH FRUIT FOR JUICE DURING SEASON
3. START OVER AT END OF WEEK

PERPETUAL CALENDAR
Lunch Menus

MONDAY	TUESDAY	WEDNESDAY	THURSDAY	FRIDAY	SATURDAY	SUNDAY
Tuna salad	Peanut butter	Deviled egg	Salami and	Hot soup	Hot dogs or	Grilled cheese
sandwiches	and jelly	sandwiches	cheese sand-	(thermos)	pizza	sandwiches
Potato chips	sandwiches	Apple	wiches	Orange	Fruit salad	Carrot and
Brownies	Carrot sticks	Cookies	Pickles	Crackers	Ice cream	raisin salad
	Cookies		Cupcake	Cookies		Ice cream

1. MARKET ONCE A WEEK
2. USE FRESH FRUIT IN SEASON
3. PACK THE LUNCHES THE NIGHT BEFORE
4. START OVER AT END OF WEEK

PERPETUAL CALENDAR
Dinner Menus

MONDAY	TUESDAY	WEDNESDAY	THURSDAY	FRIDAY	SATURDAY	SUNDAY
Beef Bourguignon Noodles Green salad	Vegetable soup Cold artichoke French bread	Tamale pie Green salad Carrot and celery sticks	Broiled chicken Baked potato Sliced tomatoes	Cheese soufflé Green peas Mandarin salad	Hot dogs Baked beans Molded fruit salad	Meat loaf Pan potatoes Salad
Cold meat loaf Apple sauce Cabbage salad	French onion soup French rolls Green salad	Steak sandwich French fries Vegetable salad	Fettucini Alfredo Tossed salad	Quiche Fresh fruit salad Hot rolls	Hamburgers Buns French fries Jello salad	Turkey and stuffing Green beans Mashed potatoes
Sliced turkey gravy Potato cakes Molded salad	Turkey sandwiches Vegetable salad	Macaroni and cheese Tossed green salad	Poached fillet of Sole Baked potato Green beans	Spare ribs Fresh vegetable Scalloped potatoes	Spaghetti Green salad Garlic bread	Baked ham Sweet potatoes Waldorf salad
Cold ham and cheese Sliced tomatoes Sliced cucumbers	Scalloped potatoes and ham Green vegetable	Split pea soup French rolls Applesauce	Lasagne Green salad	Fried chicken Baked potato Vegetable	Tacos Refried Beans Cold slaw	Beef Bourguignon Rice Salad

1. SHOP ONCE A WEEK
2. CHOOSE SEASONAL VEGETABLES AND FRUITS
3. VARY MENUS DEPENDING UPON WEATHER

school lunches the night before. I don't want to scare you by sounding like a top sergeant; it's just that any time you can eliminate indecision, you are making room for yourself. Any time you can streamline an essential task you are getting ready to move ahead. Any time you can *save time* you're proving that there *is* time to pursue your goals.

Since it is often easier to *see* something than to read about it, I've made a sample chart for our friend Janet, mother of three and full-time career woman. Since her children are nine, thirteen, and fifteen, it can be assumed they are fairly adult in their food tastes. You will notice that I have planned a substantial meal on Sundays. That's because I've always done my own charts that way. I love to cook and as a working woman I have enjoyed fixing a traditional Sunday dinner. We also had a family rule that no matter who went where on the weekend, being at home for Sunday dinner was a must. That way I could be certain that the homework was completed and a good night's rest assured.

Children who visit fathers on the weekend sometimes arrive home frazzled and tired. Knowing you want the children home for Sunday dinner can be a relief to a father. He has to go to work on Monday, too, so it's hard on everyone concerned if he arrives on your doorstep at ten-thirty Sunday night towing tired, unfed, unbathed ragamuffins.

You will also notice that I've skipped desserts for Janet. She can do as I did and turn this responsibility over to her fifteen-year-old daughter—or stick to ice cream or fruit. I feel that the sooner you can get away from the whole idea of pie/cake/pudding, the better it will be for you *and* your children. Try to avoid that old demon sugar, which plays such havoc with your weight, your complexion, your teeth and . . . well, you know about *all* that. . . .

Housetime. After setting yourself free forever from the daily indecision of meals, the next area to attack is the housework. I am assuming that like Janet, you have a job of some kind. Therefore you can't take the day to make your way leisurely through your chores. You have to fit them into your already crowded schedule.

Most married women without jobs take an unconscionable
amount of time to do their housework. In fact, very few of us
are efficient in this area. Let me give you an example. It's Friday night and you and the kids have just finished dinner. The
dishes are in the sink; the laundry is piled up beside the
washing machine ready to be sorted; papers are strewn across
the living room rug; you didn't make your bed this morning because you overslept. The flowers on the coffee table died two
days ago and the couch cushions are so lopsided they don't look
as though they're on the right couch.

You and your daughter are playing backgammon and your
son is in the garage working on his car. The phone rings. It's for
you. A man you met last week at work is calling to ask if you
would like to have a cappucino with him at this new coffeehouse he spotted. He's a very attractive divorced man and you
would *love* to go for a cappucino with him. Wonderful. He'll
pick you up in twenty minutes.

Chaos! Pandemonium! Instant panic! You quickly send
your daughter out to the garage to fetch your son to do *something* about the kitchen. You assign your daughter the job of
whipping the living room into shape. As you toss out the dead
daisies and throw the laundry into the machine, you yell out to
the kitchen for your son to please vacuum the front hall after he
loads the dishwasher. Returning to your room, you spread up
the bed, then dash in and turn on the shower. As the water
heats, you pull a print blouse and black slacks out of your
closet, search under the bed for your boots, and plug in the
electric curler. When the doorbell rings, you—bandbox neat—
open the door and invite your new friend into your attractive
living room to meet your two delightful children. When you
come home from the coffeehouse and your friend asks for a
drink of water, you take him into your sparkling kitchen.

You know what I'm saying. When you and your kids *have
to*, you can move like an invasion force! But you just don't do
it often enough. As Professor Parkinson said in his book,
Parkinson's Law, the job expands to fit the time allotted."

Lady, you have to get organized—and so do your children.
There can be no more waiting for emergencies, no more beg-

ging or cajoling, and no threats. Starting right now, *everyone* is going to have assigned tasks at assigned times.

Dividing the Work. It is now time to make another chart. Go back to the daily schedule we discussed at the beginning of this chapter, the one you made detailing your day. Take a pencil and fill in those *other* jobs that seem to keep you frantic: dusting, vacuuming, mopping the kitchen floor, changing sheets. You know the jobs I mean. Find a place for them somewhere on your weekly chart.

Next, take a separate sheet of paper for each child. Yes, even your three-year-old. She'll feel left out if only the big kids get a schedule. On separate sheets of paper make a daily schedule for each child. You can ask the children to participate in the planning if you feel this would make them more co-operative. I find that if I have the charts completed *before* I call a family conference, it saves a great deal of time and argument. I certainly do not mean for you to just hand out the charts and say, "This is it, gang." You must have a discussion *after* the charts are completed. Half the fun is swapping chores.

On each piece of paper, list that child's schedule as it now exists. Then go back to your schedule and see what job or jobs you can switch over to them. Here are sample charts for Janet's three children to give you an idea.

Kimberly   Age 15

7:00	Get up
7:00–7:45	Shower, dress, make bed
7:45–8:00	Breakfast
8:00	Leave for school
4:00	Home from school
7:00	Dinner
8:00	Homework
10:30	To bed

There is a three-hour span from the time when Kimberly gets home from school until dinner. She has to be at home because she is the baby sitter for her two younger brothers. There is no reason why she can't perform some household tasks during that time. Go through your own list and switch over *one* chore per day to her. Monday: Dust living room. Tuesday: Mop kitchen floor. Wednesday: Change the sheets, etc.

Douglas Age 13

His schedule is basically the same as Kim's except that he likes to shower at night and sleep an extra fifteen minutes in the morning. Since he has that same pocket of time from 4:00 until 7:00, he also gets some chores switched over. Monday: Vacuum the living and dining rooms. Tuesday: Sweep the front walk. Wednesday: Strip the sheets off his bed, etc.

Kevin Age 9

Kevin is the baby and has not had to accept many responsibilities. That is going to change now. Kevin can learn to pick up his room and make his bed. Give him the job of policing the living room at night to see that all balls, mitts, schoolbooks, etc. are put where they belong.

Along with their jobs, your children should receive allowances on a regular basis. It's no fun at all to work without pay. Dock them a certain sum per job for chores left undone.

Eliminating Work. A friend of mine was helping me change the sheets on my bed when she started to giggle. I asked her what was so darn funny about changing sheets. She said, "Nothing. I was remembering when I was married and used to spend half a day carefully ironing the sheets and pillow cases."

I laughed, too.

It's ridiculous to go through these routines any more. Whenever and wherever you can, buy no-iron, drip-dry items. I would also suggest that you box any small collections requiring dusting and put them away. If you have decorative silver like candy dishes, cigarette boxes, rose vases, wrap them in plastic and put them away! Put up smart blinds instead of ruffled cotton curtains. Streamline your life.

USING YOUR NEW TIME

The purpose of organizing your time is to find those hours you need to pursue your goals. Janet has decided that she is going to try for law school! As she said, she can always come down in her ideals, but why not aim for the top. Let's see how she does it.

The A,B,C System. In order to go to law school, Janet must first finish college. That will be her A Priority. After investigating, she found out that she can attend night courses four nights a week and, by going summers, get her undergraduate degree in English in two years. (She went to college for two years before her marriage.) Janet will now take another piece of paper to give A,B,C ratings to her life.

All tasks relating to her school will get A ratings. So will her children's doctor's appointments, and her job. B ratings will be all those tasks that have to be done, but only after all A's are completed: Marketing, washing, children's activities. C's are those activities with the least priority: Cleaning, social engagements, shopping etc. The reason marketing is a B and shopping a C is because everyone has to eat while shopping can be postponed. Social engagements are a C unless they are important.

The purpose of the priority list is to fix your goal clearly in mind. You should still follow your charts, but when interruptions occur and you only have a certain amount of time left in the day, you give it to an A. Janet should *always* do her homework in preference to washing or shopping. If she finishes early, then washing has priority over shopping. (The children need clean jeans.)

You will have to be flexible. It is going to take a great deal of experimenting to work it all out. Right now you probably aren't sure of your goals, so you can't rate your priorities. By the end of the book you will be able to.

Life Plan. Goals, in order to be realized, must have time limits. It's exciting to have great successes to look forward to! Your life plan is a five-year look at where you want to be, and what you hope to accomplish. To give you an idea of how it works, here is Janet's.

1 month	Enroll in college.
	Open savings account for vacation.
6 months	Lose ten pounds.
	Have $150 saved ($25 per month).
1 year	One year of college finished.
	Have $300 saved.

3 years	One year of law school finished.
	Buy new living room couch.
	Kimberly graduates from high school.
	Have $900 saved. Take kids on trip.
5 years	Three years of law school finished.
	Douglas graduates from high school.
	Sell house and rent apartment.

When Douglas graduates from high school, Janet plans to sell her home and move with Kevin into an apartment. She plans to quit her job and use some of the money from the house sale to support herself while she studies full time and prepares to take the bar examination. It is a wonderful life plan! She will look at it once a month and revise it from time to time. It will become the focal point of her self-directed life.

When you write your life plan it has an excellent chance of coming true. Without it you are back to cause and effect living. I urge you to aim high. Give yourself bonuses. When you complete a six-month plan, treat yourself to a present such as a new blouse or a belt or pair of earrings. On the first day of each month review your chart. It will give you a burst of energy.

Other Aids. Before you begin all your chart making, treat yourself to some colorful aids. Buy a package of construction paper in mixed colors and a couple of felt tip pens. Write out each child's chart on a different colored paper. Letter them carefully so they are pleasant to look at. Tack them up in the kitchen or buy a cork bulletin board.

Buy yourself a fabric-covered binder or make one by covering an ordinary notebook with contact paper. Section the book with markers. In it keep your copy of all the charts, your lists, your priority page and your life plan. It's also a good place to keep your phone numbers.

Speaking of phone numbers reminds me of one of the jobs my children all shared: phone duty. Each child was assigned to answer the phone for a week. This meant that as soon as he or she came home from school it was up to that child to answer every call and to take *written* messages. The messages were then put in a dish on the hall table. If the child on phone duty had to go out one night, it was up to him or her to find a replacement.

For the messages I bought one of those pink tablets like those they use in offices, which have a place for the name, caller, time called, etc. The children loved them because they were so businesslike!

Plan rewards for your children as well as yourself. Mine always felt that to go out to dinner in the middle of the week was a huge treat. Putting surprises in their lunch boxes and under their pillows was another winner. Letting them have a friend stay over on the weekend was another. I believe in the award system. I rewarded good marks, honors, home runs. Some child psychologists might disagree. Well, that's their problem.

Are you exhausted by all this talk of jobs, charts, lists, and plans? Try not to be. The dividends are so fantastic that *any* effort will be worth it! The definition of courage that I have taped on my typewriter is:

COURAGE IS HANGING ON ONE MINUTE LONGER

Whenever I see that, I type one more page, or answer one more letter, or read one more article. Think of how this definition can apply to your life: jogging one more block, studying one hour longer, passing one glass of wine.

Courage! Remember that a little will power creates a *lot* more will power. Strength of character gets easier.

3

Work

and the Divorced Woman

Today's divorced woman is *expected* to work. The national trend, as you well know, is *away* from alimony. A good many states have eliminated it completely or replaced it with spousal support. Spousal support is designed as a *temporary* measure to help support a woman while she trains to enter or re-enter the job market. Gone are the days when an ex-wife could expect to be supported until remarriage or death.

This is not all bad. In many ways it's a blessing. Only by getting out and into the mainstream of life can a woman *build* a life. Running your own show, earning your way, planning your future—this is the way to happiness and success. No longer will you be a financial and emotional prisoner dependent upon the *whim* of a man. You're all yours now!

Support Payments. Before we go on with the world of work, let's talk about support (i.e., money from your ex-husband). If you are one of the few (very few indeed) who was granted spousal support (alimony), don't count on receiving it. Consider it a marvelous miracle. Each month when the check arrives, kiss the envelope and run, do not walk, to your bank and deposit it as fast as you can fill out the deposit slip. Then go back to your job or your training class.

No, I'm not a cynic. I'm a realist. You should be, too. Simply because some well-meaning judge has said you *should* receive so much money per month is absolutely no guarantee that you *will* receive it. Ex-husbands just hate to pay alimony. They will withhold your check for any reason that seems logical to them. Some just withhold it. Period. When this happens you will have to sue. This takes time—and costs money. It also leaves you with unpaid bills and a nervous stomach.

An ex-husband can always go back into court and try to prove that his circumstances have changed and he can't afford to pay you any longer. (Remember, the national trend is *away* from alimony.) Or he can disappear. There has been a recent *sharp* jump in runaway husbands. Yes, you can try to track him down, but then what? When a man runs away from his obligations you know he's going to do it again and again. As I said, the current disposition of justice in this country favors him!

I have heard women say they can't work because it will weaken their case in court against their ex-husband. The theory behind this statement is that if a wife demonstrates by working that she can support herself she lessens her chances of getting alimony or increases her chances of having her existing alimony reduced. If this is the advice of your lawyer I'm not advising you to go against it. What I am suggesting is that a court order is meaningless if the other party won't comply. When your support comes in the form of a check from your ex-husband, it comes at his whim.

A far better way to get your support money is in the form of a trust, or in real property. This way you maintain some control. I would not recommend staying in a business or company with your ex-husband. Get him to buy you out, or you buy him out. Some formerly married couples work together quite well. You may be one, but why take the chance? Take the money instead and start a business on your own.

Child Support. Child support is money awarded by the court to be paid to the custodial parent by the non-custodial parent. If you have custody of your children, your ex-husband must pay you a certain number of dollars per child each month. No matter what he pays, I know of *very* few cases in which it covers all the needs of the children. The remainder—or bulk— of their support is your responsibility.

Child support is always negotiable. As the children grow, their needs increase. You can always go back into court to try to get an increase in your child support payments. Your ex-husband can also go into court to try to get them reduced. Since child support is based on the needs of the children *and* the father's ability to pay, the court will take a hard look at your ex-husband's income before it grants an increase—or a decrease.

Should your husband fail to make his support payments, you can get a judgment against him and attach his wages. That is, if you *know* where he works. If he is in another state which has reciprocal child-support laws, you can go after him through your district attorney. You can also hire a lawyer in the state in which your ex-husband works, get a judgment, and attach his wages there.

Often when a woman remarries, her ex-husband feels he no longer has the obligation to support his children. Even if a woman's new husband is delighted to accept the financial responsibility for her children, she should still insist that her ex-husband contribute—for his sake as well as the children's. Money from one's own father is an important link and should not be broken. When a father does not contribute to the support of his children, he often stops seeing them.

In today's financial picture it almost takes contributions from two households to raise children, obtain proper medical and dental care, and see them through college. As I said in the beginning of this chapter, today's divorced woman is expected to work. You say this is so unfair? Well, dear heart, nobody ever *said* divorce was fair. Lamenting your circumstances will never change them. Getting off your backside and *doing* something, will.

FINDING OUT WHAT YOU CAN DO

You absolutely must approach the world of work with an open mind and a desire to succeed. As William James said: "Our belief at the beginning of a doubtful undertaking is the one thing that insures the successful outcome of the venture." You must *believe* you are an achiever and the deed is half done. It's exciting to think about widening your horizons, meeting new people, and starting a new life—a life that is *you-oriented*. It's heady stuff.

The world of work doesn't have the limitations that "socializing" does. In a married life your friends are generally your husband's buddies from work and their wives, your sorority sisters and their husbands, your neighbors and your family. When you step into the world of work *you* choose the people you want to see. They can be anyone.

Martha is a grandmother in her late forties whose husband left her for a younger woman. During her married life she and her rancher husband lived in a valley town in Central California. After the divorce Martha moved to San Francisco, rented a pleasant two-bedroom apartment so her children and grandchild could visit her, and enrolled in art school. Her income came from generous spousal support. After all, she had been married twenty-seven years and her husband was suffering from enormous feelings of guilt.

Everything went swimmingly for a year. My friend did extremely well in her classes and had the social life she had always dreamed about. Artists, designers, gallery owners filled her living room to drink wine and have marvelous discussions. Abruptly the money stopped. Martha's ex-husband met business reverses and could no longer send her anything. Martha was devastated. She dropped out of school and began to take care of elderly patients just to eat and pay the rent. She babysat on the weekends and worked afternoons in a gallery, all the while sinking deeper into a depression.

One day I asked Martha what she wanted above all else in the world. Her answer: to be a commercial artist. "All right," I said. "Then make *that* your goal and fit the rest of your life around it." She said she didn't see how she could *possibly* do that. She had to work to stay alive. We had many discussions, then I finally said that she had *better* try because the way she was going she was killing herself!

The next day she went back to her school and inquired about scholarships. The faculty were delighted to see her and arranged an interview. She got the scholarship! It paid her tuition and supplies. Next she asked about jobs available and was appointed mailroom "grandmother," a "position" which involved answering the phone and sending out information about the school, a job which she handled with ease and excellence.

Her next hurdle was her rent. She decided she didn't want to go to the trouble and expense of moving to smaller quarters, so she put a notice on the school bulletin board advertising for a roommate. The first person to approach her about the ad was a young *male* student in one of her classes whom she liked enormously. The idea appealed to her instantly and he moved in that weekend.

She now had her school, enough money to feed herself and to pay half the rent, and as she said, utter, exquisite joy! She also said she got far more out of her art school because *she was paying for it*.

Three months after this happy experience, an old girl friend from the valley came to visit her. Martha later told me she hadn't realized how "different" she had become! Her friend was "appalled" at her eating habits, "intimidated by her kookie friends," and "shocked by her gay roommate." My friend said she will probably became a legend when the stories of her life get back to the valley.

One of the greatest deterrents to a woman's success is the belief that she is "too old." This kind of thinking can keep you wedded to a dull, dead-end job. It can also keep you from asking for any job at all. This is nonsense.

You are *not* too old to learn—to start over. You are as *smart* as you choose to be. There is no set time when your learning ability decreases. It only decreases if *you* say it decreases. Look at the discoveries made by people over sixty, the books written by people over seventy, and the astute business decisions made by people over eighty.

A perfect example is the life of D. K. Ludwig, who is one of the wealthiest men in the world. Last year and the year before he had forests planted of trees which won't mature until he's one hundred! Now in his eighties and still going strong, he will probably be there to supervise the making of the pulp into paper.

So make a pact with yourself to become the most interesting, most vital, most alive person you know. Start your adventure with the work that you do—or would *like* to do. Following is a step-by-step method for reaching your full creative and productive potential. Doesn't that have a nice ring to it?

1. *Investigate You.* If you are a woman who has never worked or worked briefly before your marriage or before your children arrived, then your first step is to determine what you can do. Take a piece of paper and a pencil and at the top of the page write Education. Under this, list each school you attended and the courses you particularly liked or in which you excelled. Don't forget dancing school or modeling school or cooking school. Next, list your trade schools, such as business college. Last list your college and/or university training. Don't just list your majors; list all the courses you took in various fields.

Next, write down the words Work Experience. Starting with your very first job as a baby sitter, list everything you have ever done for which you received pay. Think back and be specific. If you worked in a dime store, which counter did you have? If you typed, how many words a minute? If you worked for a veterinarian, what type of pets did you handle?

Your next category is Volunteer Experience. No matter how trivial or meaningless you think it is, write it down. Collecting for the Heart Fund; being a Girl Scout leader; manning the refreshment booth at Little League; Red Cross work; museum guide. If you helped your husband in his office, that's "volunteer" work. Put down exactly what you did. If you kept the household accounts or managed property, put that down.

After Volunteer Experience comes Hobbies & Interests. This is what you *like* to do. Tennis, needlepoint, refinishing furniture, Chinese cooking, gardening, collecting bottles, flying a plane. Now is the time to think of all the things you've ever *tried*.

The last category is Personal Data. Here is where you list all your sterling qualities. You are slow to anger. You are well groomed. You are a hard worker. You are punctual and co-operative. You can speak in front of a crowd, drive a car, and you have a good sense of humor.

Now spread these lists out in front of you and see how many possible jobs you can list that would make use of your particular talents. A good way to do this is to go right down each list and try to think of one job for every entry. Baby sitting—day nursery. Cooking school—caterer. B.A. Art History—gallery saleswoman. Collecting for the Heart Fund—professional fund raiser. Put down everything you can think of, even if you wouldn't consider doing it. Remember, there is *no* such thing as a *menial* job.

Do you see what this is accomplishing? It is getting you to think about work in terms of yourself. You *do* have something to offer. Everything you have *ever* done in your life is *experience*. So never let yourself be heard to utter those dreadful words: I have no experience.

From all the possible jobs you listed, make a list of Possibles. Those are jobs you *know* you could handle. This is your hot list. Beside each Possible put the name and number of prospective employers; names of prospective companies; leads from your friends; and all the bits and pieces of information you will accumulate in your search.

2. *Résumés and Interviews.* Every prospective employer will want a résumé—a neat, tidy résumé. If you don't know how to type, find a friend who does. Then have professional copies made either by mimeograph, multigraph, Xerox, or offset printings. Use standard-sized typing paper while remembering that the first rule of business is Time Is Money. So keep it brief, *not* over two pages.

Résumé Form

A. In the upper left-hand corner list your name, address and phone number.

B. On the upper right hand side indicate the type of job you desire. (You could give a couple of choices in a related field.)

C. The first reading is Work Experience. In reverse order list

your last three jobs, beginning with the most recent one ·
held.

1. State name and address of company, date of employment, name of your supervisor (person you reported
   to) and title of job you held.
2. For each position you held tell exactly what you did;
   layout for ads, typing and dictation; buyer for junior
   sportswear; greeted customers; conducted tours.

It doesn't matter if these were paid or unpaid jobs.
You had the responsibility for seeing that *something* was
accomplished.

D. The next heading is Education. This should be a sum-
   mary of all the schools you attended. Follow this with a
   list of the special courses you have taken since you left
   school: flower arranging; Chinese cooking; real estate
   school; French. If you have received any on-the-job training,
   list that.

E. After Education comes Volunteer Activities
   1. List name and address of agencies, institutions or groups
      you served. Be specific. Museum guide—French Im-
      pressionists 1963–65. Region 6 Heart Fund Chairman
      1971–72
   2. Give name, address, and title of someone familiar with
      what you did.

F. Personal Data. Put your status (divorced) and number
   and ages of your children. I do not feel that you have to
   give your age. It's fairly easy to calculate from your education. Next, state the geographical area in which you
   prefer to work and if you are free to travel. If you have
   a driver's license, put that down. List any other licenses
   such as real estate, pilot or practical nurse.

G. Personal References. Give the name, address, and phone
   number of three members of the community, in good
   standing, who know you and would give you a good
   recommendation. Choose your doctor, minister, school
   principal, banker. Do not list anyone mentioned in
   Work Experience. These are your personal or character
   references.

Once you have completed your résumé and had it professionally reproduced, the serious business of job hunting begins. It will be the A Project in your life, so plan to devote several intensive hours a day to it. A good way to begin is to go through your address book and alert your friends, family, neighbors, and club members that you are looking for a job. Tell them the areas in which you feel qualified and the types of jobs that particularly interest you. Offer to mail them a résumé, or mail the résumé wherever they suggest. It always helps to be able to say on a note, "I'm mailing this to you at the suggestion of our mutual friend, Bob Crowley, who thought you might be having an opening soon. I should appreciate the opportunity to meet you in person." Give the letter time to arrive, then follow it up with a phone call.

The next step is a visit to your local State Training and Employment Service. You can find them listed under your state government offices in the phone book. Their services include counseling, testing, retraining, and placement. There is no charge for any of these services. In many areas this employment service maintains a special office for women seeking professional and managerial jobs. Because these offices are part of a national network, they can give you information about job openings across the country.

In addition to the State Department of Employment, there are hundreds of private agencies. These agencies charge a fee, either paid by you or by the employer. Look in the yellow pages of your phone book and pick out two or three agencies which specialize in your area of interest. Drop in and see them. Discuss job opportunities. These people can be a source of a great deal of information. When you find an agency which you think will be of help to you, register with them. But *do not* pay any sort of fee until they have secured a job for you.

Be sure to check the want ads in your newspaper. Employers who place ads are looking. They need help now. Read all the ads. You never know what you'll find. You can also determine from the number of requests which areas of business are actively seeking people. If you can't find a job with the qualifications you have, you can consider training in this field. In addition to your daily papers, check your neighborhood or weekly publications.

If you live in a large metropolitan area, go to the major employers and check in with their personnel offices. Check with schools, hospitals, insurance companies, government agencies. Go to the local YWCA. They have bulletin boards listing job opportunities and offer courses in employment tips. Watch the business section of the newspaper for new companies or stores opening in your area. Be alert. Job hunting is an attitude. *Expect* to find a job. Keep telling yourself that the job you are seeking is seeking you, and only *you* can fill it.

One day it clicks and you have an appointment for a personal interview with a prospective employer! Here are some guidelines to help you make the most of that interview and land that job.

A. *Do Your Homework.* Before you arrive for the interview, find our about the company, what they do or what they make. Know whether they have branch offices or statewide connections. You can drop by the office a day or two before the interview and pick up pamphlets or brochures. These will give you all the information you need.

B. *Be Prompt.* In fact, be early. If you are not certain where the office is or exactly how long it will take you to get there, "ride the course" the day before. That means take the bus or your car and go to the office exactly as if today were tomorrow. Then on interview day you won't have the worry of not knowing where you're going. If you have planned two interviews for one day, schedule them at least two hours apart.

C. *Dress Well.* I don't mean dress up, but to dress a little better than you would for the job. This shows that you care. If you ordinarily wear glasses, then wear them. Don't try a new hairstyle or new makeup. You know how to look your best. Above all, don't try to dress "young." That produces the absolute opposite effect. Park your chewing gum, please, and don't smoke.

D. *Be Supplied.* Have at least two copies of your résumé. You'll need one to refer to as the interviewer reads his or her copy and asks you questions. Take a small note pad and ball-point pen to make notes. Have your social security number handy so you don't have to plow through your wallet.

E. *Filling Out Forms.* If you are given an application to fill out, read the *entire* form before you begin to write. Consult your résumé so your dates and names will be correct. Watch your spelling and punctuation and write or print legibly.

F. *Don't Oversell.* In your nervousness, be careful you don't start spilling out your problems to the secretary while you're waiting. Be businesslike. If you gush or plead, you weaken your case. Remember that they need you as badly as you need them. But they don't need or want your problems. Be prepared for this question, "Why do you want to work for us?" Have a good, sound reason. Needing the money may be your real motivation, but the employer wants to hear why you have chosen him and his company.

G. *Benefits.* I would suggest that you don't ask about vacations, benefits, coffee breaks, or retirement plans on your first interview and I would wait for the interviewer to bring up the salary. If you are asked *what* salary you expect, you could answer by inquiring what the firm has been paying people in similar positions.

H. *Timing.* At the end of the interview ask when you may call back. If they say they'll call you, it's quite all right to question the time involved. If the indications are that it will be *quite some time,* ask the interviewer if he or she knows of another company who could use your services. Leave promptly and do not linger. Thank everyone who has spoken to you. Good manners are a sign of intelligence.

It may take several interviews before you find that job. Use these interviews as training sessions. After each session go over in your head the questions that were asked and the answers you gave. This is the way to improve your presentation. Interviews also acquaint you with different businesses and how they work. Every time you learn something you are moving forward. This can be an exciting time in your life. You are getting your feet wet in the real world.

3. *Temporary Jobs.* If you find you don't have an immediate prospect for a permanent job, consider taking a temporary job. Being a temporary secretary can provide a terrific learning period. By working in different offices you learn what types of jobs you like and which you don't. You may find that anything to do with banking and finance bores you to tears. Temporaries replace women who have gone on vacation. The employer you get may decide you do a better job and put you on permanently. Working temporarily within a company allows you to snoop around other departments to see what else is available.

Liz, a woman just turned fifty, had to get a job after her divorce but decided her secretarial skills needed upgrading. She joined a temporary office help agency in Los Angeles. Her third assignment was to go to the home of a scriptwriter, high in the Hollywood Hills, and type his manuscript. While she was there, he had two important visitors drop in at noon. Rather than disrupt his writing schedule by going out to lunch, he said he would fix them a snack. As he fumbled with saucepans and canned soup, Liz came into the kitchen and offered to take over. Obviously relieved, the writer returned to his visitors and Liz put together an impressive improvised meal.

The next day the writer asked Liz to shop for a wedding present he had to send. The day after he asked her to plan a dinner for eight for the following weekend. Within five days the writer asked her to be his permanent assistant. During the next year she not only typed his scripts, but redecorated his house, planned all his entertaining and spent five weeks in France doing research. As she describes her job, it is an absolute dream come true.

4. *Training Programs.* Many companies like to train their staff and offer very comprehensive courses to persons willing to take the training. Certain large banks have this facility. Find

out if such a bank operates in your area. Banking today is an excellent field for a woman and offers career potential. Bank officers know that women customers entering a bank like to do business with other women.

Large department stores often conduct buyer-training for those who want a career in merchandising. You earn while you learn. The salary is generally not very high, but you are receiving your training. In addition, you are trained the way the store specifies which gives you great job stability and opportunity for advancement.

5. *Trade Schools.* If you absolutely cannot find a job with the training you have, consider going to a trade school. Give careful consideration to the occupation you choose because you will be investing time and money in it. Try to arrange for a loan to cover your expenses while you learn, with the understanding that you will pay it back in monthly installments. (Actually, the new support laws were designed for this purpose, but if you are one of the many *not* receiving help from your ex-husband, you will have to do it on your own.) Many vocational classes are conducted at night, which would enable you to hold down a daytime job. It doesn't matter *what* kind of a job, since you are training yourself for something better.

Here is a partial list of schools that are readily available. Before you choose one, see if you can determine the demand in your community.

Real Estate	Secretarial
Hair Dressing	Market Checking
Chef Cooking	Dental Hygiene
Decorating	Practical Nursing

6. *Finishing an Education.* If all you need to become a teacher is two more years of college, by all means try to figure out a way to do it. If you want to go back to school to become a psychologist, a C.P.A., a dentist, an architect, or a lawyer, do it! It doesn't matter *what* type of work you accept in order to finance your education. The important thing is to do it. It may take you five years to complete a three-year course, but so what! This is your life and you should be doing what you want

to do. Once you have decided, commit yourself to a course of action and do it!

The hard thing in life is not *getting* what you want. The hard thing is *deciding* what you want. Once you have determined what it is you want above all else, *nothing* can stop you. I know this to be a fact and I urge you to believe me and to put this faith and determination into your life. No, it isn't easy or fun all the time. It's hard work. You will face experiences that seem like trials. Sometimes you will feel as if you were being tested. Do not be daunted. Hang onto that mental picture of what it's going to be like when you get there!

Beware of the distractions, the temporary lures that keep you off the track. When you rush to satisfy short-term wants, you run the risk of losing long-term goals. Distractions are a waste of time and energy. When they are over we feel disappointment in ourselves and wonder if, in fact, we'll *ever* amount to anything. So choose the right way, even if it's hard work, because a victory over temptation gives an added spurt of vitality that nothing, save victory, can match.

ON THE JOB

Securing that first job is just the beginning. Now you have the opportunity to prove yourself; the opportunity to learn; the opportunity to advance. You notice I don't use the word *chance* because I don't believe in chance. I believe in the word opportunity which is the *opposite* of chance. To believe in chance is to believe in an illusion; to believe in opportunity is to believe in a realism. Chance is a quick flash in the pan, it's over and out. Opportunity is constant; it flows like the ocean; it is always available. You can miss a chance, but you can always have another shot at opportunity.

1. *Attitude.* Whatever your job may be, your *attitude* toward it determines your success or your failure. It is a beginning, an opportunity to build toward a career that will support

you for the rest of your life. Even if your job is mopping hall-ways to pay for your training as a dental hygienist, be grateful for that mop and that hallway. This job is a means to an end, a channel, a way to get you where you want to go. Be the best mopper in the town!

When Sarah decided she wanted to go into advertising as a copywriter, she knew she would have to go by a circuitous route. She had no portfolio, no past experience, and no former jobs in a related area. So she took a job as a secretary to the creative director. The company hired her, she thinks, because she was over thirty-five and looked reliable, because she was so eager for the job, and because she agreed to a salary that was less than secretaries were then making.

Part of her job was answering mail. Sarah's boss would call her into his office and dictate several letters, one after the other. Sarah had only learned Speedwriting, not shorthand, so she had a terrible time getting everything down. On the fourth day she said, "Since I open the mail and have a general idea of how to answer it, why don't you let me type up replies in rough form, you correct them, then I'll do them in final."

Her boss was delighted with this idea. It saved him a great deal of time, and it developed that Sarah was an impressive let-ter writer. Within a month, he had turned 60 per cent of the correspondence over to her.

Another part of her boss's job was interviewing prospective copywriters and artists and reviewing their portfolios. Sarah soon learned what he looked for in new creative talent and she took over the reviewing of the portfolios. This taught *her* how to write copy. Within three months she submitted an idea for a very difficult but small account that nobody particularly en-joyed working on, and the account was turned over to her. She learned; she advanced; she made more money. She never com-plained or tried to do less. She tried to do more and more and more. When she was ready to become a copywriter, she asked for the job and she got it. If Sarah had been turned down, she still could have taken her experience and tried elsewhere.

2. *Advancing.* Once you have a job, start forming your goals. It's time to make that list of what you hope to accomplish

and how long you think it will take. These are your A Priority goals. Let's say you have taken a job as a teller in a bank and your goal is to become an officer of that bank. What separates you from that job? Knowledge and experience. You are getting the experience and some of the knowledge you need right now, but you need more.

The best way to learn about a business is from the experts. Go to your local library and check out some basic books on money, finance, and banking. You will be overwhelmed at what's available. Then check your local night schools to see what courses are offered in adult education. Each time you widen your scope of interest and add to your store of knowledge you are advancing.

Another way to advance is to switch jobs within the company. When you know a better position is going to be available, go after it. Let the right people know you're interested and what you've done to prepare yourself. If you are in sales in a department store and want to become a buyer, start a campaign. If you are a secretary in a large insurance company and you want to become an underwriter, find out the qualifications. It's not where you begin in a business that matters, but what you *do* with that beginning.

Another way to advance is to familiarize yourself with the companies doing business *with* the company where you work. Because you know one business, you are often valuable to another.

Keep your goals clearly in mind. Review your priority list once a month. Don't forget to add those rewards such as: three years: take two-week vacation in Mexico; four Years: have $8,000 in savings account; five Years: buy first piece of income property. Believe me, it is the only way your goals will become realities. Singlemindedness of purpose is your most powerful weapon to defeat confusion, lack of nerve, self-doubt and bad advice.

3. *Dead-end Jobs.* It's true that there are some jobs that have absolutely no future. The only reason you should even consider such a job is because you need the money while you

obtain training for a better job. Sometimes you don't realize a job is a dead end until you've been on it a couple of months.

What classifies a job as dead-end? The best definition is a job where you will be doing exactly the same thing as you are doing now for the rest of your life and you hate it. The last part—the hating it—is what makes it dead-end. Some people are so in love with what they are doing that they want to be doing it for the rest of their lives. Even with the love of doing it, there *still* should be an elevating wage scale or it is dead-end. An artist should receive more money for her work as her proficiency increases.

A dead-end job could be a position in a company where you *know* you'll never be advanced. This could be due to the fact that all of those above you are young, or because the business is family-owned, or because the company is prejudiced against women. The first two of those reasons you can't do anything about, but the third you can. That is, if you have the time, money, and statistics to fight it. If you are the sole support of three children, I would simply quit and move on. Let the younger, single women fight the battles. That may mark you as a traitor to the women's cause, but I don't think so. Anyone who knows how hard it is to raise three children will understand. And what if they don't? It's *your* life.

4. *Big Jobs/High Stakes.* What about that glamour job? What about an acting career or writing the Great American Novel or entering the diplomatic service? Well, why not! You are only in competition with your own potential. The cardinal rule to observe here is what it costs you.

Karen is a young divorced mother with three children who has always wanted to be an actress. She had a couple of good parts in her college plays, but then she married, had children, and you know the rest of the story. Now, suddenly a divorce has given her the opportunity to pursue an acting career. But how can she support her three young children in New York while she begins the hard job of looking for parts? Obviously she can't.

Karen's husband is remarried and living in New Jersey. He would like to have custody of the children. After a fierce struggle within herself Karen relinquishes custody and goes off to New York. If her acting career is truly that important to her, then she has done the right thing. The children will certainly be better off with their father in a family situation than living with Karen and sharing her sketchy life. But what a price to pay!

Not all so-called glamour jobs require such sacrifice. Writing, for instance, is something you can do *while* you work. Because glamour jobs *are* what they are, you must be dedicated and willing to give everything you've got. Perhaps it's the monetary rewards that are the attractive part. Remember, there are a hundred easier ways to make money than by writing or acting or singing, so don't be lured by the promise of wealth. Only go after a glamour job if you feel in your heart of hearts that this is what you *must* do.

STARTING YOUR OWN BUSINESS

Never say anything is impossible. That's the most certain way in the world to keep yourself wedded to unfulfilled living. There are in all of us hidden dreams, undeveloped talents, suppressed desires. They *remain* where they are because we keep them there. No, we say to ourselves, that's impossible. No, I haven't the time or the talent or the money to do that. I'm afraid.

Fear. That's the greatest barrier of all. Fear of change; fear of failure; fear of making fools of ourselves. When we fear, we *fail* before we even try. The antidote to fear is courage, with a dash of faith and a jigger of trust.

Every day women all over the country are renting small stores, climbing up ladders, and painting ceilings. Every day women all over the country are putting extra phone lines into their homes, listing themselves in the yellow pages, and sending out announcements. These women are Open for Business. What separates them from you? Nothing but attitude. If you have a special dream to start an Italian restaurant, open a knitting shop, teach yoga, then bring it out in the open and look at it. It's possible to do *anything* you want to do.

1. *Working In or Out of Your Home.* You can stay home and earn money. How? By offering or selling a service. Some services require a license; some don't. Ask your lawyer or call the Better Business Bureau. If you are going to take care of children you would need a license and extra insurance. If you are going to teach piano, I don't think you would, but, as I said, ask an expert.

What business can you operate in your home? The list is wonderfully long and varied. Here are a few suggestions:

Cooking classes
Teaching music
Teaching a language
Giving Art lessons
Displaying and selling a product
   (clothes, gifts, cosmetics)
Teaching flower arranging
Doing bookkeeping and tax forms
Secretarial work
Child care

Once you decide on the service you wish to render and you've checked with your lawyer or city hall about licensing, the next move is advertising. The most inexpensive form is by word of mouth, but this takes time. I would suggest a simple flyer mailed to the residential community; notices on school and store bulletin boards; or a small ad in the local weekly paper. You can't sell if the people don't know where you are.

You can also conduct a business out of your house, using your home as the contact and work center. For instance, a catering service or a plant-watering and dog-walking service for vacationers. Or a shopping, decorating or baby sitting service.

Perhaps the most unusual service I've heard about was organized by two women in Southern California and called Knowledge Swap. What they did was put people who wanted to teach what *they* knew in touch with people who wanted to teach what *they* knew. For instance a woman who wanted to learn to drive a car was offering to exchange Spanish lessons for driving lessons. A man offered to teach chess in exchange for learning how to make bread. A teen-ager was willing to teach guitar in exchange for scuba diving lessons. Any person wanting to swap skills paid five dollars to be listed in their register. When a "matching person" could be found, they would be put in touch with each other.

I've always thought that the same kind of swap could be organized with skills—I'll do your ironing if you'll do my mending or I'll wallpaper your powder room if you'll make my living-room drapes. The same file system and registration fee could be used.

Whatever your endeavor, be businesslike. Keep books and records. Keep definite hours and be dependable. Have someone answer your phone when you're out, or buy an answering device. Since you are in business to make money, have set prices for your services and be consistent. If you give a discount to a friend it is certain to get around and your other customers will demand the same price.

2. *Opening a Business.* Who hasn't had a dream of opening a business of her very own? I am a frustrated innkeeper. I would like to have a small, elegant place in the country that caters to discriminating guests. Superb food would be my forte with individually decorated guest rooms done in flocked wallpaper and Victorian antiques. What's your dream? Why not bring it out in the open and look at it. You probably have an idea that could very well support you.

Two divorced women in Houston, Texas, bought a monogram machine and do a thriving business. Their clients are not only sophisticated customers who desire individualized linens, but also stores which are unable to fill their own orders. The women came up with one idea which has made them a great deal of money: personal pillows. These are pillow cases monogrammed with wedding dates, birthdays, and love messages. They also do the usual towels, blouses, bathroom and table linens.

A divorced woman in Denver operates a plant rental. Her clientele are business offices who don't have the time or the manpower to care for the plants in their lobbies, reception rooms, and offices. She brings in the plants, rotates them, and keeps the areas looking green and lush. I can't tell you how many divorced women operate boutiques, gift and antique shops, decorator studios, restaurants, and camera shops. The list is truly endless.

How do you open a shop? Yes, you need money for inventory. How much depends on your stock, rent, equipment and help. The best source of information is others in the same business. Talk to bankers. The more *research* you do, the better your chances of success. Once again, consult your lawyer as to the permits or licenses you will need. Scout several locations before you rent your space. Know how many stores of your kind are in the area. Find out about parking. Find out if the area has a high crime rate.

There are also courses you can take through adult education on this very subject: How to Open a Small Business. The federal government in some instances will help with the financing. If you *want* to do it you can. Businesses are opening daily and doing very well. Just remember, however, that the more homework you do, the better your chances of success.

THE HELP YOU NEED

Help is available. A hard worker, dedicated to an idea, is a contributing member of society. You can find the financial help you need. You can also find the emotional help you need, but let's talk about the financial aspect first. Banks are not *all* unfriendly. Properly used, your neighborhood bank can be your best friend. Once you have researched your idea, try it out on a banker. He or she is trained to ask the piercing questions. He or she is also willing and able to bet the bank's money on you and your business. If the first bank you approach is of no help, try another. And again another.

It often seems that the state and federal governments only help those on welfare, those who cannot help themselves. Truthfully there *is* money available to help people like you, winners who want to succeed in the American tradition of free enterprise. The money is often hidden down long bureaucratic hallways, but it's there. Pretend it's a scavenger hunt and you have to find the hidden treasure. Just keep asking and asking until you get the right answer.

Externals, however, are not enough. As I've said so many times before, you have to have the right attitude and *faith* in what you are doing. Whenever you are tempted to rely completely on externals, remember the story of Noah and the Ark. Imagine a man building an enormous boat on dry land without a drop of water in sight! Why did Noah do this? Because he had a message from God to *survive*. There was nothing happening in his life to indicate he wasn't going to survive, but he had enough faith in himself to believe his instincts.

Noah did not wait around for God to send him a boat; he relied on himself to build one. And what happened when the floods did come? The greater the amount of water that he faced, the higher the Ark rose. The message is, of course, that within you is this same ability to stay afloat. If you are inspired to do something, do it! It's God's plan that we *all* succeed to the degree that we are willing to try.

1. *Day Care Centers.* If you have small children, you need a safe and secure place for them while you work. If there is no day care center in your neighborhood, organize one. The best place to start is with a local church. Churches have nurseries, playgrounds, and elderly parishioners who would love the chance to work and feel needed. It wouldn't take much effort to organize such a center. You could also work it out to have the mothers rotate the lunch responsibility. It has always been my feeling that the way we use churches and temples, one day a week, is a supreme waste. Since the facilities are there, they should be used. It wasn't too long ago that the church was the center of the community. You can make it happen again.

2. *Nursery Schools.* The same is absolutely true of nursery schools. If you can't find one, organize one. Here would be a terrific job for one or two divorced mothers. They could keep the children of working mothers who would pay a fee for each child. We have a tendency in this country to wait for someone else or for the government to *do* something for us. It is far better if we do it for ourselves.

PLAY IS THE REWARD OF WORK

One of the great joys of working is that is makes play so much more fun. Now that we have your world of work all organized, let's talk about play. Play is that carefree time you treat yourself to when you have worked hard. It's weekends, holidays, and vacations. How you use this time should be as well thought out as work time. Don't groan. You'll have a far better time if you *plan* your hours rather than just letting them happen.

1. *Weekends and Holidays.* If you have children, plan your weekends and holidays to include them. They can be the best companions in the world. As a working mother you probably don't see as much of your children as you would like to, so here is your chance to discover each other.

If the weather is right, consider a day-long bicycle ride. Plan your itinerary so you know which roads you will be taking and the points of interest you will be covering. Not only is this a good way to be with your children, but think of what it does for your waistline.

How about an overnight camp-out? Find out where in your area you can pitch a tent and build a fire. An overnight requires minimal equipment. If you don't want to buy or rent a tent, you could rent a room in a lodge for the night.

There are any number of all-day outings such as a trip to the museum or an art gallery. You could take in a matinee at the opera or ballet or you could attend a lecture on a foreign country or visit an historical monument. Check your Sunday paper. It should be full of all kinds of captivating ideas. Last Sunday our paper contained a story about a family who takes long Sunday walks. At breakfast they open the phone book to a page at random, then count ten names down from the top. They look up the address on the map and that's the destination of their Sunday walk. If it is a terribly long distance, they figure how to do part of the trip by bus.

2. *Vacations with Dividends.* If you spend weekends and

holidays with your children, you may want to treat yourself to a learning or "becoming" vacation. Last summer I went to a language school and lived in a house with a group of people studying the same language. It was a fascinating experience. Another friend of mine treats herself to two weeks in a spa. A third friend goes to a tennis ranch. These are all vacations in which you learn, or in which something beneficial happens to you.

You can also stay home and spend your vacation taking a two-week course in photography or jewelry making. Because this is a complete departure from your work, you not only stir the creative juices, but you rest and relax. A vacation is best if it is beneficial. Some people like to loll in the sun for two weeks. This to me lacks imagination and inventiveness. If you want two weeks in the sun, why not be collecting rocks or learning to weave blankets or picking grapes?

3. *General Travel Pointers.* To the majority of divorced women, travel is a luxury. Therefore I would say the first rule of the road is: Make It Meaningful. I recommend that you plan your trip far in advance, which makes it last a long time. Read about the area you are going to visit. Write to the Department of Information to request material to read. Ask about dates of specific feasts or festivals; ask about access to private collections; ask for recommended field guides. You will be amazed at the answers you will receive.

If you can get up the courage, travel alone. I know it sounds frightening, but once you've done it, you'll never go any other way. (Except, perhaps, with someone you love very dearly.) If you can't get up the nerve to venture out alone, take one of your children. I hesitate to suggest that you travel with a girl friend because you will be severely limiting your experiences.

Be inventive in your mode of travel. You can bicycle through Scotland; take a barge in Germany; and rent a car in Spain. I met a thirty-eight-year-old divorced woman who took a series of buses from Katmandu to Turkey. It took her three months, but she said it was the best three months of her life. I favor exotic places off the usual travel path. You can have far more of an adventure for less money.

If you can, give your travels a purpose. I know a woman who

collects antique playing cards. All year she corresponds with dealers around the world. When she takes her two- or three-week vacation, she visits these dealers and is often invited to stay in their homes. Another woman in New Mexico collects recordings of folk music. She is in contact with governments as well as universities and private citizens. She has been the special guest at many folk festivals and feast days.

Collecting can also be profitable. One of our local stores features a collection of jewelry from the Middle East brought back by a friend of mine. She told me she always pays for her trips from what she makes on the sale of her jewelry.

I happened to be in Italy after my cookbook was published and with me I had a list of names of the most unusual small restaurants. My editor had given me the list. Each time I went into one of these restaurants I would tell the owner that I was collecting recipes for a *new* book and ask to see the kitchen and meet the chef. This invariably led to a tour of the wine cellar, a good bottle, a special meal and many delicious memories.

4. *Where Not to Go.* As a traveling single woman you want to meet people, especially interesting single men. One place they are *not* is on giant cruise ships. The chances are that all you will meet on board are other single women. I would avoid ski resorts in December. Go instead in January, especially during the first week. It's much easier to meet people when it isn't a mob scene. A chair lift is a good place to strike up a friendship. Your chair mate is your captive audience for fifteen minutes. You can cover a lot of ground in that time.

Other places to avoid are Honolulu and Las Vegas. These areas are overrun with available cupcakes. Why enter *that* competition? Any well-known and overcrowded resort area is not going to work to your advantage. After all, you're not interested in numbers. A select few are always preferable to a mob.

5. *Travel Etiquette.* The first rule of the road is: travel light. I have finally learned to take *only* what I can carry at one time. That includes a suitcase, over-the-shoulder flight bag and over-the-shoulder purse. I long ago rid myself of that boxy encumbrance known as a cosmetic case. In fact I've all but eliminated cosmetics. I take just a small zipper packet containing my

favorite lipstick, lipstick brush, eye liner, and blusher. I leave *all* bottles and jars in the medicine cabinet and buy a bar of face soap, a small jar of moisturizer, small liquid make-up and small hand cream *after* I reach my destination. I have yet to go anyplace in the world where I can't find these items. I've been to some rather obscure places including the sheikhdoms of the Arabian Gulf. Can you believe that I found Elizabeth Arden in Abu Dhabi and Vaseline Intensive Care Lotion in Rasal Khaimah!

Invest in a good foolproof haircut before you leave—one that allows you freedom from rollers and electric curlers. Leave wigs and hairpieces at home. This is a vacation, remember. If you wear glasses, take two pairs. Have your nails done before you leave, then again during your trip. Leave those dangerous bottles of nail polish and remover at home.

Clothes, naturally, are determined by where you go. Keep your wardrobe limited to one basic color scheme. Shoes are bulky, hard to pack, and add pounds. Another trick is to stick to solid colors. You can do more with them than with prints, stripes and flowers. Taking one long jersey dress is always a good idea. It can take you anywhere at night. Slacks, skirts and turtlenecks are perfect for daytime. Wear something attractive when you travel. Don't save everything pretty for your arrival. Why get on the plane looking frumpy? I don't know who started the idea that you have to travel in old clothes, but it is certainly a silly notion.

There are two schools of thought about your wedding ring. Some women say it's a blessing to have it on as it discourages the undesirables. Others say it discourages everyone. I've always traveled wearing a wedding band and I personally think it's a good idea. I've been followed into hotel lobbies and turned to my unwanted admirer and said, "Did you wish to see my husband? He'll be here in a minute." My girls, who travel the world by themselves, say I'm old-fashioned. When they have a problem, they just turn on the man and tell him to buzz off. If this doesn't work, they head for the nearest policeman.

The main ingredient to happy travel is to smile and radiate good cheer. Talk to people. Be friendly. Ask questions. And when things don't go right, be a good sport. Nobody enjoys a complainer. I've found out that the more seasoned and sophisticated the traveler, the less fault she finds. People who travel the world don't break their stride over muddled hotel reservations, late buses, unexpected rainstorms or lumpy beds. Make the best of it; that's part of the fun of life.

6. *Traveling with a Man.* When I wrote *The Divorcée's Handbook* ten long years ago, I was very adamant about a great many things. One was traveling with a man not your husband. I thought no self-respecting woman should put herself into that position. You know what I mean—that awkward standing by the elevator trying to look blasé while he scribbled a phony Mr. & Mrs. in the desk register, or looking over your shoulder in the restaurant to see if you knew anyone in the crowd.

No one cares any more. No one. Not the hotel, not the desk clerk, not the waiter, not your ex-husband. But wait, what about you; do you care? Of course you do. Why? Because we're not of the swinging singles set who change bed partners as easily as they change eye shadow. We belong to the era that *did* care, does care, and our values are hard to part with. So what can you do?

If you are invited on a trip with a man, and he is paying for everything, and you are terribly fond of each other, I can only say to do what your heart and head say to do. Remember, however, that he is of *your* vintage and shares your values. If you do in fact go, don't be coy about it. Let someone know where you are going and how you will be registered. If you have small children, the baby sitter should know how to reach you. If your children are grown, leave them a number.

Traveling is available to everyone. You don't need to wait for a man—or for anyone—to invite you. Invite yourself. Don't be afraid. You'll be absolutely amazed at what good company you are once you take the time to make friends with yourself.

4

Money

and the Divorced Woman

The first thing that can be said about money is that there is never enough. Ever. Whatever her economic level, the divorced woman always seems to have problems making her income match her outflow. There are only two tested ways you can help yourself; you can cut down on your spending and/or generate more income. It's exactly like all those fad diets. There are still only two sure ways to lose weight: eat less and exercise more.

Worry. Before we examine the ways in which you can cut your spending, let's talk for a minute about worrying. We probably, as a people, spend more time worrying about money than about any other problem in our lives. A great many of us feel that if we had more money it would solve all the *rest* of our problems. I cannot say that it wouldn't. I can think of half a dozen people right this minute whose lives would be immeasurably enhanced by more money. I can also tell you—and them—that worrying about it isn't going to make any difference whatsoever. Careful planning is.

My classic story is about a man who has a great many legitimate worries. Yet he has worked out a thought pattern that allows him freedom to live a very active life—something he couldn't do under a heavy work load. Every morning this man lies in bed and thinks of the *worst* thing that could happen to him. Then he says to himself, "No one is trying to shoot me; no one is trying to put me in jail; I have no serious illness. Therefore I shall now leap out of this bed and challenge the day."

Absurd? Probably, but not if it works for him. So if you think it will help you, then imagine the worst. You'll find that your "worst" isn't really all that bad. And better yet, it's curable. By action, *not* by worry.

SAVING MONEY IN THE KITCHEN

I have a French friend, an elegant woman, who says most American women put their mink coats down the garbage disposal. What does she mean by this? Simply that as a thrifty housewife she feels American women waste food. By careful food management they could save enough money to buy what they now consider unattainable luxuries.

In many ways my friend is absolutely correct. We have been "programmed" to buy the item requiring the least amount of time, whether it's packaged food, no-iron shirts or plant seedlings for the garden. We must also have those other time-savers: An electric coffeepot, an electric can opener, blender, and crockpot. In the bedroom an electric blanket, heating pad and shoe buffer. And in the bathroom are our electric curlers, or hair dryer, our Waterpik and our shaver.

No, I am not going to suggest you give all luxuries up in the interest of saving money, repair bills and energy. It's too late, isn't it? But you can think about them, and realize that they *may* be timesavers, but you are paying dearly.

SAVING MONEY ON CLOTHES

I can just hear you moaning, "But I don't spend *anything* on myself." Face it, dear, you *do* buy clothes, so why not listen to a few hints painstakingly collected.

Clothing Sales. I know that you are supposed to be able to buy that designer gown for 40 per cent off at the big post-holiday clearance sale, not to mention shoes, slacks, and handbags. I used to go down each year clutching my sale announcement in my hand. But I got tired of finding hostess dresses in size 34½, slacks in size 6, and shoes in 8AAA.

But then I'm not a shopper. I don't spend enough time in stores to know the merchandise and to be able to tell, in fact, if the sales goods are a bargain at all. Here, however, are the secret battle plans of a friend who is an A Number 1 first class sale shopper.

1. *Know your salesgirl:* Visit the stores you like often enough to know the merchandise and make friends with a salesgirl or buyer. When the sale day arrives, your friend can have your garment spotted—or even partially hidden —so you won't lose it to a quicker arm.

2. *Try it on:* Remember that sale items are not returnable. One size ten can be cut differently from another, so try everything on. Bring the shoes you plan to wear with the dress or skirt to see how they look.

3. *Check other sizes:* Often a garment is on sale because it was mis-sized. You can tell by looking whether something might fit you. That twelve might be a ten. Look at the tickets, not at the rack indicator. Sales are busy times and garments quickly get hung in the wrong place.

4. *Check the designer floors:* The more expensive the garment, the greater the sale value. Half price on a wool suit is a much greater saving than half off on a cotton blouse. Don't be intimidated by the "French Room" or the "Designer's Boutique." March right in. What are they going to do, throw you out? That haughty saleslady is not trying to embarrass you. She probably looks that way because her feet hurt.

5. *Have alterations done elsewhere:* If you buy slacks that need shortening or a jacket that has to be let out, take it to your neighborhood tailor or dry cleaner. They are usually far less expensive than the store's alteration charges.

Sometimes you can have the store fitter pin the garment for you at no charge. It depends upon how much of a con artist you are.

The great disadvantage to sale shopping is buying that non-returnable impulse item. I have the most gorgeous electric blue evening shoes you've ever seen. But to wear with what? I have a print silk designer's blouse that doesn't match another thing in my closet. Before you head for the sales, know what you want *before* you get there.

The Junior Department. Another secret to department store shopping is to buy from the junior or college section. Sweaters, turtlenecks, slacks, lingerie, shoes—practically any item you can name—all cost less money than comparable merchandise in the women's section. This goes for basement merchandise, too. In the basement you can find near duplicates of a great many garments sold upstairs for one-third more.

Factory Outlet. If you live in a big city (e.g. Los Angeles, New York, Chicago, Dallas) look in the Yellow Pages of your phone book under "Clothing Manufacturers." These local manufacturers usually have a nearby retail store where they sell their seconds (damaged goods), overcuts (too many cut in one style) and end-of-season unsold numbers. It will amaze and distress you to see a sweater for four dollars that you paid twenty-four dollars for in your local uptown department store.

Sewing. If you know how to make your own clothes, you are way ahead of the woman who has to rely entirely on the retail outlets. You can further reduce your spending by buying your fabric on sale. Remnants are another saving. Wholesale fabric companies often have retail outlet stores. If you sew you probably know all these things already.

I do, however, have a message for the home sewer. Do not sacrifice style and chic. Too many women who make their own clothes fall into the gimmick trap: covered buttons, contrasting piping, bows, fabric belts, matching hats—you know what I mean—that loving-hands-at-home look. Put attractive leather buttons on a wool dress; a narrow gold stretch-belt on your slacks; a straw hat with your summer suit.

Thrift Shops. I was initiated into the cult of thrift-shop shoppers by an English noblewoman who was my house guest. I had always felt that the moment *I* walked into the Symphony Resale Shoppe I would see someone I knew. Then what would I do? My British friend had the perfect answer. "Why, you say good afternoon, of course." Of course.

Every large city—and small town for that matter—has a Junior League or Assistance League thrift shop, a private or Catholic school bargain store—not to mention the private entrepreneurs offering seconds-to-go. These stores are treasure troves once you decide to venture in. Most of the dresses, skirts and suits are in there because the hemlines went up or down, but there's nothing wrong with the slacks, sweaters, evening dresses, and hostess skirts. Check the scarves, handbags, jewelry, and active sports clothes such as ski pants and tennis dresses.

Real Thrift Shops. My youngest son, who is a thrift shop expert *cum laude,* says that the *real* buys are at the Goodwill, Salvation Army, St. Vincent de Paul, and at garage sales. He prides himself on the fact that nothing on his person cost over twenty-five cents. Before you turn me in to the juvenile authorities let me say that he is nineteen and this is *all* his idea. On his way back to college after Christmas he decided to take a train to the town nearest his college. From there he planned to go on by bus. (He really is a different kid.) His train was delayed on a siding for ten hours. When he got to the bus station, he had to spend the night there. Being aware of the part of town in which they locate these stations, I was frantic when he told me this on the phone.

"Not to worry, Mom," he said. "Some of the old guys in there gave me great tips on where to get some clothes."

I'm certainly not recommending that you look like a ragamuffin. I mention these stores only to those of you who can go in freely, with an air of abandon, jauntily finger the goods, and not say in a loud voice, *Who* would wear such clothes! These stores serve a very necessary purpose. Maybe yours.

Your Own Style. I have found *my* secret to dressing. I've developed my *own* style that doesn't depend on Paris, Seventh Avenue, *Vogue*, or *Women's Wear Daily*. I couldn't afford to be *haute couture* anyway. My style could probably be called "Ethnic Abandon." I like articles of wearing apparel from other countries which were not necessarily designed for the purpose to which I put them. I'm talking primarily about non-working or after-hours clothes. You *still* have to conform to standard office regalia during the day, but once you're out of that office, what you put on your back should be "you." For me, it's long thoubs and djallabs that I have bought in the souqs (open markets) of Arabia. My job takes me to the Middle East, and I have some treasures that I've picked up for five and ten dollars. Only once have I paid over ten dollars for a caftan, and that was when the American ambassador invited me to dinner in Abu Dhabi. I was awed to the point of spending forty dollars for an incredibly beautiful sky-blue dress all embroidered in white but which would certainly have cost triple that price anywhere else.

A great deal of my ethnic clothing was originally made for men. I bought the shirt and pantaloons the Pakistani workmen wear, and the tight pants the Indian houseboys use. I bought a white disdash—the Arab man's national dress—and wear it as a housecoat.

You don't have to go to Arabia to find terrific ethnic clothes. Most big cities have Mexican and South American stores, and don't forget Chinatown and Japantown. Those stores also have satchels and totes that you can use as handbags. I used to carry a school lunchbox for a purse—until my insecure teenagers hid it from me. Now they would think it was kitsch.

I have another friend whose style is "the forties." She has made a study of the era and knows just what funky stores cater to "forties freaks." There she buys her wide-shoulder suits and crepe dresses. Another woman I know always looks like a Parisian waif. You know *that* look. You don't have to pick a category; you can create your own. It takes a little time, but it also takes little money. Why not develop your own style? After all, you're not dressing for "him" any more.

Swaps and Hand-Me-Overs. If you have a good friend (preferably in another town) who is your size, arrange to swap certain articles of clothing with her. You get the same lift from wearing your friend's sweater as you would from a new one. After all, it's new to you. Another way to save is to ask a well-dressed married friend (your size) what she does with her old clothes. Why not? She's your friend and she will be flattered. More important, she'll probably send you some things you can really use.

Hand-me-overs are particularly helpful when you have growing children. When mine were small they went to a church school and we had a "uniform swap" that was a life-saver. You might even organize such a swapping service in your town. Most youngsters outgrow their clothes before they wear them out.

SAVING MONEY IN THE HOUSE

It always frosted me to read the glossy home magazines and see a sparkling green-and-white living room with the caption: "How She Furnished This Room on $1,500." When you read the small print you find out that marvelous coffee table is made out of a campaign chest they "found" in the attic; that the bookcases were made by the husband with his power tools in his basement workshop; that the Tiffany light came straight out of a kit and a class at night school; that the shag carpeting was a mill end; and that the antique wicker furniture had been a garage sale bonanza they carted home and sprayed white.

The divorced woman reading this snickers to herself. All she recovered in her attic was a nest of spiders. As far as those swell bookcases are concerned, well, even when she *had* a husband, he wouldn't have known a power tool from an electric mixer. And who has time to make a Tiffany lamp or drive clear down to the carpet mill to get that super remnant! Wicker furniture at a garage sale? That must have been *some* neighborhood!

The point of this is, of course, that for me to point out how you can save money furnishing your home is ludicrous. You'll have to make do with what you have because *few* divorced women's budgets allow for new or even used furniture. My one big tip is to get a clever friend in to cast an eye on what you have. Just a new arrangement of your living room furniture can give you a lift. Another no-cost hint is to change rooms. Put your two daughters in your big bedroom and take their smaller room. Or let your son have the dining room and put a table in the kitchen or living room. In other words, make your house fit *you*—not the other way around.

Household Purchases. The time does come when you will have to replace sheets, towels, dishes and so forth. Do this during the after-Christmas sales. A great many stores send out catalogues which show you pictures and colors as well as give prices. To avoid the temptation of the impulse item, order by mail or over the phone. This is also a terrific timesaver. If you can't wait for sales, buy seconds. This could be a sheet with a barely discernible flaw. Or shop the basements of the large department stores.

For dishes, pots, and pans, try garage sales in the neighborhood. I've found iron skillets that you can't find anywhere else. And teapots. And measuring cups. And breadboxes. Also try the thrift shops and junk stores. As they say: "One man's junk is another man's treasure."

Household Repairs. Nothing wipes out the old budget like a washing machine repair or a leaky roof. This requires the services (costly) of someone who knows what he is doing. When I was a homeowner I got my best plumbers, electricians, and painters through our local fire department. Many firemen do these jobs in their off hours and for less money. You may get a flat "no" when you call, because not *all* firemen moonlight. In such a case, check with your neighbors for their recommendations.

College students also are a valuable source of help. What one can't do, his or her friend can. I am amazed at the skilled young people who are reviving so many of the ancient crafts:

leaded glass and stained-glass windows; fine custom cabinet work; hand-made furniture; hand painted pottery. I think it is in some ways a reaction to our terribly materialistic culture. At best it represents a return to doing work you love rather than accepting a job because it is "impressive."

If you do happen to remodel your kitchen or add a bathroom, let me suggest that you visit the wreckers to look for the fixtures. You can find perfectly good ovens, toilets, towel bars, light fixtures and hardware. It's a great experience if you've never been to a wrecker's retail yard. You can often find marvelous antiques such as claw-foot bathtubs and French doors.

Another good source of such items is carload sales. Here an entire shipment from the manufacturer is offered at reduced prices. But just as with buying clothes, you should shop around first so you will have something to compare.

Saving Money on Yourself. Practically every town of any size has a beauty school. There, on certain days, you can have your hair done free. Sometimes the set isn't the last word, but so what. It's a pleasure to lean back and have someone else wash your hair. On other days the services are not free, but they are always way below the market. Treat yourself to a facial or a manicure. At the prices they charge, it's a great bargain and good for your sagging ego.

If you have a dental college in your town you can get your dental work done quite reasonably. The instructors supervise, so you are not going to get drilled in the wrong tooth. If you have a child who needs orthodontia, see if you can get it done through the college. The county hospitals with a large staff of interns give medical aid for a reasonable price. Each area varies, so be sure to check it all out *before* you need help.

Another sure way to save money on yourself is to avoid your problem zone. Each one of us has an area of spending that could almost be deemed foolish. For one woman it's a passion for shoes. She will buy a pair of shoes when she knows she can't truly afford them and doesn't really need them. Another woman woman simply can't pass the cosmetic counter without buying that new jar of wrinkle cream or the latest face bronzer. For another woman it's cookbooks, house plants, or needlepoint kits. You know where your weakness is, so the best defense is to avoid it.

SAVING MONEY ON TRANSPORTATION

One definition of a car could be: a machine that eats money. Certainly it is a grand convenience and a joy to have, but it also can be more trouble and expense than it's worth. If you live in an area with good local transportation, seriously consider selling your car. Not only would you be saving on the gas and repair bills, but just consider how much you would save on insurance and parking tickets!

Even if you are a person who can't possibly imagine life without a car, you can cut down on its use. Save all your errands for one day. Teach your children how to use the bus. Designate certain days as No Car days and leave Old Nellie in the garage. Gradually you will ease off on your dependency.

How to Market Without a Car. Walk or take a bus to the market, then call a cab to take you home. (Remember, you shop only once a week now.) Some markets will deliver free if you come into the store, pick out everything and pay for it. A market which both selects and delivers usually makes it up in the prices it charges.

When I lived in Los Angeles I arranged a market car pool with three friends. Saturday morning the four of us (in one car) would drive to downtown Los Angeles to the huge central market, which is a collection of independent vendors all under one roof. We would split up because we each had our favorite fruit and vegetable man, our favorite butcher and our favorite cheese stall. At noon we would meet at the Mexican restaurant next door for tostados and cold beer.

You can call a friend in your neighborhood and do the same thing. It turns a boring event into an outing—and keeps your car in the garage. If you don't have a car, offer to pay for a cab on the day it's your turn to drive. Another idea is to hire a teenager with a car to do the marketing for you.

Helen is a divorced woman without a car, living in New Jersey. She has solved her marketing problem by arranging to shop at night with a date. The man has to market, so she simply suggests they do it together. Since most single men hate the task, they welcome her company. She can tell them which pears are ripe, how to pick out a chicken and what to do with an eggplant. She also knows the best places to shop and where to find the bargains.

How to Shop Without a Car. Catalogues are marvelous periodicals. You can buy anything by mail except liquor, firearms, and regulated drugs. The Sears, Roebuck catalogue used to be called The Dream Book, and to a large segment of the population I'm sure it was. The modern equivalent of the giant catalogue is the store mailer. You can order all your household needs and children's clothing without leaving your living room.

Newspaper ads are another way to shop without a car. Simply call up and have whatever you want sent out. Shopping by mail or phone helps you buy *only* what you need. You're not tempted by the new summer handbags on your way to the towel and sheet department.

If you work in a downtown area, shop on your lunch hour. Walk through the stores instead of having that salami and Swiss cheese on a French roll. Most large stores deliver, so you can have your purchase sent to your home.

How to Get Around Without a Car. After having written a novel which deals with the energy crisis, it is my feeling that we all may eventually be required to use public transportation, so why not start now? If you can't quit driving "cold turkey," do it gradually. Learn the bus routes. Start a marketing co-op. Take the train into the city. Send your kids to the dentist by bus. Take a cab to a dinner party. No matter what you spend on public transportation, it can't be equal to what you spend on a car.

MANAGING MONEY

Managing the money you have is often more difficult than earning it. To get the maximum from every dollar is an art. We often hear "saving" referred to as an "old fashioned" virtue. With today's society based on the plastic charge cards and the revolving payment plans, we are encouraged from every corner to spend, spend, spend.

Debt is a debilitating state to be in. When you owe money you simply are not your own woman. You are hampered in your work by the worry of payments. You are paying dearly in interest. You feel defeated. If you have serious debt problems, I urge you to sit down with someone whose financial judgment you value and work out a budget plan. Living on a money budget gives you a sense of accomplishment. If you know *where* you stand and *where* you are headed, you absolutely will get there. Without a plan you could quite possibly wallow in the never-never land of instability for the rest of your life.

Savings Accounts. If you don't have an account with a savings and loan, open one immediately. Choose one that is near your home and has postage-paid saving-by-mail, free traveler's checks, free banking (at a nearby bank) and free safe deposit boxes. If you can't get all of these services, get as many as you can. Some services require a minimum balance, but you'll qualify eventually, so you want the services there when you're ready for them. Check around. The important thing, though, is to decide on one and open the account. Get a pass book and a mail-in envelope.

The habit of saving money starts gradually, but soon you get enchanted by seeing all those little five- and ten-dollar deposits add up. Soon you would rather make an entry in your savings account than buy yourself a new lipstick. At least that's the hoped-for result.

After you open the account, decide on a given amount that

you are going to deposit from each pay check. If you get paid weekly, then make it a small amount, say five dollars, but that means *every time* you get a paycheck you are going to send a five dollar check to your account at the S&L.

When you make up a household budget, make a pact with yourself that if you spend less in one area than you thought you would, the money goes in the savings account. Ask your family to give you money instead of presents for Christmas and your birthday. If you get a raise, stick to your same budget and put the extra money into the account.

Treat that money as if it didn't exist. It is there for a grand purpose—not to be pulled out for even a minor emergency. That's one reason you shouldn't choose a S&L near your work. It's too handy. Having it near your home allows for that genuine emergency. Most S&L's are open until six and on Saturdays.

Charge Accounts. As some great sage once said: "We are mastered by our gadgets, victims of our luxuries and prisoners of our debts." Therefore I suggest to you—close all charge accounts! Immediately. If you can't bring yourself to do that, at least take all those demon plastic cards and hide them somewhere . . . between the springs and mattress of your bed . . . between the pages of your dictionary . . . in the back of your linen closet. Anywhere where it will be an effort to reach them. It's when they are in our handbags that the trouble starts.

Just think what a great freedom it would be each month *not* to have to face that stack of window envelopes. No more: IG-NORE THIS REMINDER IF PAYMENT HAS BEEN SENT. An end to the lethal: STOP! YOU MAY NO LONGER USE THIS ACCOUNT! We have become almost immune to the dun of the credit office. We pay a little, very little, on the account giving us the most trouble, and plan to use a *different* card the next month.

The stores love it! Do you know that most department stores get 18 per cent interest? Selling anything is almost a sideline. They are the new moneylenders in front of the temple. Remember this the next time you push through that revolving door. Revolving credit is designed to make you pay once-and-a-half for an item that was probably not worth once!

Credit Cards. If you are in a business in which you take people to lunch and need records, obtain a Master Charge, Visa or American Express credit card, but use it only for business. Don't be tempted to put those home or personal items on it. You will be starting that same vicious cycle of the revolving payments.

One good feature of the credit card is that it is most helpful when cashing checks. For this reason alone it is worth securing. If you have a job with a dependable income, you should be eligible for a major credit card. If you have any problems or are turned down, ask to see the manager of your bank. Tell him or her your problem and ask for suggestions and help.

The woman's movement has called attention to the unfair practice of denying women credit. No one wants the publicity of being called "discriminatory." Remember this when applying for a credit card. If you are a working woman you have a *right* to the same privileges of credit as a working man.

PROVIDING FOR YOURSELF

You are now the lady of the house. There is *no man* of the house. You are solely responsible for you: today, tomorrow and a year from tomorrow. You have to know how to take care of what you have. You have to find out how to protect yourself. You have to have some idea of how to plan for the future.

Insurance. Most divorced women operate on such a day-to-day existence that when someone mentions insurance they throw up their hands in horror. Insurance! Who understands insurance? Well, you should, for one. Do not be baffled by insurance. Nobody says you have to know *all* about it. There are dozens of insurance agents out there who know all about it and will explain it to you.

Your Home. If you own your own home and it is not paid for, the mortgage company frequently requires you to carry casualty insurance on the house to protect their investment. Find out if this policy covers your personal property: furniture, art, jewelry, clothing. If it doesn't, talk to an insurance person and find out the least expensive way to increase your coverage to include these items.

There is a policy you can take out called mortgage insurance. In the event of your death the remainder of the mortgage on your home will be paid in full. This may or may not be worth the extra premium. If you have children, the house would probably be sold anyway in the event of your death.

Your Car. If you are buying your car on time, the loan company requires insurance coverage to protect their investment. The state in which you live also has minimum insurance regulations. Find out what they are. Shop for auto insurance. Because we are so fearful of being sued it is easy to get "overinsured" and strap ourselves with large premium payments. Carry insurance in keeping with *your* net worth. Don't insure yourself as if you were Mr. Rockefeller.

Your Health. The *best* medical plans are the ones privately handled by your employer. When you *accept* a job, ask about medical and hospital coverage. If you are in a job where this type of plan is not available, you might consider joining one of the national organizations. Investigate several, thoroughly, before you sign up.

A good person to ask about medical plans is your doctor. Or better yet, your doctor's nurse. She is the one who fills out the forms, so she knows which companies pay and which don't.

Your Life. There are mixed feelings about life insurance. Personally I feel it's a good idea for a husband and wife to insure each other. When one dies, the other has some immediate help. I wonder, however, how valid it is for the divorced woman to insure herself. Certainly we all want to leave our children something, but not at the expense of a financial burden on ourselves. Raising children takes a tremendous investment of time and money. If we give our children a good childhood and help through college, I feel we've done our job financially.

To hear the argument in favor of life insurance, I suggest you read one of the many books available on the subject of women and money. I also suggest that you talk to two or three agents. You are as intelligent as the person selling the policy. If he or she can understand it, so can you. Do not be intimidated. Ask all the questions you can. Yes, even dumb, stupid questions. Remember, you're the *buyer!*

Wills. Before we move on to the depressing subject of wills, let's talk about attitude. Too many divorced women put off all this planning and investigation because they feel it's only a matter of time until they are remarried and then *he* can worry about all that. Don't let this happen to you! Nothing is for certain in this world. Put your house in order yourself because it's *your* house, *your* life. Even if you do remarry, you have a vital interest in this aspect of your life and you should know what's going on. It's ironic how easy some of these things are once you break through the mystique of money. The more competent you become, the less risk you will run of remarrying for the *wrong* reasons.

Now for wills. Everyone needs one. Go to the lawyer who handled your divorce—or some lawyer you know and have dealt with—and tell him you want a will drawn. The procedure and form are simple when you do it through a lawyer. It is also official.

YOUR ESTATE

If you are a divorced woman who has inherited money or been awarded a substantial divorce settlement, I assume you have people close to you who can advise you. Listen to what they say but do yourself the biggest favor in the world. Get smart about money. Learn to handle what you have yourself!

Stocks and Bonds. If you have a portfolio of stocks but you are not intimately acquainted with the stock market, call the largest broker in your city and ask when they will be giving the next seminar on the stock market. If they don't offer this free service, ask them who does. At this point, if the person on the other end of the phone is on his or her toes, you will be invited into *their* office to visit their counselor. Go. It's all free and informative.

Check your local night classes. There is usually one given on investments. I was checking out our local city college the other day and they even offered a class in How To Read *The Wall Street Journal*. It is truly amazing what is available. There is absolutely *no reason* to be uninformed today on any subject that interests you.

Real Property. It used to be that in a divorce the wife was awarded the home. Today the trend is toward "dividing" the house, which means it has to be sold in order to split the money. If you were fortunate enough to receive your home, then you own "real property." Now it's up to you to support it. If you can't keep up the payments, taxes, and insurance from what you make, consider selling your home. You certainly don't want to go into debt to support your life-style.

If you do decide to sell your home, do *not* spend the proceeds. Invest it in another piece of property or put it in your savings account. Lump sums of money are *very* hard to come by and once they're gone . . . they're gone. You should live on what you earn. If you don't, then you had better cut back because you are living over your head. When you use principal— or accumulated money—you are in essence going into debt.

I am certainly no financial genius, but it seems to me that owning income property is a desirable aim. The world of real estate investment, however, is one you do not understand overnight. It takes time to learn. Your best teacher and ally is a good real estate broker, but don't stop there. Augment what you learn from your broker by reading at least one good book on the subject.

Owning an apartment house, a store, or a medical building is one of the best insurance policies in the world. You are now in charge of your life and it is up to you to plan for your future. When you invest in income property and let the payments go toward reducing the loan, you are creating an endowment for yourself. When you retire, the income from the property can help support you.

This is not wishful thinking or a dream with little reality. It is possible, entirely possible! Don't put limits on yourself by saying what you can and cannot do. Of course you'll start small, but the important thing is to start. You know why so many women don't accomplish anything? Because they don't aim. You have to *plan* success. It happens to very few unexpectedly—or overnight.

Eleanor is a divorced woman in Michigan. Because of the duration of her marriage she was awarded the family home. Her two boys were in college at the time of her divorce and she was teaching school part time. She decided that she would sell her home and get a smaller place. She began reading ads and going to open houses. One Sunday she visited a small, two-bedroom home that she particularly liked and started talking to the saleswoman who was "sitting" the house.

From this chance meeting came a new life for Eleanor. The real estate saleswoman was herself divorced and she suggested to Eleanor that she consider a duplex or a triplex. This way, she explained, part of the monthly payment would be carried by her tenants. Eleanor became fascinated with the idea and spent a great deal of time looking not only at duplexes but at all manner of income property. After she made her choice, a charming old home that had been converted into five small apartments, she decided to go to real estate school and become a licensed saleswoman.

Eleanor did extremely well in school, joined her friend's firm, and quit teaching school. When her youngest son finished college he joined the firm. A year later, her older son, who was dissatisfied with his job, suggested that the three of them open an office together. Eleanor said she wanted to call their firm Burroughs and Mother, but the boys decided on Burroughs and Sons. They have all done extremely well and over the years Eleanor has parlayed her five small apartments into a twelve-story building.

Money. If you received a cash settlement in your divorce, run, do not walk, to the nearest savings and loan and open an account. Do not touch the money if at all possible. Pretend it doesn't exist. Organize your life as if it wasn't there. Plan your budget based on your salary and live on it. If you don't have a job, get one.

When you feel you are on an even keel, then, and only then, should you think about what to do with the money. Consider buying certificates of deposit; look into municipal bonds; consider investment property. But don't *do* anything until you have given it a great deal of thought. Above all, *don't* spend it.

Money and Men. Now we come to a knotty problem that most women with money—a little or a lot—hate to face. A motivated working woman with assets is a target for hustlers. That may be the wrong word, because you can usually spot the obvious hustlers. The men I mean are the ones who will do any manner of deed to part you from your money. They will wine you and dine you to try to sell you something: stocks, bonds, insurance, real estate, a boat, a car or a smart little condominium in Baja. The only defense against this "legitimate" salesperson is knowledge—knowing of who *he* is and the worth of what he's selling. Even then, do *not* accept business dates. Tell him you'll see him in his office.

Less obvious is the man whose lot in life is not as secure as yours. His apartment is not inviting. Yours is. He hates to cook. You happen to be a gourmet chef. He doesn't have a car, but you do. He's often short, so you pay. And pay. And pay. If this describes a relationship you recognize, then understand it for what it is. You're independent. He's dependent. And it is *not* going to change. As long as you *give* he will *take*.

To me this is a high price to pay for companionship. I'm talking about the chronic sponge, not the man who has had a bout of bad luck and is trying to put his life in order. There is a big and obvious difference. The man who sees you as a soft berth—a patsy—is a user and is after a share of what you have.

Frances is a decorator for a large department store. She is a very attractive woman in her middle fifties. Her constant companion is a man named Stewart. No one is quite sure what he does. He is always in evidence at her parties, uses her car while she's at work, and charges his clothes on her account. One day I asked her why she allows herself to be taken advantage of by this man. She seemed surprised at my question and said, "But Stewart never asks for money!"

Clever Stewart. He's getting plenty without committing the fatal blunder of asking for cash money. That usually wakes up the tigress in any woman. He is playing a game that allows Frances to lie to herself in order to live with herself.

If a man should ask you for money, a loan, a sum to tide him over, absolutely refuse. Tell him you've known too many friendships that were ruined by borrowing and lending and you have made it a rule never to do either. This is a rule you have lived by for a good many years and you never abridge or amend it. Period.

Children and Money. What mother hasn't sacrificed to give her child something he or she wants, or needs, or greatly admires? We all do it. It is a joy to be able to *give* to our children. There is, however, a tendency in some children to be con artists and work their mothers for all they're worth. To let yourself be taken advantage of is just as wrong for the child as it is for you.

Carol is a nurse in Chicago who makes enough money to support herself. She lives in a nice home outside town which she received free and clear in her divorce settlement. Her one son, Jeff, is twenty-two. When he entered college, at eighteen, his father paid his tuition and books. With his part-time job and an allowance from his mother, Jeff has managed to live. But not on the scale he thought he deserved.

At twenty, at the completion of his second year, Jeff told his father that he was not going back to college unless he received more money. His father replied that he couldn't do more than he was doing. Jeff went to his mother. He told her he wanted to quit his part-time job and enjoy his college life, move into a fraternity house and be like the other guys. Unless he could do this, he said, he was going to drop out of school and join the Army.

Jeff played on his mother's guilt. He told her that if she had stayed married, he wouldn't have to be "working" his way through college. It wasn't fair that he was being punished for something that was not his fault. Can't you just hear him saying all those words that break a mother's heart? Carol's solution was to rent her home, furnished, with all the things she loved, and take a small room near the hospital. The rental money she gave to Jeff. Has she helped him? Of course not. He will always be running back for more. She is robbing him of the chance to stand on his own two feet.

In closing the grand subject of money, let me say this: *Security is the great illusion.* From childhood, a girl is reared with the idea of marrying a fine boy with ambition, because that is security. No, madam, it is not. No man is security. Every man is as vulnerable and as susceptible as every woman. A rich man can lose his money. A talented man can be fired from his job. A healthy man can be injured or disabled. A man can change his mind or lose his mind. A man can be run over crossing the street.

The only security in this world is your ability to take care of yourself! Not only is that security, but it is the greatest freedom of them all.

5

Living

and the Divorced Woman

How anyone else is living is of no concern to you. From now on you are going to pick a life-style that is all yours. Certainly how and where you live is going to depend on the ages and number of your children, your job, your finances, your health (both mental and physical) and your inventiveness. One thing you should *stop* doing, however, is living in the future. It is so easy for the divorced woman to defer living until her children are grown, or her job improves, or she remarries. I'm reminded of a woman I met, Alicia, a very attractive woman of forty-two with five teen-agers. At the time of her divorce she lived in one of the nicest sections of Los Angeles. After her divorce she decided to take her children and move back to the Bay Area. Instead of picking one of the communities within a reasonable distance of San Francisco, she picked the last house on top of the highest hill in Marin County, which is across the Golden Gate Bridge.

What happened to her is that she became a chauffeur. Every errand, every appointment, every social engagement her children arranged meant that she was forced behind the wheel of her car. Her older two children now have licenses, which has helped, except that she constantly finds herself stuck on top of her hill without a car. I met a very attractive man who had dated her twice and although he told me he enjoyed her company, he said he found her G.U. (Geographically Unacceptable.)

When I asked Alicia why she had put herself in this situation, she said she felt at the time of her move that it would be simpler and better for the children if they were raised in the country. But she didn't pick "real" country, which I could have understood. She picked a very married community of lovely homes, each on their own acre of ground. There was not an apartment house in sight. So naturally there were _not_ going to be any single men or women within miles. She is not only G.U. for a social life but she is G.U. for a job, for enjoying the many cultural activities of San Francisco, for meeting a wide range of people from various age and interest groups. She is "deferring" _her_ living until her children are all off to college.

No one can criticize a mother's desire to do what is best for her children. In Alicia's case, hers was an unnecessary sacrifice. It is my feeling that a woman who has a business life and a social life of her own makes a more interesting and competent mother. The stay-at-home mom often loses contact with her children. She becomes a drudge, a fixture around the house who cares more about the condition of her kitchen floor than the condition of her local government. In other words her spectrum of involvement is limited. This type of woman isn't any more interesting to children than she is to adults.

Alicia is not a typical divorced woman. She has income from private funds which allows her to sit on her mountain top. I only mention her to illustrate that if you are contemplating arranging your life solely to benefit your children, don't do it. For _their sake_ as well as yours.

There is really no truth to the phrase "in the right place at the right time." The secret to successful living is to make where you are the right place and now the right time. There also are no rules any more about how you _should_ live. Women have always had a tendency to manipulate—and be manipulated by—approval. It was always known to our mothers, aunts, and grandmothers _which_ was the best section of town. Fathers, uncles, and husbands were pushed to make more money to go into that part of town. And once there, the ground rules were strictly adhered to.

I sincerely believe we are on our way to outgrowing these notions. Today we tend to live where we want to—and the way we want to. When we lose this neurotic need for approval, this fear of censure, we will have taken a giant step forward. As a divorced woman you are the head of your household and you don't have to justify, explain, or defend how you live, how you operate, how you spend your time.

CREATIVE LIVING

Your main thrust now is to *expand* your life. By taking on new interests you increase your potential in every area of living. New people pass into your life. You increase your ability to work, to earn money. You add to your children's storehouse of knowledge and increase their opportunities. You open the way for even *greater* development.

All creative living begins with imagination. Why do you suppose the romantic Gothic novel is so popular? Because it plays on our suppressed emotions. We, the readers, supply the missing link; the power to visualize and imagine! Pretend for a moment that you are the writer of one of these novels and in it you are going to create your imaginative dream world. Think about it. Just how *do* you picture yourself? Surrounded by luxury? Living in a foreign country? Owning a town house in Georgetown? Well, that won't do. If you are going to *write* a description of your ideal life, then you have to be specific. The same thing applies to living it.

I learned the basic rule of fiction writing when I wrote my first novel. That rule is: There Are No Birds. There are robins, eagles, swallows. There are two white doves on the slate roof of the cathedral not a couple of birds on top of the church. You see what I mean? All a novelist *has* is words. All you have is your one lifetime. So specialize. Don't live with the birds; live with the peacocks and the parrots.

How do you specify your life? The same way you classify a bird. To go back to your description of your ideal life, how do you see yourself? Define it. Do you see yourself living in a seventeen-room villa in Palm Beach, or owning a six-unit apartment house or baking bread in a mountain lodge. Think about *what you want*.

If you picture yourself living in a foreign country, which country? Spain, Sweden, Australia? Do you sincerely want to move out of the United States or were you just being colorful? Be specific. Now sit down and start writing again. This time from the heart.

When you develop your own imaginative way of living, doing the unexpected or unusual, caring not for fads and fashion, it may be said that you have developed style. Style depends far more on imagination (*that* word again) than on money. You aren't breaking rules; you're ignoring them. You aren't seeking after the pace setters; you're too busy projecting your own individuality.

I realize that the freedom to arrange your own life is an awesome responsibility. Just look at it this way. Divorce is a jolt, a jolt that should break up your chain of frozen ideas. To help you decide on that perfect life-style, let's examine the options open to you. They are truly limitless.

Do read through these descriptions with an open mind. Remember you are setting the pace and where you live is *your* decision. Later we will discuss the pros and cons of moving, but for now pretend you are researching a life-style for your heroine.

1. *City Life.* By cities I mean large metropolitan areas with bookstores, coffeehouses, and French restaurants, a Middle Eastern deli, boutiques, cheese stores and poster shops. All the wonderful places that make up for the lack of a garden, no parking, bad schools, high crime, and much noise.

Cities offer a wide range of jobs, training schools, and cultural activities. They also offer streamlined apartment-house living. They offer good metropolitan transportation and the opportunity to be *really* different. You can live in an old Victorian house in San Francisco, a studio in Greenwich Village, a town-house apartment in Philadelphia.

I would not suggest a move to the city if you have very young children. If you have teen-agers and can find a good public school[1] or afford a private one, I see no objection. If you have high school or college-age children, they'll love the city as much as you will. If you have no children at home (or no children), I assume you're already there!

2. *Suburbs.* Suburbs are basically small towns located within commuting distance of a large city. They offer the same job opportunities as any small to medium town: teaching, nursing, medicine, dentistry, law, accounting, secretarial work, sales, real estate. They have some good restaurants, branches of the big department stores, adequate-to-excellent schools, movie houses, bowling alleys, ice cream stores, and nurseries.

Housing consists of the full spectrum of houses, cheap to outrageous, some nice apartments, condominiums, and converted barns and carriage houses.

3. *Country Life.* Country life means living on a farm or a ranch, or in a small rural town not within commuting distance of a large city. If you are on a ranch or a farm your work is predetermined by what you grow or raise: cattle, sheep, chickens, pears, grapes, walnuts. In today's real estate market, people who know say that it is practically impossible to buy an existing ranch or farm and make money. The price of the land is high, high, high. So unless you are already on such a piece of land or will inherit same, you are better off not to attempt this type of life.

That doesn't eliminate the possibility of living in the country. You can rent or buy a house with little land but which borders on a large spread. Or you can live in the rural town. You get the same magnificent feel of spaciousness, clean air, and quiet nights.

The job opportunities would be the same as the suburbs but on a much smaller scale. Let's say you're a third-grade teacher in Detroit and you long for the quiet country. You should certainly investigate teaching in Loveland, Colorado, or Rockland,

[1] Some cities often have one or more excellent public schools.

Wyoming. If country is your prerequisite, there's a lot of it there.

Schools are usually quite far apart in the country and you would have to plan on your children's taking a long bus ride. Small towns have handy schools which are frequently excellent. Opportunities to meet people abound, it's just that there are not too many to meet. Most entertaining is done in homes, so you find few restaurants. Your social life would have to come from church, school, job, and married friends. But believe me, any time there was an available man, you would get to meet him. The people may live far apart, but news travels fast.

4. *Resort or Planned Communities.* This category includes beach communities such as Miami or Malibu: desert communities such as Palm Springs or Scottsdale; mountain communities such as Vail or Stowe. It also includes the new, planned communities in which your rental or purchase price includes golf course, swimming pool, sauna, tennis courts, art lessons, square dancing, and twenty-four-hour security.

Let's discuss resort living first. These communities depend on tourists and second-home people. There is a terrific onslaught of people during the season and an exodus the minute it's over. The support community, however, remains and usually has a very good time off-season. Your job opportunities are relatively the same as they are in the suburbs except there are far more restaurants, dress shops, beauty spas, and bookstores. These jobs could be in jeopardy during the slack months unless, of course, you were the owner of the business.

Schools in resort areas are the same as they are anywhere else. Your social life could pick up during the season, but that could be devastating. Remember those stories we read when growing up, about "summer romance"? Well, you're never too old to be a victim. I don't recommend resort life unless you're a certain kind of woman looking for a certain kind of man. We'll go into that later.

Planned communities started for the young swingles and the retired folks. Now they encourage everyone except people with children under fourteen. Here your entire life is by the numbers —if you want it to be. You can play bridge in the clubroom on

Tuesday night, take lessons in decoupage on Thursday, square dance Friday, go to the barbecue Saturday and take the charter bus to the ball game on Sunday. In addition you have use of the golf course, tennis courts, gym, and sauna. It's a full life.

As for a job, you would have to secure one in the nearest town and hope that your social life didn't leave you too pooped to put in your hours. If you have a set income for life and don't need a job, you might look into one of these communities. I know several people who live in them and absolutely wouldn't live anywhere else. If you have a good job in the community and want to live in that type of environment strictly to use the facilities on your own time and not participate in the group activity, then it can be an outstanding value. Your older children will enjoy it too. Up to a point. It is "programmed communal living" and no matter how hard you try to get away from it, it creeps over into your life.

5. *Big Opportunity Living.* If you are a woman who doesn't care *where* she lives as long as it is in an area with great economic potential, then let me make these four suggestions: Los Angeles, Denver, Houston, Atlanta. According to my in-house financial expert, these four communities are enjoying unprecedented booms. In a boom *all* business flourishes. If you're in an area of high unemployment, it would be worth a trip to any of these four places to check out jobs in your field.

If you are a professional woman and your main goal in life is to get to the very top, then you eventually will have to go to the capital of your field. Publishing—New York. Film—Los Angeles. Advertising—New York. Modeling—New York. Theater —New York, etc. When you have a burning ambition, such things as schools, local transportation, community life always seem to work out because you *want* them to work out.

Another way of approaching where to live is to go where you are needed. I had a woman write to me more than eight years ago to say that she was a trained psychiatric nurse with a great deal of additional experience in the operating theater. When she was married her husband took her to live in a small town in Oklahoma. She went to work in the hospital there a couple days a week just to keep her hand in. When she and her husband were divorced she began working in the hospital full time, but she felt she just wasn't using her capabilities in that very small facility. Her letter to me was asking my advice.

I wrote to her and suggested that she pick out a town or city which she had enjoyed visiting, one that had a large modern hospital, and go there, check into a hotel, walk around the town, then drop in at the hospital and ask to be shown around. If she liked the town and the hospital, I suggested that she apply for a job.

She didn't answer my letter for a month, but after one quick reading I understood why. She had chosen a city in New Mexico. After she toured the town she visited the hospital and when she finished her tour and the head nurse learned why she was there, she rushed her into a washup room and into a uniform. They were desperate for someone with her skills! She stayed for ten days, then went back to Oklahoma to get her sixteen-year-old daughter who was staying with a neighbor. We corresponded for years and the last I heard she had married a scientist in the space program and was completely fulfilled in her work.

6. *Living in a Foreign Country.* Unless you have a job that is sending you to live outside the United States, I would say you have to have a *secure income* (dependable) to chance it on your own. Jobs in foreign countries are hard to find and don't pay very well as a rule. But if you have the income and want to pick up the kids and spend a year in Greece—go. This kind of an experience will benefit all of you. I know a divorced woman from San Diego who took her two children to Italy and lived near Rome for two years. She met a professor on his sabbatical, married him six months later, and went to live in a town in New England. She was ready for whatever life had to offer and went out to meet it head-on.

If you are a divorced woman with no children or grown children, and you would like to work outside the country, you could go to one of the several hundred large American companies with offices around the world. Somehow an "unencumbered" woman is more employable for these jobs than one with children.

HOW TO LIVE

Deciding on the locale is just the first step. Now you have to decide *how* you are going to live.

1. *House.* A large percentage of divorced women with children were living in a house at the time of their divorce. It used to be that the woman almost automatically got the home. As I said, the trend now is to sell the home and divide the money. Unless you are one of the fortunate ones to be awarded the home, you will be looking at alternate modes of housing.

A home is a very nice thing to have if you're married, if you have a good income, or if you own it free and clear. It is a beast to have if you're divorced, struggling to make ends meet, and have mortgage, insurance, and upkeep to pay. On the other hand, you may find that these payments are less than rental payments would be. In addition, you are building equity in your home. Furthermore, inflation is increasing the value of the house enormously. Now might not be the time to sell.

If you have been awarded your home and would like to remain in it, you could consider sharing it with another woman in your similar circumstances. You not only share the expenses but the work and even the babysitting. If you don't think you could handle that type of arrangement, you could rent a room to a college student or retired person. Or you have the option of generating more income to be able to support the house by yourself. Nothing is impossible if you want it badly enough. Remember our heroine. You can design *your ideal* life. That's the first step toward getting it.

2. *Renting a House.* It is easier to rent a home in the suburbs and in small towns than it is in the city. Before you go to the expense of moving, be certain that you have at least a year's lease. It's not just the moving costs, but hooking up the washer and dryer, buying curtains and blinds, bathroom rugs, shelf paper, and all the other expenses.

3. *Apartment or Flat.* With children and dogs, rentals are al-

ways a problem. The first consideration is the neighborhood. It has to have adequate schools and transportation to your work. If possible, try to get near a park or playground. When you arrive home after the children do, it helps if they have someplace to play.

Older buildings and flats have larger rooms than new apartment houses do. You don't get such a cramped feeling when you have high ceilings. Sunny exposures also are good for your mental health. Finding just the right place is a matter of looking and looking and more looking. I don't know anyone who has had much luck with rental services. The best way to do it is by looking at the newspaper ads or simply combing the neighborhoods in which you want to be. Knock on managers' doors and leave your name and number.

4. *Mobile Homes.* Trailer parks (as I keep calling them) have come into their own in California. They are being built with tennis courts and swimming pools and for the most part are beautifully kept. The streets are paved and the lawns mowed. The way most of them operate is that you buy (or rent) a trailer and the park owner rents you space. Sometimes you can rent or buy a mobile home already in place. Like the structured communities, many parks will not allow children under fourteen. But those who will have safe places to ride tricycles. And you could certainly find available baby sitters.

5. *Boats.* In some harbors you are allowed to live on your boat, with certain restrictions. Most dock owners require that you use showers and bathrooms on shore. I've known several single men to live on their boats and love it. For a while. I also know a couple in their sixties who sold their home and all their belongings and moved on board their sailboat. They think it's the most fun they've ever had and can't imagine why they waited so long.

I don't feel that this would be a safe place for small children. Older children would object to the cramped quarters, and not being able to play their stereos at all hours. Noise carries on the water and your neighbors are one jump away. But if you are a boating person and happened to win custody of a thirty-six-foot

Chris-Craft, why not move aboard? It certainly cuts down on the housekeeping! And think of the interesting people you'd meet.

6. *Houseboats.* I covet a houseboat I saw for sale in Sausalito, California—an absolute dream of an A-frame with a loft bedroom and deck above, and a big living room and bar-kitchen below. It was anchored in a long row of houseboats with a wide lawn in front and a locked iron gate. What a place, I thought, for a lady writer with grown children away in college!

Houseboats are not readily available in most areas, but where they are, do check into them. They may not be a place for small children and they are usually too small for other than weekend visitors. The initial cost of a houseboat is low. You will, however be required to pay dockage, just as you do for a boat. But no property taxes!

7. *Other.* There are still other options: mountain cabins, communes, or tents in the desert. It's up to you. You don't have to answer to anyone any more. Remember that.

HOW TO DECIDE IF YOU SHOULD MOVE TO A NEW LOCALE

The advantages of moving should outweigh the disadvantages, or at least equal them. It would be rather foolish to abandon your present location on the off-chance that it will be better somewhere else. You can't run away from problems, loneliness, or sad memories. They go too. Moving should always be *toward* a goal, not a retreat from a loss.

One way to test your reasons for moving is to make a list of all that you would be leaving behind:

1. Your present home
2. Your friends and family
3. Your children's school and their friends
4. Your job

5. Your familiar surroundings
6. Your community identity
7. Your lawyer, dentist, and doctor
8. Your church
9. Your local merchants and service people
10. Your ex-husband

These are all valid reasons to stay where you are. If you have family in the area, you will miss their company and the help they give you. It's always a chore to leave a settled home and enter the world of crates and packing boxes. You'll miss your friends and your children will miss theirs. It's hard work breaking into a new job, new routines. You also know your way around where you live, which freeway gets you out of town, which cleaner hand-blocks sweaters. Your bank knows you. Because you were president of the PTA two years ago, the community knows you. You have an understanding gynecologist, and your son is an altar boy at church. The produce man saves ripe avocados for you, and the washing-machine repairman said he could keep your machine alive another year.

This brings us to item 10—your ex-husband. Let's discuss him for a minute because you need to be lucid and level-headed on the subject. As much as you wish never to see him again, as desperately as you wish he would get a heart attack for dating that twenty-two-year-old model, he is your ex-husband and the father of your children. He may strongly object to your moving or he may be equally glad to see you leave. Remember that you are adding a big expense item to your lives and that is transporting the little darlings back and forth. You run the danger of his not going to the trouble of seeing the children because *you* moved them out of town. It's a known fact—out of sight, out of mind. You may also have added difficulty getting your support checks. This doesn't mean you can't move. Of course you can. Just beware of exactly what you are leaving behind.

Now let's look at what you are moving to:

1. A better or more interesting place to live
2. A chance to meet new friends or be nearer your family

3. A better school for your children and an opportunity for them to meet new friends
4. A greater career opportunity
5. A more interesting and varied environment
6. A chance for greater involvement
7. Expanded medical and dental services
8. A new church
9. Diversified shopping
10. Leaving the old boy to his cupcake

TESTING THE WATER

If you have gone over these lists and feel that you can definitely improve your situation by moving, check out your proposed new town or city *very carefully*. If you have three or four possible candidates, do the same for each location.

Plan to go the area and stay with a friend or check into a hotel. If it's within driving distance of your present residence, by all means drive. You'll need your car. If it isn't within driving distance, rent a car there. This is in the interest of saving time; later you'll want to depend on public transportation if possible.

On your visit check out the job market, school situation, and available housing. Walk up and down several streets. In other words, try on the town. Moving is a big step, especially if you have children. You *have* to find out if you can get a job or if training is available to get you a job. Better career potential is a sound reason for moving.

I met a divorced woman who moved with her three children from California to Indiana, of all places. (It's hard for us Californians to believe that anyone leaves here.) She was interested in a certain social life that involved horses, also she quite openly wanted to remarry. She had checked out several locales by a very ingenious method. In each town she was considering she would call the local newspaper and invite the women's editor out to lunch. No one ever turned her down when she said she wanted to interview them! And interview she did. She said that after a two-hour lunch and a bottle of chablis she learned everything about the town including the availability of eligible men!

Simply talking to people is *always* your best source of information. Talk to the principal of the school you're considering for your children. Walk into a real estate office and discuss neighborhoods. Go into an unemployment office and ask about jobs. If possible try to have your new job lined up before you move. That way you won't get too far behind with money.

SMOOTHING THE WAY

There are several people in your old town who can help you in your new one. Ask your doctor to recommend a new doctor and to send him your medical records. Ask your minister, priest, or rabbi to write to his counterpart in your new locale introducing you and your children. Go to your drugstore and get your prescriptions. Ask each of your friends if they know anyone in your new town. If they do, get their names and phone numbers. Prevail upon your friends to write or call them first. It makes all the difference in the world to *know* someone in a new area.

If you have a houseful of furniture and it is a major move, remember that the movers are at their busiest between June and September. If you can move during the winter months you will get better service. If you shop around a bit, you can probably get a reduced rate. Get boxes from the movers and do your own packing of dishes, silver, vases, linens and anything you have in closets. If your move is fairly local, solicit your friends' help in moving anything they can, such as pictures, mirrors, lamps, books, plants, and clothing. This helps on the price of labor.

Have an idea where you want your furniture placed in your new residence. With wide masking tape and a felt-tip pen, mark the furniture and the boxes: living room, south wall, back bedroom, against the wall; in kitchen, etc. You can't believe how much time and agony that will save.

IN YOUR NEW DIGS

If you have decided to make that move, do it with a sense of happy anticipation. Move joyfully. Don't lament what you are leaving. Keep telling yourself and your children what an exciting adventure awaits you.

1. *Your New Home.* Put everything away as soon as possible so you are in a functioning environment. Nothing clouds the mind like disorder. Start your job absolutely as soon as possible, put the kids in school, and begin living. Don't buy anything for the house, apartment, or flat for at least four months. If you have windows which need covering, go to the local variety or hardware store and buy white shades. They always cover, look nice and fit in with what you do later. If you have young children, let them draw or paint pictures on their shades. After you have settled into the house you can begin to buy those items that make it more to your taste. You may discover after four months that the neighborhood is impossible, the transportation is not reliable or the school is not all you hoped for. In this case you haven't invested any money in the home and you can look for a new place to move when your lease expires.

2. *Your New Job.* In your enthusiasm to get started, don't set a pace you can't maintain. If you start out as an overeager boomer then slacken off, you leave a bad impression. Accepting more of a work load than you can handle leads to a great frustration that can affect your productivity and your mental health. You don't have to drag your feet, but be certain you understand each and every direction. Don't be afraid to ask to have things explained two or even three times.

When I first went to work in an advertising agency, the man who hired me showed me my desk and assigned me the job of creating a print ad for a new scotch. He assumed that because I was a published writer I could just go into a room and start creating. I was too frightened to ask for directions and for a month I was a nervous wreck. I went to other copywriters and got them to show me the kind of paper to request from the mailroom. I watched the format they used and tried to copy it. I talked to people in production, in media, in art and in music. I spent hours looking through volumes of previous ads. I got to work an hour early, seldom took a lunch break and stayed until they locked the doors at night. What I was desperately doing was trying to learn advertising.

When I finally got up enough nerve to explain how lost I was, I was switched to assistant copy chief. Here I checked over other people's writing and found I had a very good editor's eye. What a difference! I was in a job I could do and which I enjoyed enormously. Had I been more open in the beginning and asked questions instead of wandering around on a hit-or-miss basis, I would have been given the indoctrination (as I was later) and accomplished twice as much in half the time.

3. *Your New Friends.* Anxious to meet people and make friends in a new area, we are often not as careful as we would be in our old surroundings. Wait awhile before you make commitments with people you don't know. Discriminate is not always a bad word. There are people you want to socialize with and those with whom you don't. There are people who are bores and time wasters, drinkers and carousers. There are people who will take advantage of your newness and aloneness. Be careful.

Caution your children in this area. Tell them to take their time picking a new best pal. In their newness and aloneness they are eager to belong. A bad choice of a new group could keep them out of a gang much more to their liking. Children can be far less forgiving toward someone who runs around with a fast crowd than adults are. Getting off to a bad start can affect their school work, their social life, and their attitude around the house.

4. *Moving or Staying.* Whether you move—or stay put—your life as a divorced woman is going to change. Don't lament this change. It can and should be a very exciting time in your life. You have been living with yourself a great deal longer than anyone else has. By now you should have an idea of what activities you truly enjoy and those you don't. You know when you

have met someone who appeals to the inner you, and you know when you're being surface polite. You know which work absolutely thrills you and which is a drudge. You know when you are being you and when you're being that someone *someone else* thinks you should be.

About fifteen years ago I met a woman at a park tennis court who was married to a lawyer, her "second lawyer" as she put it. She was living in a two-story Spanish home in Palos Verdes with a swimming pool and a view of the ocean. She had four children; two hers, one his, one theirs. She played tennis as if she were trying to kill the ball forever.

We played tennis about once a week on my lunch hour and became the type of initimate friends which such an anonymous setting breeds. We freely told each other all sorts of personal private secrets. One day she announced that her husband had asked her for a divorce. She seemed relieved, as if the frantic demon within her had finally been stilled. She took time with each tennis shot, ate her sandwich with measured bites, and leaned back against the fence as if she were pleasantly exhausted. "What are you going to do?" I asked her.

"Go and be me for the first time in my whole entire life. I've promised me no more living for my father, my lawyer husbands, their business friends, or even my children. I'm leaving tomorrow. I've lived in a fantasy world for so long that I know exactly where I'm going. I'll send you a letter."

She took all the money out of her bank account, the stocks out of her safe deposit box, emptied her savings account and left her husband a quitclaim deed to the house and furniture. She put her three children, the dog, and the cat in her station wagon and headed north. She had all the catalogues from a college in Northern California and she drove right to the campus and enrolled. The kids and the animals played on the wide lawns while she walked around and looked in every building. She was going to get her master's degree in English Literature.

From the campus she drove out to the coast, about a thirty-minute ride, to a small town where a great many crab fishermen lived or kept their boats. Within an hour she had rented a six-room cottage. For beds she and the children went down to the sporting goods shop and bought cots, and sleeping bags. The cottage had a stove, ice box, table and chairs.

They are all still living there in that cottage except for one change. Her ex-husband's son came up to live with them. Later she bought the cottage and added a second story and balcony overlooking the bay. My friend now teaches at the same college, is writing her second children's book, and I'm certain, being herself every minute of every day.

I have had many conversations with divorced women whom I consider enormously successful human beings. It is quite amazing how many of them have said they knew they were capable women but that they felt insecure and inadequate the minute the marriage dissolved. Even though many had been carrying half—or more—of the financial load, they felt their life only had meaning when the husband was there. He was the physical, touchable, acceptable presence that allowed them entrance into the established world. This ridiculous misplaced responsibility keeps women leading half-lives. Your creative living cannot begin until you learn that you simply do not need a man to make it all all right.

Breaking the inherited tradition of the man-woman family unit is not easy. Accepting the responsibility to determine your life-style is even harder. This is why living with a fantasy, as my tennis playing friend had, can ease the transition. When you make a dramatic change you can experience a loneliness like no other. What is worse, you become terribly depressed and full of remorse. What you left behind begins to loom large and lovely. You remember all the good things and build them up out of proportion. This depression can be quite dangerous to you physically and mentally.

Do your changing a step at a time. You'll know what works and what doesn't. Don't be discouraged if you make a few false starts. That's called experience. Be leery of those people who will accuse you of running away or of lacking the initiative to stick to one thing. You can run if you like, and who knows if sticking to one thing is the answer to life. There is truly nothing more exciting in this world than living! Grab it! This is the big chance you've been waiting for!

6

Children
and the Divorced Woman

Chapter Five of *The Divorcée's Handbook* was entitled "Bless the Children," and it started this way. "If your marriage was blessed with children, repeat after me: 'My children are my greatest asset.'" This *still* seems like the best way to begin a discussion of your children. You are a very rich woman if you have children, and I urge you to think about that at least once a day. A good time is when you are about to lash out at them with an angry statement that is more the result of your anger, frustration, or loneliness than the act they have just committed.

A divorce has a way of making us selfish women. It forces us to pay a great deal of attention to ourselves. Suddenly *our* needs become overwhelming and our hurts deep. The best cure for this condition is to change our focus to concentrate more on our children. This thrust of affection can cure two pains at once—yours and theirs.

It is an awesome responsibility to be the one full-time parent. It is up to you to choose where you live and how you live. It is up to you to be the disciplinarian as well as the dispenser of tenderness. You are the former of ideals and the pacesetter of standards. You are the final authority on matters which you're not sure about either. At times you want someone to tell you what to do instead of always having to make decisions, decisions, and more decisions.

WHEN DIVORCE IS DAMAGING

Divorce doesn't damage children. Parents damage children. The act of divorce creates the anxieties, the hurts, and the hostilities that trigger parents into saying the hurtful words. A child can adjust to a divorce amazingly well if he or she is not made to feel that it is in any way his or her fault. When parents try to justify their actions by directly or indirectly indicating that the child had something to do with it, they will indeed end up with a damaged child.

Another danger is telling children more than they can handle. Kids do not like to be told your problems, nor do they like to be told your grievances against their father. It's unfair to unburden yourself upon them at any age. I'm guilty of thinking my college-age children are ready to be sounding boards for my anxieties. My youngest daughter finally said to me one day, "Hey, lighten up. Don't lay your heavy trip on me. I've got my own problems."

It's a very tempting explanation to blame all the family ills on the divorce. You've heard a harassed mother say, "Of course my daughter is timid! After all, her father deserted her." Not only is this unfair to the daughter now, but it reinforces her timidity and gives her an excuse for continuing to be a timid person. Let's say the father did in fact desert, went to another country, changed his name. This action on his part is the very *last* thing that should be related to any behavior of the daughter. She should try to forget him completely and you should go out of your way to see that he is in no way a part of her life.

On the other hand let's say (as is probably closer to the truth) that this woman had a common garden-variety divorce and the father just doesn't happen to see his daughter as often as he should. The mother *still* should not call attention to his behavior or relate it in any way to the daughter's behavior. They are entirely separate problems and should be handled as such.

An equally damaging reaction is to suddenly smother your

children in affection. This makes them wary that something *terrible* must be wrong. All extremes are unsettling to children. They are creatures of habit. Aim for the middle road— moments of paying attention to and listening to them and moments of leaving them by themselves. After all, isn't this what everyone craves?

BE TERRIFIC IN THE MORNING

One time of the day that should be filled with attention and lavished with good cheer is—the morning. Don't groan and say you're a grouch until noon. You can no longer afford that luxury. I shall now quote from myself again. (You can't imagine what an odd sensation this is.) "Remember, children wake up each morning with a whole new set of cells that have to be trained. Learning, we know, happens when an idea or concept is changed from the unreal into the real. A child racing down the hill to the school bus should not be carrying anything but his sweater, his books, his lunch pail and anticipation. If he has spilled his orange juice, and you in your nervous state call him stupid and clumsy, he carries *that* with him. When the teacher starts to explain how an adjective modifies or describes a noun, and he doesn't get it on the first go round, he says to himself . . . 'I don't get it. I guess I am pretty stupid.' What a mental message for this child to send himself! A child should only be punished for a principle, not an act, and certainly not an accident."

Consistency. The more predictable a routine a child has in his life, the safer he feels. This is not a great medical pronouncement; it's just something I know for a fact from having raised four children. It also seems to be something they do not easily outgrow. My brood, who now range from nineteen to twenty-four, still have their Christmas stockings. They will probably scream with embarrassment if they read this, but even when they have Christmas with their father, they eventually make it to my house at some point during the holidays to collect the goodies from their stockings. Each year as their grandmother and I fill the stockings we think that surely *this* is the last year. But that's ridiculous. My sister and I still have stockings.

These traditions, as well as house rules, are especially important to the child with divorced parents. Keep as much routine going as you possibly can. Plan an hour a night—"The Children's Hour"—to sit and talk with them about their day. Try to turn your children into talkers. It's great therapy for all of you.

Set up a specified time to do homework. (You already know how I feel about TV.) *See* that the homework is done if you have doubts that it isn't. Check report cards carefully. They are not only a barometer of how your child is doing in school, but how your child is *doing*. A sudden drop in grades could be indicative of a disturbance that should be looked into.

One area where I do not feel consistency is necessary is in the selection of a school. I feel that if a child is unhappy in a certain school or has gotten in trouble there and doesn't want to go back or simply wants to try something new—let him change. I was allowed this choice growing up and I appreciated it, so I passed it on to my children. Two of mine have gone to school in Europe; one had trouble with a faculty member and changed schools; and three of them at different times tried boarding schools. My oldest son went four years to the University of Wyoming, while my oldest daughter switched from the gigantic campus of the University of Colorado to Briarcliff, a small private girls' college in New York simply because she wanted to see what it was like to go to school in the East. Why not? I don't feel that anything is gained (or learned) by forcing a child to stick it out someplace he or she is not happy. Learning is a delicate matter and can never be forced.

THE WOMEN'S LIBERATION MOVEMENT

A great deal of good has been accomplished by the women's movement. A *great* deal. It also has had some disturbing side effects which I think should be mentioned. One out of eight households today is headed by a woman. Heading or leading a household can't help but do something *to* that woman. One mistake I feel a great many liberated mothers make is trying to replace their role as mother. They tend to want to be the pal or the peer of their sons and daughters.

One woman comes to my mind. She is divorced, the mother of three teen-agers, and working in the library of one of our state colleges. From the back it is hard to distinguish her from her fifteen-year-old daughter. She wears Levis and turtlenecks, platform shoes, and long hair. She's a trim 124 pounds. She also smokes marijuana. I'm not going to get into a big discussion on the legality of pot, because it's not relevant. The issue is that she does it in front of her children. Why not? she says. She has a right to her own life and she wants her kids to see her as she is. She has a great many friends among the students and her Friday night parties feature guitar music, pizza, wine—and, sure, grass.

The neighborhood children are openly envious of this hip mom, while her kids are secretly embarrassed. The mother is "doing her own thing," but at the expense of her children. When I had my own radio show in Los Angeles, I went through a brief craziness when I bleached my hair (I am a *dark* brunette) and wore very short skirts and white boots. (I shudder thinking about it.) One day as I was jauntily swinging out the door to the studio, my youngest daughter, then twelve, stood blocking the doorway, her hands on her hips. "Mother," she said in her deep adult voice, "just who are you kidding?"

It was a great relief to all of us when I became normal again. That doesn't mean that I let my hair grow gray and wore housecoats. I just quit acting "childish," which I think is the key word.

Manners have been a casualty in the women's rush to the well of equality. Today's mother feels foolish showing her daughter the correct way to sit in a chair. We don't sit any more, we lounge—legs dangling over the arm of the sofa. And what of our sons? Do we still tell a son to walk on the curb side of a women, light her cigarette, and hold open the door for her? He's liable to get a hit in the mouth. But one tradition you can safely teach both your boys and your girls is how to shake hands: very firmly while looking the other person directly in the eyes. Don't be talked out of *that*, because it's an important thing for them to know.

As the resident parent you fall heir to all the questions about life. You will be quizzed on more subjects than "Meet the Press." Don't be afraid to say you don't know if you are truly stumped. But when it comes to human biology—defer. At least with your boys. I firmly believe it is your ex-husband's responsibility—and privilege—to have *that* discussion with his sons. We should simply *not* be that unisex about it. Leave the men their maleness! If your ex-husband is not in the picture, enlist the aid of your brother or father or a family doctor. Do not ask a male friend. That brings up all kinds of questions and possibilities in your son's mind.

There are various theories afloat that homosexuality is caused by a domineering mother. Certainly a great many men do feel threatened by today's liberated woman. She seems to know who she is and where she is going, and that's a challenge to any man. Some take it the right way and realize that a self-possessed woman is a better wife. Others ignore the challenge, and the woman. We've come a long way, baby, but I hope *not* to the point where we think we can be both mother *and* father to our children.

Discovering Your Children. With children, you need never suffer from acute loneliness. Certainly you want the companionship and physical attention of a man, but you don't have to sit around moping about it. You don't need to wait for a man to call to get out of the house. Nor do you have to go alone. Right under your roof are the best dates in the world—your children.

Date Your Children. At any age—say over three—a child or young adult makes a terrific date. If you have more than one child, taking each one out by his or herself is one of the most beneficial things you can do. Each one needs to be alone with you some of the time. Invite your son to take you to a ball game or a movie. Ask your daughter for lunch and a Saturday stroll through the museum. Go on bike rides or long walks. My oldest son asked *me* out the other night to go to a disco. We had a fabulous time on the dance floor. There was no embarrassment nor feeling of duty—just fun. When we sat down for a delightful ice-cold beer he reminded me of the times I took him to the Italian restaurant and a movie on Friday nights. He said he always felt so grown-up ordering the pizza or spaghetti, paying the bill, and buying the theater tickets. That had to be ten years ago!

Date with Your Children. Many of the men you date will have children of their own. Why not suggest you all do something together? A great many fathers are stumped as to what to do with their kids when it's their weekend to have them. Packing a lunch and going for a picnic is always a winner. Take balls and mitts, a Frisbee, a jumprope, and a deck of cards or dominoes. If either you or your date has a backyard, suggest a Bingo or Monopoly tournament and a barbecue. Let the kids plan the menu, make the salad, build the fire, and set the table.

If you are dating a man without children and he invites you sailing or to the beach when it's a glorious Saturday, ask him if you can bring your son or your two daughters. Why not? All he can say is yes or no. If he says yes, but only one child when you have three, tell him that is fine but you will have to do something with the other two the next weekend. It's good to split up the children so long as they *all* get equal time.

One of the best times we had when my children were in their pre-teens was a week we spent at Catalina Island. I was dating a man with four children. He rented a large power craft for a week and took his four and sailed the boat from Los Angeles harbor to Catalina, where he dropped anchor. My four and I stuffed our sleeping bags with shorts and bathing suits and flew over in the seaplane. At night every inch of the deck on that craft was carpeted with sleeping bags. During the day it looked like a floating diving platform and towel laundry. We had disputes and disagreements, but the eight children remember only a "keen" time.

Travel with Your Children. When it's time for your vacation, consider taking it with your children. Rent a mountain cabin for a week or go camping. I know a divorced man who takes his son and daughter on a bicycle trip every year. There are detailed books on the subject and even organized tours you can take. Most airlines will take your bike with your luggage so you can literally go anywhere in the world.

Kids have no trouble meeting people. You'd be surprised how your social life can improve when you're traveling with your children. Try taking them skiing with you or to the park to play tennis. They'll march right up to a couple and turn your singles game into a doubles match.

It doesn't take a lot of money to think of something inventive to do. If one of your children collects rocks, you might consider a trip to the desert. They all must study American history at some point in their education. How about a drive to Washington, D.C., followed by a trip through the battlefields of the Civil War? In California a marvelous trip is to trace the steps of Father Serra by visiting the missions. You have no idea how much such an adventure will improve their grades in school. You will have made history come alive for them.

If your children are away in college or working in another city, visit them on your vacation or on a long weekend. When I go to New York on business, my favorite date is my daughter. We go to dinner, then she takes me with her to the college hangouts. I'm certainly not interested in a date with a Princeton senior, but I do immensely enjoy talking to these young people. I find them much better company than a great many people "my age."

Last year I spent a week in Paris with my daughter who was attending the Sorbonne. I had never been to France so she was *my* tour guide. She made reservations at an inexpensive hotel near the family with whom she was living, and we did all the typical tourist things. I became intimately acquainted with the Métro and quickly learned the best bakery at which to buy our bread for lunch. We always had one or two of her pals along and it just couldn't have been a better vacation!

You may be waiting to see Paris in the springtime on the arm of your lover. I can't fault that. It just may be many moons away. In the meantime why not sign up for one of those relatively inexpensive package tours and take your son or daughter with you as their graduation present? The sooner you get over the notion that you *have* to travel with a man, the sooner you will travel. You *meet* people traveling. All *kinds* of people. And that's what you want. Break that couple-mold right now. The whole world is outgrowing *that* nonsense. Springtime in Paris is delicious all by yourself, sipping a *citron pressé* on the rue de la Paix. I was in my forties before I got to Europe for the first time. I'm not one to look back and regret—yet I wish it hadn't taken me so long.

Working with Your Children. As a mother who works, it is only fair that you ask your children to share the responsibilities of the home, i.e. chores. We talked about time charts for each of your children in Chapter II. If you are not already on a schedule, do start one immediately. You will have fewer disciplinary problems with your children if each one knows exactly what is expected of him or her.

I firmly believe in a system of allowances. Each child should know exactly how much money to expect each week. I also believe in the gig system: chores left undone result in decreased allowance. We are not a welfare nation (as yet) and no one in the family should receive money unless he or she earns it. Set the gig scale so there will be no argument over how much you deduct.

Having a goal in life is one of the healthiest forms of activity. It sharpens the senses. If you can encourage your children to save their money toward some major objective, you will have taught them a valuable lesson. Suddenly as a nation we are becoming aware of the great sadness that we have *not* taught our children how to save. We give them skis and stereos and rob them of the pleasures of achievement.

Saving money just to save it is a hard lesson to teach anyone. But to save for a personal goal gives the project a beginning and an end. Once a child has accomplished a major saving feat, he is sometimes loathe to part with the money. This is a good sign; it means that he is learning the value of money.

When you encourage your child to save for a project, be sure it is a realistic venture. One child I know saved to buy a horse. When she finally purchased the animal she had to double her work efforts to make enough money to pay the feed and board bill. She had to work after school and on weekends. Soon she had to take a job one night a week on top of all her other chores. Her grades began to suffer. Her mother and even her younger brother helped out, but the horse was draining their extra resources faster than they could accumulate them.

It was finally resolved that the horse be sold and the money be put into a savings account. The girl took a job exercising horses on weekends and quit her other jobs. Her grades went back up. She was still around horses, which was where she wanted to be. She said that by the time she buys another horse she will have saved enough money for an Arabian champion.

Lessons. There is always the child who wants to take ballet lessons so she can have a pink tutu like the girl next door. Or there's the boy who knows he'd have more friends if he could just play the guitar. As a working mother you do not have the time or the money to give your children paid lessons. That's exactly what you tell them when they ask. "Sorry, but that's the way it is." On the other hand, if they want to take voice lessons at school or swimming lessons at the park pool or pay themselves for karate lessons, then you should be all for it, providing they organize it, find the time for it, and pay for it.

That doesn't make you the meanest mother on the block; it makes you the most realistic mother. It also determines who genuinely wants to learn what—and at what price. It is a revelation to find out what is available through Girl Scouts, Y's, park departments, and schools, and for very little or no money at all. Encourage your children to discover what's available and help them work it into their lives. I said to help them—not to do it for them. They must still keep up their grades and do their chores. The rest of their time is their own. It's amazing how diligently a boy practices that guitar when he has bought it himself, takes the bus to his lesson, and pays the teacher with his own money.

Money, Money, Money. I wonder if there is a day in the life of a divorced mother when she doesn't worry about money—not that worrying does any good. I finally got so tired of being dunned by my children that I made them put all requests in writing. It worked wonders. I put a card tray on the console in the hall which was where all requests were left. Just the simple act of putting them in writing separated the genuine needs from the pesky "I wants." A typical week's collection might contain a request for "shampoo, herbal"; "shoe laces long enough for my hiking boots" (a marginal item because hiking is extra-curricular); "turtle food"; "red ink marker." My youngest son always waited until the last minute and his notes were frantic. "Hurry. Emergency. My teacher says if I don't have a gym suit by Monday I get a pink slip!"

I recommend the magic note pad. You can't imagine the arguments it saved. If you feel that the requested item should be in the child's budget or you simply don't have the money for it at the time you can write "request denied," or "not this week, try next," and put the note back on his or her bed. The biggest service the note system performs is eliminating blame-passing. Without the note, your son can say it's *your* fault he got a pink slip because he *told* you last week that he had to have a gym suit. Under the note system there is no contest.

Extra Help. A working mother with a houseful of young children needs additional help. If you have a bedroom to spare I suggest that you get some sort of live-in help. I don't mean a paid full-time maid unless you can afford that luxury. I'm talking about a college student who wants room and board in exchange for chores and baby sitting, or a pensioner who wants a nice place to live. Both are available.

College students can be found through the employment office of your local college or by placing an ad in the school paper. When you interview them find out their schedules. Often they are going to school during the hours you need them most. A theater arts major usually has long labs in the late afternoon or evening, which would mean she could stay with the children while you worked. If your children go to nursery school, you need a student who would be there in the late afternoon. It is a bonus if you can find a student who drives. You can buy the gas in exchange for running the children to school or doing the weekly marketing.

With a student, however, you are adding another young

person who needs rules. Here you have to be quite firm. No boy friends staying over. No parties when you are away. No drugs, and that includes marijuana. You don't have to be nasty about it any more than you would be with your children. Those are simply your rules and anyone who lives under your roof lives under your rules.

Pensioners or senior citizens can be an ideal solution, almost like a live-in grandmother. You can find these marvelous ladies through churches, the Salvation Army, and Catholic Welfare. Remember that they are not maids to be given chores; they probably had their own homes and would resent such treatment. But you must sit down in the beginning and *clearly* decide on their responsibilities. Certainly, watching the children is number one. But does that include evenings and weekends, and, if so, how many nights? Will they help with the cooking or the ironing, and, if so, how many hours and which meals? Don't leave anything open-ended or you both will be unhappy. You'll think she's not doing enough; she'll feel overworked and exploited.

There may be those times when *you* need extra help, mental help. Reach out because help is available. Most cities have parent stress lines that you can call when you are simply not coping. The Y has discussion groups where you can share problems with other mothers. If you need help with your children remember Big Brother; and I think there is now a Big Sister organization.

Use your church. More people should. Take yourself into your minister's office and tell him you need a shoulder to cry on. Ask your priest to dinner and encourage the kids to tell him what's bugging them. Ask your rabbi if he would please have a talk with your ex-husband to get him to see his children more often. These are good people, God's people, and their mission is to help and to heal. So let them.

Visitation. Theoretically a divorce decree stipulates the visitation rights of the father. This could be one weekend each month, two weeks in the summer, and half of every holiday. Some agreements simply state "reasonable" visitation. If you both are reasonable people this method works very well, at least until one or the other becomes unreasonable. I don't know which way you have worked it out, but I do have some suggestions as to how to handle the inevitable problems that arise.

Daddy's Day. When father is picking up one or more children for the day, find out from him his E.T.A. (expected time of arrival.) This doesn't mean that's when you'll see him, but that's the time you'll have the children ready. Ask them where their dad is taking them and see that they are dressed appropriately: jeans for the park, bathing suits for the beach, good clothes for going out to dinner. If the children don't know, call their father and ask him. If he gets upset and shouts, "How the hell should I know. It's only Tuesday for Christ's sake!" then ask him politely to call you when he does know. You've done your part. If he shows up Sunday to take them to his parents' for dinner and they are in cords and sneakers, it's his problem.

As they leave, ask for an E.T.R. (expected time of return.) This, too, is only fair. You need to know if you have time to go to a movie or take the train into the city or go to dinner with a friend. Then if he brings them home early he will have to sit with them until you return at the appointed time. A good rule always is: get it settled up front.

The Children Staying Over. Today's children of divorce spend a great deal of time on freeways and in airports, in sleeping bags and on front-room couches. They have to know how to handle Dad's new wife, as well as stepbrothers, half sisters, and kids from previous marriages who nobody knows what to call. They may be staying over with their father under strained conditions. Be ready to answer their questions on how they should act. You should do all you can to give your children that extra measure of confidence. They *really* need it.

Packing. It's Easter and Dad's turn to take them for a week. Find out where they are going. Skiing? If they are actively engaged in this sport and have boots, poles, parkas, ski pants and thermal underwear, fine. Get out the suitcases and help them pack. Joyfully. Don't be mean and say things like: "Well, if he's got enough money to pay for all those lift tickets, then why can't he raise my child support?"

That is *not* at issue here. Remember, the divorce wasn't *their* idea. If you have genuine grounds for increased child support, take it up with your lawyer.

If, however, none of your children has ever been skiing, and you own not a ski nor a pole, to say nothing of the clothes, I feel it is up to the father to outfit them. This might be a one-shot trip and you and the children will be sitting there with hundreds of dollars worth of gear and nowhere to use it. Believe me, anything to do with skiing is expensive. Everything you need could be rented, but I still feel this is the father's responsibility.

Let's say Dad is taking the children on a motor trip to the Grand Canyon. It is certainly reasonable to assume that they will have jeans, T-shirts, warm jackets, tennis shoes or boots, and dress clothes to go out to dinner. If one of your sons has outgrown his tennis shoes, don't force him to wear them in the hope that his dad will buy him a new pair. You buy them before he leaves. That's what I mean by giving self-confidence. Don't make your son start a happy adventure by having to *ask* for something, or worse yet, struggling through the week in shoes that pinch.

Packing is an art and the first rule of the road is: keep your gear together. Show your children how to arrange their suitcases so they can comfortably live out of them for a week. Don't load them down with too many changes. A good traveler travels light. Be sure that you have name tags on *every* item of clothing including both *socks* of each pair. When everything gets taken to the laundromat at Yosemite, it will ensure that your group get all their clothes back. After all, you do not know who is going to be on that outing.

If your ex-husband lives a considerable distance from you, and the children must fly or take a train or bus, buy them one-way tickets. It is up to the father to supply the transportation back. If he doesn't, and the children call frantically, wondering what to do, wire them money or a prepaid ticket to return home. Don't make the problem worse by yelling at them and saying what a selfish rogue their father is. Don't demand that they *sit* here until he buys their tickets. It isn't their fault. Bring them home, but the next time the father wants them to come visit tell him (or have your lawyer tell him) that they will come when they receive their *round-trip tickets* in the mail.

Swapping. If your ex-husband calls and asks if he can switch weekends with you, and it doesn't upset any plans you have already made, for heaven's sake switch with him. Anything—and I mean anything—you can do to facilitate and encourage visitation, you should do. You *want* the children's father to continue his interest in them. Having his good will doesn't hurt you either. You may want to switch a weekend with him, or get him to take them two weekends in a row so you can get away a full ten days. Life is simpler and far more pleasant when you get along with your ex-husband.

This brings up Christmas. I know more than one child who spends the better part of Christmas at the airport because two fanatical parents insist the child's time be equally divided. One year the child spends Christmas Eve with the father and Christmas Day with the mother. The next year it's reversed. It doesn't seem to matter to the parents that the child, after spending Chrismas Eve with one parent, must get up at the break of dawn to catch a plane to spend Christmas Day with the other.

What truly works best is to alternate Christmases—one year with one parent, the next with the other. That gives the Christmas parent one full week. Or have two Christmases, one before the twenty-fifth and one after. Try to keep in mind what is best for the *child.* I can't imagine that Christmas in the airport would be it. Some children, mine included, think that two Christmases are great. That's one of the pluses of divorce. They've never felt deprived at all. Both their father and I have established traditions, and the children have felt doubly fortunate.

The Rest of the Family. The persons who sometimes suffer the greatest loss in visitation rights are the grandparents and the aunts, uncles, and cousins, especially on the father's side. Far too many mothers forget that their ex-husband's parents would dearly love to see their grandchildren. I recommend that you call your ex-mother-in-law and ask her if she would like to have the children over. If she's in another city, write and ask if she would like to have them visit her.

Family life in our country has been under a terrible assault. It's not just the mushrooming divorce rate that is to blame. We have become a very mobile society, changing jobs every five years, moving from state to state. The old-fashioned family, gathered around the turkey at grandmother's house, is rare indeed. Make every effort to keep in touch with whatever family you have, his or yours, for the sake of your children. It's their birthright.

RULES OF THE ROAD

There are some rules of behavior you should remind the little darlings about, besides the simple etiquette of "please," "thank you," and "I had a nice time at your house." There are special rules which are indigenous to children of divorced parents.

1. *Telling.* A feeling of almost conspiratorial brotherhood develops among brothers and sisters of divorced parents. I feel that this represents a healthy need to belong which should be encouraged. Once in a while you'll encounter a bad egg who can't wait to get to his dad's house to rat on his sisters. This represents another kind of need, a need to feel big, a need to endear himself to his father. To guard against this kind of activity, it's a good idea to have a chalk talk on family loyalty before their departure. It can be as simple as:

"You are all going to your dad's to have a good time, so leave any bad news behind. What happens in this house isn't really anyone else's business anyway."

You are not trying to hide anything from their father. They should all know by this time that any great mishap will be relayed to him by you. Don't you become a "teller" either. Don't be the kind of mother who says, "Listen, if you do that one more time, I'll call your father," or the kind of mother who calls him on the sly with behavior problems so he can mete out justice when the unsuspecting child arrives. It's up to you to handle behavior problems. If you can't, you should tell your son or daughter that you love them very much, but their problem has become too big for either of you, so you think it might not be a bad idea to get their father's advice.

2. *Gossip.* Gossip has to do with your social life. "Who does your mom go out with?" "Where was your mom when I called up on Friday night?" Be candid with your children and tell them that it's all right for them to answer these questions. This way they won't worry during the entire visit that they have been disloyal to you. If you *don't* want the children to answer this type of questions, tell them not to lie, but to say, "You'll have to ask her, Dad. She asked me not to tell you, and a promise is a promise."

That, of course, may get your child in trouble with his father. He may call it arrogance and punish the child. It's a tight spot for a child. That's why I favor the honest approach. Either way, tell them not to *volunteer* information.

3. *Quizzing.* Okay, it's your turn. The children have come home from their father's and you bite your tongue for a day. When you can't *stand* it any longer you ask:

"What did you do at your Dad's? Is his new apartment nice? Was anyone *else* there?"

Come on, be honest. We've *all* done it, and don't think the children aren't on to us. They'll come back at us with:

"Sure, I had a good time. We went to the movies and had dinner at Dad's apartment. It's nice. Really nice. No, Dad didn't cook. His friend did. Yes, a woman friend. Sure she was nice. Kinda young for Dad, though."

One of the most difficult tasks the divorced mother faces is not to be judgmental of her ex-husband's life. He has to find his way just as you do. When the kids come home with tales of how they had to sleep on the floor, or there wasn't any milk, or Dad's girl friend came back awfully early in the morning, bite your tongue. This is *all* allowable. But if the kids tell you that he left them alone in his apartment until three in the morning, then you have an honest gripe. Take it up with him, not them.

When you feel that you have reason to complain to their father about his actions, you might call him and in an unhysterical voice discuss it with him. But remember what this does to the kids. It marks them in his eyes as tattletales. He's liable to deal harshly with them or even stop seeing them. You don't want this to happen, so before you call, weigh the consequences.

It is very tempting (sometimes) to wish that your ex-husband *wasn't* in the picture; to wish that you had the children all to yourself. Besides being detrimental to the children, you are cutting yourself, and them, out of some emotional and financial help. He *is* the father of your children. If you can encourage him to *act* and *be* the father, perhaps he will help more. College comes along mighty quickly, and today it takes two parents to put more than one child through school. As distasteful as it may sound to you, you *need* each other—at least as far as the children are concerned.

4. *When He Doesn't Show Up.* Many a child has sat in the living room, all dressed up, waiting for Daddy. And Daddy didn't make it. These are the experiences that break your heart. These are the times you would do anything to spare that child such a devastation. But you can't. It's a fact of life now, so what do you do? If it's not too late at night, *you* take that child somewhere. It won't be the same, but it will be something. Take along a best friend, but don't tell the friend what happened.

If you have an ex-husband who is habitually late or absent, make a rule that your children will be available for one hour and one hour only. If he does not appear during that hour, you and the children are free to make other plans. Be certain that the children understand that it is their father's problem and does not reflect on them. Keep it light, almost a joke, or they will begin to feel rejected. "You know your dad. He probably thinks today's Wednesday instead of Friday." If he arrives more than an hour late be sure your child has something else to do and is *out* doing it. A child has a right to be treated fairly, and waiting around for an errant father isn't fair.

DAD'S NEW WIFE, MOM'S NEW BOY FRIEND

Well, it's true. Ex-husbands tend to remarry before ex-wives do. (Some of the new wives are the girl friends from *before* the divorce, so what can you expect?) The only time you will have to deal with her is when it concerns your children. Be pleasant. You might as well, because you've got to go through a lot together—graduations, weddings, christenings, to say nothing of the months and months of visitation. She'll probably be the one dispatched to pick up the children and bring them home. As I said, be polite. That doesn't mean you have to invite her in for coffee.

I have heard some bizarre stories of divorced couples getting together with their new spouses for Thanksgiving dinner. I have a friend who always has her ex-husband and his wife to dinner when they bring her children home after summer vacation.

A good relationship is far better than open hostility. Remember that you cared enough about this man to become his wife and bear his children. Try to remember some of his good points. (One of his good points?)

It often happens that your children will genuinely like your ex-husband's new wife. Don't take this as a personal affront. Be delighted they like her. (I know it's hard.) My girls were reminiscing about their "early days" of visitation and they decided that having their dad married, as he is now, was far superior to the parade of girl friends that passed into their lives. Then my oldest piped up:

"But you know, I'll *always* remember Robin. She bought me my first bra."

Don't you wonder, sometimes, how our children will all turn out? They are living such totally different lives from anything we could possibly have imagined. I have talked to so many young people from "broken homes" and most seem to have landed on their feet. Of course all the results aren't in yet, and probably never will be. Can you imagine yourself coming into the living room after dinner to meet a man who was going to take your mother out to a film? Your mother! A *boy friend!* Absurd, yet our children face that over and over.

"Say good evening to Mr. Smith, dear." "You remember Mr. Whitman, don't you, Pam?" "This is Mr. Billingham from my office. We're going to dinner now."

You notice I say Mr.; so should you. When your children have been with a male friend of yours on several occasions, and it's all right with your friend, let them call him by his first name. Never have them call him Uncle or any of those other ridiculous nomenclatures which divorced mothers think up for their boy friends. Stick to Mr. as long as you can, for several reasons. Number one, it's proper. The second is that it doesn't unnecessarily *involve* the child with the man. You may see him three times then decide he's a dud. When he's not around any more, your child will say, "Whatever happened to Mr. Whitman?" not "Whatever happened to Bob?" It's easier to dismiss Mr. Whitman than it is Bob.

Some children, especially children who don't see enough of their father, will search for a dad in your male friends. That's why you should strive for an impersonal air. Your son doesn't need another disappointment in his life. Certainly you can all be friends and do things together, but then Mr. Smith goes home to his own life.

After your children have met a man you're dating, don't ask them what they think of him. They'll probably tell you, but asking calls for them to concentrate on how they *feel* about this particular man. In other words, it's another involvement. If they don't happen to like the man in question, then what? Are you going to quit dating him? Are you going to be afraid your children will be rude to him? You also don't want your children to think they have the power to determine your social life.

Children can be monsters if they take a strong dislike to someone you're dating. Here you have to be firm and demand that they be courteous. Never allow your children to be impudent or sullen. It's a miserable habit to break. If they can't be civil, they should be told that they are not welcome at the dinner table when he is there.

Often a child will have an uncanny way of spotting a phony before you do, so there is no harm in listening to what a child volunteers. In your great desire to meet people, to go out, you will sometimes miss—or overlook—a man's faults. The only time to listen *seriously* to your children's opinion of a man is if you are thinking of marrying him.

Etta is a divorced woman who has been single fourteen years. At the time of her divorce her son was seven. Shortly thereafter she met a man who was absolutely everything she ever wanted or admired in a man. They dated for a year, then became engaged. When she told eight-year-old Donald that she was going to get married to Mr. Oldham, he threw a fit. He cried and screamed and had nightmares nearly every night. When Mr. Oldham would come to the house he would charge at him and kick his shins. Then he would run and lock himself in his room so that his mother wouldn't leave him with the baby sitter. Within six months the engagement was off and Mr. Oldham moved away.

This Christmas, when he was home from college, Donald said to his mother, "You know, Mom, you should get married one of these days. I worry about you. I still don't know why you never married that Mr. Oldham. He was such a great guy. I liked him a lot."

Do you think if Etta told Donald the truth he would believe her? Of course not. Children remember only what they want to remember.

WHEN YOUR EX-HUSBAND HAS CUSTODY

Traditionally, custody of the children was usually awarded to the mother. Not any more. More and more fathers are demanding custody—and getting it. Today the court takes a long look at both parents and decides which one it feels is best for the child. Another phenomenon is the number of mothers today who voluntarily relinquish custody. This is very hard for me to relate to because I can't imagine the conditions under which I would have done this. However, mothers whom I know personally have told me that they knew themselves well enough to know that the father would handle the children better.

Edith is a young woman of thirty-two, living in Los Angeles, pursuing an acting career. Her ex-husband is a life insurance salesman, remarried, living in nearby Garden Grove. Edith told me she knew it would be better for her children to live in a home with a father and a stepmother than living the unpredictable life she has chosen. The last time I talked with her she had landed a small part in a series that necessitated her shooting until two in the morning three nights in a row. "What life," she said, shrugging her shoulders, "is that for a child?"

If you do not have custody, use your visitation privileges lavishly. See your children every time you possibly can and under all kinds of conditions. Don't just pick them up and take them to the movies. Bring them to your apartment, no matter how small it is, and let them feel they are a part of your life. Introduce them to your friends, your associates at work and the men whom you date.

Do *not*, however, allow a man to "sleep over" when your children are in residence. As a mother without custody, you have to make the children understand that you did not leave them for another man. This would make them feel abandoned. You can only make your children feel loved and cherished by the way you treat them. Words are only words, and in no way are they a substitute for warm arms and happy afternoons.

Young children will not understand that what you did was forced upon you by the court or done because you felt it was right. You are gone—and *that's* what they understand. The only solution to their confusion is to be with them as much as possible. As they grow older and understand more, you can have deeper conversations with them, but don't explain too much too soon. They simply are not ready for it. They probably will not completely understand until they are grown and have "big life problems" of their own.

Write to your children as often as you can. Really force yourself to get a letter off first thing every morning while you have your coffee. You tell me who doesn't like to get a letter. In your letters you can offer a great deal of good advice because the person reading your letter is your captive audience. Think about that a minute. Whenever you read a letter, the writer has your full, undivided attention. The same is true when *you* write the letter. Say all the loving words you don't have time to say in person. Be chatty and full of news, but also tell them how often you think about them and how proud you are of them.

WHEN THEY LEAVE THE NEST

No matter who has custody, you or your husband, somewhere between the ages of forty and fifty, you will lose your role as active mother. Nothing grows faster than children, so make each day, starting with today, a contribution to their future life. Love is the magic potion. To love a child in just the way he or she needs to be loved at *that* particular moment can alter a life. I remember visiting prep schools with my oldest son when he was fourteen. As we walked through the dormitory that was later to be his, we stopped and looked into one of the rooms. It was a mess, with the bed unmade, clothes on the floor, books spread out on every flat surface. On the wall over the desk was a handmade plaque which read:

WE ARE THE FUTURE LEADERS OF OUR GENERATION
HOW DOES THAT GRAB YOU?

I laughed. You would too. It was a funny scene, yet how absolutely true. These children we yell at and pick up after and coerce and love *are* the future. Ours as well as theirs. I look at this son now, ten years later, a freshman in law school, and I know he's been through a lot, an awful lot. But he has made it as a person, and that's what counts. You can't hold them back; you have to urge them on. And out of the nest.

I've lost my active role as mother. My four are all in college, but it is not an unhappy time for me. I have a career I love and a fascinating life hand-chiseled out of disaster and hard won by work. Yet I look at their baby pictures and wonder how it happened. When did they grow up? Where was I? When I go to visit them or they come home to see me, it's a marvelously exciting time. When they leave, I'm dreadfully lonely for a while. But as I put the stereo back on my station and sit down at my desk to work, I can truthfully say that I'm glad it's over. And that's the way it should be.

7

Beauty

and the Divorced Woman

An artist friend of mine said to me as we sat together at a sidewalk cafe:

"You know, I can always spot a divorced woman."

I asked him how.

"Because of their discontent."

When I asked him to define his use of the word discontent and to explain his remark, he said:

"Discontent shows in your eyes, they reflect your agony. The mouth sags at the corners and the shoulders bend forward, almost into a slouch. Discontent takes the bounce out of your walk and the mellowness out of your voice."

I began to wonder if *all* divorced women are discontented. "Surely," I said to my friend, "some are satisfied with their lives."

"Aha," my friend answered, "satisfied is one thing and contented is another. Satisfied could be a temporary compromise while contentment is deep pleasure with the way things are."

If, then, we accept my friend's definition, it would indeed be difficult to find a contented divorced woman. We will, therefore, have to *do* something about not letting this show in our faces, our voices or our posture. We have to begin our beauty treatment by looking at our lives and how our lives determine our looks.

BODY HABITS

It is quite true that the human body is a machine which responds to stimuli. Different parts of the body—heart, stomach, eyes—react to different stimuli. What are these stimuli? You know them well: food, noise, disease, cold, harsh words, fear, love—the list is endless. Our bodies are bombarded daily and forced to react to this never-ending onslaught.

Whatever can we do about it? One thing we can do is to start each day by taking command and reporting to ourselves that "generally, all is well." That's a mini-armor, but it's a beginning. If said often enough, it's habit-forming. If we listen to my artist friend, that would be the first step toward erasing the look of discontent. We can't go on to any other beauty hints until we take this first step because *that* look would spoil the whole effect.

Another step toward bodily control is to learn to predict our weaknesses. We each have a fairly accurate idea of what sends us into a depression dive: trouble with one of our children; lack of money; being slighted by a friend; not hearing from the man of the moment. If we *know* these truths about ourselves we should be able to take charge of the situation and to say:

"Look, self, I *know* he should have called by now, but he hasn't. Now, am I going to let this discontent *show* on my face for the world to see, or am I going to reject his stimulus and create my own?"

If you care about your looks, you'll create your own.

How do you create your own stimuli? First you reinforce your mini-armor by saying, "all is well," then tick off a list of things that *are* going well in your life. Then you say to yourself, "Look, it is absolutely *stupid* to let someone else determine *my* bodily reactions!" Then you smile (go on, *smile*) stand up straight and walk as if you didn't have a care in the world.

This isn't a foolish pantomime; it's a training session. Remember, the human body is a machine, a fine hand-crafted machine, which can be re-programmed. Since *you* are the person spending the most time with you, the programmer should be you, not him! Not them nor it! This isn't going to be an instantaneous transformation. You will have to have several of these training sessions.

A third step toward bodily control is self-suggestion. Over the years I have read an enormous pile of books on autosuggestion, hypnosis, and mind power—all in the interest of learning about self-control. It baffles me how we allow ourselves to be victimized, tyrannized, and ruled by our emotions, feelings, and reactions. It certainly can't *all* be the fault of divorce or we would be cured by the pounding of the last gavel. "Divorce granted. You are free to run your own life." Like hell, I say.

It's a constant battle to assume control of your own life. It requires vigilance to keep your cells in line. These training sessions *will* work if you keep them up. They are not going to *solve* all the problems, but they are going to improve your mental and *physical* state. Not only should you have these talks with yourself at the time of the bombardment, but you should conduct auxiliary training sessions at night. After you are in bed and have finished a chapter in the book you are currently reading and begin to feel sleepy, turn off the light. Now, in a natural voice, start giving yourself orders:

"When the kids are cranky tomorrow I will not scowl and yell at them. I will smile. I will speak in a normal voice. I will be in charge."

This nighttime training session is a mild form of self-hypnosis. What you are trying to do is to get through the conscious mind to the *other* (or unconscious) mind. When you are drowsy your conscious mind doesn't put up the defenses it does in the cold, hard light of day. You can slip suggestions to yourself. This is a good time to work on *any* problem area such as smoking too much, indulging in self-pity or lack of confidence.

In order for your training sessions to be doubly effective, you have to start bringing out your own good features. If you don't, your body will get very tired of being told what not to do. You'll be at a standstill. You can't take a negative out of your life without replacing it with a positive.

I've always had an aversion to books or articles that talk about a "new you." Whom do you know who ever changed herself into a "new person"? I don't care how you may diet or exercise; what plastic surgeon or psychiatrist you visit; or which beauty salon or dressmaker you patronize. There are parts of you that will still be hanging around. This is not meant as discouragement, but as encouragement! You've got a lot to work with already. You don't need a major overhaul, but just a few adjustments or a tune-up. After all, in marriage we *all* have a tendency to let go. Well, you have to begin holding in your stomach again. Furthermore, you'll like it.

THE EIGHT AREAS OF CONCERN

You may be starting to wonder what all this has to do with beauty. We shall get on to eye shadow and face lifts next, but none of *that* does any good if you haven't paid attention to the inner self. Good looks by themselves cannot sustain anything; they're skin deep, remember. What you are after—what we are all after—is a deep beauty that will stand all tests, especially the test of time. Following is a brief listing of eight areas of concern.

1. *Objectivity.* There is nothing quite like a divorce to put you on Stage One. The tension is fierce, the drama high. You have meetings with your lawyer and phone calls from your friends. It's a very you-centered, unnatural existence. You can think of nothing *except* the divorce. Everything that happens in your life is immediately translated into how it will *affect* the divorce. Divorce, divorce, divorce. You, you, you.

There is probably no one more unattractive than a non-objective person. You meet them all the time. You say you enjoyed the film and they say it reminded them of their trip to Italy. You say your job is getting you down and you're thinking of quitting. They say they have a month until their vacation. You say you think it might rain tomorrow and they tell you about the new roof on their house. Do you know what that is?

They won't let *you* talk about *you* or about what you think, feel or care.

Listen to yourself for a day. If you are *still* talking about your divorce, for heaven's sake shut up! Nobody, and I mean nobody, cares how your ex-husband mistreated you or how your lawyer didn't get you enough money or how your children still have nightmares. You are divorced. Now divorce yourself from *divorce*. That is all non-objective, unappealing chatter that keeps you bogged down, dejected and *dis*contented.

I introduced Carol to Herb at a small dinner at my home. When Herb called a few days later to thank me, I asked him how he enjoyed Carol.

"Sorry, she's a very good-looking woman, but she's a man-hater. I've learned to avoid women who run down their ex-husbands. It just doesn't make sense. When a woman thought enough of a guy to marry him why would she turn around and cut him to pieces."

I've heard this from a great many men—and women. When spouses are so terribly bitter about their ex, they tend to take it out on *all* members of the opposite sex. At least that's the feeling it conveys. As a woman do you enjoy hearing another woman "torn to pieces"? Of course not. Well, neither do men.

To remedy this preoccupation with divorce, have a training session with yourself in which you develop *new* answers to old questions.

"I understand you're divorced, Carol?"

"Yes, two years ago. I'm a physical therapist at St. Mary's Hospital. What do you do?"

You can get divorce out of your life very easily with a little effort. The reason you haven't is because it keeps the conversation on you. Be honest; it's not news, it's gossip, but it's *your* subject.

People don't actually quiz you on the personal details of your divorce. You volunteer them. Some women feel they have to explain what a beast their ex-husband is in order to *justify* the divorce. Whatever *your* reason for keeping it alive, whether it is bitterness or self-pity, it's a non-objective way to act and it detracts from your attractiveness.

2. *Sense of Humor.* You don't laugh as much as you used to, do you? I realize you have a lot of problems and not much fun in your life, or think you don't, but then you don't smile as often as you should, either. The corners of your mouth just seem to turn down constantly. You telegraph to the world that you are not a very happy person. An unhappy person promises to be no fun at all.

You can change this message that you are sending out. You start by smiling. Whenever I start to scowl or pout or perform any of the other unattractive facial contortions, I think of the Mona Lisa. Picture her in your mind. It's automatic. The corners of your mouth will go up, even if only slightly. But they *do go up.* When you look at the Mona Lisa you *know* she has a marvelous secret, a delicious insight that she shares with no one. She is appealing. She has a magnetic attraction. She *challenges* you to know her.

Can a smile do all that? Of course it can. The next time you get on a bus or a train, study the faces of those around you. Depressing isn't it? Wait. There's a child who smiled at you. What do you do? Why, you smile back of course. You can't help it. Now you try it. I don't mean to sit there with a silly grin on your face, trying first this expression on, then that. What you want is that Mona Lisa suggestion.

Now that you've got the scowl off your face, let's talk about humor. I know that my ability to laugh at ridiculous situations, and most particularly at myself, has probably saved my sanity. I sincerely mean that. My first job after my divorce was representing a manufacturer of Hawaiian sportswear. I had a showroom in the Los Angeles apparel mart, but part of my job was to pack up my samples and cart them all over the country. Unless you have wrestled with giant garment bags and salesmen's sample cases, you can't imagine what hard work this is.

About the third week I was in business I decided to give a fashion show for loungewear buyers. I engaged a nearby restaurant and started to pack up my samples, with my mother helping me. Suddenly I said, "Why should we pack up everything? Let's hang them on a portable rack and roll them over to the restaurant."

My mother took the back of the rack and I took the front and off we rolled, into the elevator, down to the lobby, out into the street. As we started down toward the restaurant, the rack began going sideways. I turned around to yell at my poor mother, who was doing her best to keep us on an even keel, and as I did, my end of the rack went into a crack, a wheel fell off, and the hangers all slid forward on top of me. I lost my balance, fell off the curb into the gutter, and the entire mess came over on top of me.

If anyone ever asked me the most embarrassing moment of my life, that would come close. Lying in a gutter on busy Main Street in Los Angeles under a pile of three dozen Hawaiian mumus is some kind of experience. For a brief moment I thought of just staying there and letting a truck run over me. Then I heard my mother say to someone:

"Yes, they're all cotton, completely washable. They make wonderful hostess gowns. No, it's my daughter's line. Just a minute and I'll find her for you."

I started to giggle, then to laugh. I laughed so hard the mumus started shaking. I laughed so hard I was immobilized. Here I was, buried in hibiscus print and my mother was selling on the curb! I was a month behind in my showroom rent; the phone bill hadn't been paid; my best numbers were now going to be soiled and wrinkled for my fashion show and I was laughing as if this were the funniest joke in the world. What was my alternative? To cry? To yell again at my mother? To kick the rack? I did the healthiest thing in the world—I laughed. Laughter has a therapeutic quality. You do *feel* better afterward, and you look better. Even when your eyes tear and the mascara runs, laughter makes you come alive.

Keeping a happy face around your children is terribly important. Certainly you should have serious conversations with them, ask their help and give advice, but temper this with good feelings. That doesn't mean good times. That's another subject. You don't have to entertain your children to create good feelings. You just "lighten up," or as my children put it, leave the "heavy talk" alone. I know your situation in life is *not* funny. Your problems are real and your needs genuine. But it helps *ev-*

eryone if you don't let the problems take over. Laugh the next time your son tips over his milk. He didn't do it on purpose and he can't pick it up. He probably feels worse about it than you do. Believe me, he'll love you for it.

I don't know a man alive who doesn't appreciate a woman with a sense of humor. He knows she isn't going to break her stride over every little problem. A woman with a sense of humor is a good dinner companion and a terrific traveling buddy. She always has a good time. She is a woman who wears well.

3. *Spontaneity.* Divorce does make you wary. It leaves you with a certain amount of distrust. It makes you hesitant to love again. It bruises your self-esteem. It makes you question actions and intentions with an unwarranted diligence. It robs you of your spontaneity.

One of the traditional signs of *age* is losing your nerve. You hate to give up the known for the unknown. You don't want to experiment or branch out. You always order the same safe items on the menu and part your hair down the middle. Your conversation is guarded and you're never game for changing plans in the middle of an evening. Your kids say you're no fun any more.

If you feel that you are beginning to lose your nerve, now is the time to check the tendency. I'm not suggesting that you commit outlandish or foolhardy acts simply to prove you're still vital. I'm talking about the small acts of daily living that require a little verve. You can start by listening to yourself. The clue words are:

"I've always done it this way."

"I don't feel like it now."

"Well, maybe next week."

You can almost hear the whine that goes with those lethargic statements. I have a close friend who was describing to me the type of woman a friend of ours dates:

"He always seems to be with a bland, blond lady."

That is *exactly* how you want to avoid being described.

A good place to start putting spontaneity back in your life is with your children. Bundle them all up and take them for a walk after dinner. Kids absolutely thrive on surprises. This is something you can do for them that doesn't cost money. My children are all great game players, competing at dominoes, backgammon, Monopoly, and gin rummy. They *still* love it when I play with them. When you see your children about to start a game, say "deal me in." What wonderful, uninhibited delight this creates in your family.

Try to find ways to put more fun in your job. Surprise your boss with flowers on his desk. Or put a plant on yours. Speak to people you don't know very well. You never can tell about that shy man behind the horn-rimmed glasses. He could have been trying for weeks to get up the nerve to speak to you.

The next time you're invited out to dinner and your date asks, "Well, where do you want to go?" pick a new restaurant or a cuisine you've never tried. Or say, "Let's go to a movie and get pizza after." Anything but, "Gee, I don't know. I guess Chez Leon again." That's bland, bland, bland.

4. *Change.* Change goes hand in glove with spontaneity. You need motivation to get out of patterns, change jobs, and move on. Divorce has a tendency to rivet you to the spot you're in. You look at the world and think, "My God, I'll never have the time or the money or the talent to get out of here!" No, you may not have time, money, and talent all at once, but you don't need them all at once. When you embark on a new venture you do it gradually. All you need to start with is the *desire* to do it.

California Highway 49 runs through the heart of the gold country. There, at Coloma, was where John Marshall made his famous discovery. All the small towns along the road, once booming, then ghost towns, are slowly being brought to life.

In one of those towns is an old inn, once again whitewashed and functioning with the smell of hot coffee and beaten biscuits wafting out the kitchen window. The owner, manager, cook, and house painter of this inn is a divorced woman in her fifties —probably late fifties.

Ten years ago her husband informed her that he was leaving their marriage to be with another woman and that she could divorce him or not according to her choice. After agonizing over her decision for eight months, her friends urged her to seek a divorce. Even her children, who were worried about her failing health, told her they thought a divorce would be for the best.

At this time the woman was still living in the family home in Sacramento. Two of her children were in college and one was married. In the property settlement the woman received a few thousand dollars and the home. She was miserable. The divorce only aggravated her unhappiness; she lost more weight and all interest in life. Her family became seriously concerned. Her married daughter came by once a week to check on her. On one of these visits she absolutely insisted that her mother come with her for a drive. They started up Highway 49. At noon they stopped for lunch in one of the small towns. Next door to the restaurant, formerly a blacksmith's shop, was an old Victorian house set back from the street and covered from sight by overgrown bushes and trees.

I don't know how you feel about spirits or ESP or destiny or any of the other unexplainable phenomena that surround us, but I have a wide-open mind and an insatiable curiosity in all these areas. When this woman told me her story I had absolutely no reason in the world to doubt it. She said that after lunch she felt a strong pull toward the old house. Without a word to her daughter she began to make her way through the bushes. When she reached the front porch she stopped, then went around to the side of the house, opened the door and walked in. The house was in dreadful condition, absolutely left to rot where it stood.

The woman went into every room on the first floor, then up the stairs to the bedrooms, back to the kitchen, and out to the barn. By this time her daughter had caught up with her, but instead of saying anything she just watched her mother. She saw a look of peace on her face that she had not seen in months and months. When the woman saw her daughter, she smiled and said, "It's mine. My house. I know it is."

You can guess the rest of the story. The woman sold her home, bought the old Victorian, and with very little help brought it back to life as a charming country inn. She said she never needed to thin the wall paint. Her tears did that for her.

She said she cried away her unhappiness until the last velvet drape was hung. Then she said a final farewell to her old life and opened the door to her new one.

Restoring old houses, bringing back villages, opening shops in out-of-the-way places often seem the domain of young people. Why have they taken to these tasks with gusto? Because they are not afraid to *change*. They don't do things the way we did. Well, we don't have to do things the way we did, either! We can experiment with life, reach out and embrace new ideas. That is one of the side benefits of divorce. It gives you freedom —the freedom to choose.

5. *Privacy.* There used to be a saying that in a divorce action the couple aired all their "dirty linen" in the courtroom. Today seventeen states have *no-fault divorce laws,* and courtroom recriminations are no longer permitted. The court does not care that he slept around or that she had a miserable temper and threw things. All the court needs to know is that the marriage has broken down. When the no-fault divorce law was written, those who sponsored it felt that the removal of an adversary climate would let the couple quietly dissolve their marriage with far less bitterness and without damage to either's character. No winners; no losers. Most states are now adopting the *spirit* of the no-fault laws if not the law itself.

The no-fault law probably does help to keep the "dirty linen" out of the courtroom. A divorce, however, is still a very *public* matter. It's news, of sorts, and certainly you can't pretend you're still married. Your family know, your children know, your friends know, the department stores know, the insurance company knows and the people at work know. You are in the public domain.

When you have done something "newsworthy" people question you. Sometimes they ask guarded questions disguised in pleasantries such as "Sorry to hear about the divorce, but then I guess you're glad it's all over, aren't you?" You can answer with a simple, "Yes, you bet," but the chances are that you don't. You probably take that ball and run with it.

"Couldn't be over soon enough for me. Of course we still have to sell the house, so I still talk to Jim. I want my half! But the minute that's done we never have to *see* each other again. Ever!"

That's nobody's business but yours and your ex-husband's. You *owe* it to him and to yourself to maintain a little privacy. Your statement infers that maybe Jim isn't honest. Maybe he'll find a way to cheat you out of your half of the house. What if this statement gets back to Jim's boss. You're his ex-wife. You should know if he's honest or not. You could damage his career. That might sound like a great idea at first, but think it over. If you have children, Jim is paying child support. If he loses his job, then what? Frankly I'd much rather have an ex-husband who's successful. It speaks better of you to have been married to a responsible man. It is certainly to the benefit of the children to have a father who is in a good job. Not only does he set a good example, but he is someone they can be proud of.

If you have been airing your gripes and grievances, it's time to change your record and start keeping your life a bit more private. One thing privacy does is to develop an air of mystery about you, which is always intriguing. Another reason to court privacy is to be able to do some serious thinking. You can't learn anything with your mouth open. You just magnify your problems by discussing them, whereas you cure them by careful planning.

We live in a society that encourages trips to the psychiatrist, participation in group therapy and membership in discussion groups. Talk it out; talk it over, we are told. Tell everything you know. I feel that sometimes we've gone too far. A divorced woman, especially, doesn't need to keep talking and talking and talking about her problems. She needs *constructive* help, and such help is usually *not* found in group therapy. Unless you are *seriously* in need of psychiatric help, I recommend that you talk less and think more. Look to specific sources for genuine guidance.

6. *Friendship.* The above lecture does not apply in the case of a very close friend. Who could function without that special person who knows us, understands us, and loves us? If you don't have such a person in your life, you should put out feelers

toward establishing this most beneficial relationship. Take your time, because good, close, dear friends are hard to find.

You probably have an acquaintance right now who could be developed into a good friend. A good friend is not someone who is there just for the sake of listening to your problems. Friendship is reciprocal. You have to do some of the listening. Favors have to be exchanged. When your friend helps you, you find a way to help your friend.

One of the interesting side effects of divorce is that it frees you from the constricting idea that your best friends must necessarily be other women. They don't. Men make absolutely topnotch best friends. They can be enormously helpful in giving you business advice. Often a man can see into the heart of a problem faster than a woman can. A man trained in business will be analytical and will be able to help you to make priorities in your life.

It is sometimes difficult for a woman (or a man) to have a friend of the opposite sex. Those of us who were so conditioned to "woman's role" often feel silly or guilty taking up a man's time. We think our problems would bore them. It took me a long time to learn to talk to a man like a friend, but once I did I found men to be very receptive to having a special friendship with a woman. My men friends look forward to talking to me as much as I do to talking to them.

You will be limited to choosing single or divorced men as friends because most married couples do not understand a nonsexual relationship outside of marriage. If a husband develops a strong friendship with a divorced woman, the wife feels threatened. Most marriages couldn't survive under those conditions. You don't need *that* additional problem in your life.

Let's talk about sex just a minute. One of my very close men friends is an attractive and successful bachelor of thirty-two. He is in a business where he meets models, actresses, and all manner of gorgeous women, whose company he enjoys enormously. Yet he will drive 350 miles to spend a weekend with me. Why is that? To quote him:

"Because I can kick off my shoes, sit in your kitchen, talk to you, then go to bed by myself."

It is a treat for him, he says, to just be able to relax and talk about his business, his life, his hopes, and his fears—and not worry about the man/woman game.

Contrary to what the men's magazines would have us believe, all men are not studs looking to sleep with every woman they can. In this age of aggressive and available women a great many men welcome a friendship that doesn't require them to "perform." Men have need of comfort and advice just as women do. So reach out your hand in friendship. That's often the most desirable part of your body.

7. *Caring.* Divorce makes us zero in on our own problems to the extent that we lose sight of the world. Revolutions and famines can be taking place and we think only of the missed support payment. Certainly the support payment is of vital concern to you, but so should the revolution and the famine be. We are members of a community, residents of a state, citizens of a country, and participants in the happenings of the world.

Narrow thinking makes us dull. An uninformed woman is simply not as attractive as a woman who is interested and up to date; a woman who reads and listens; a woman who thinks and evaluates; a woman who *cares.*

It is easy to be informed with the media bombarding all our senses. All it takes is a shift in interest. Open your eyes and ears from narrow self-vision to world vision. It helps put your life into perspective. It makes you realize that others have problems, too.

Caring should extend over into helping. There is nothing more therapeutic than throwing yourself into the task of working on someone else's problem. When I get depressed over a situation in my life and start getting that narrow vision—that self-pity syndrome—I go to my desk and work on my mail. I receive dozens of letters from divorced women all over the country asking for help, advice, and solutions to their problems. I try to answer every one in a positive manner and offer my best thinking on their particular plight. Some of these women are in such a bad way that I truly wonder what will happen to them. Some are physically abused, some are neglected, and all are in genuine need. Believe me, helping someone else makes your problems pale by comparison.

Your children need a great deal of love, reassurance, and caring. When you are weighed down by the burden of despair, you are restricted from giving them what they need. When you pull them into your arms it gives you a magical lift—not to mention what it does for them. Love is a curative. Haven't all great religions stressed the power of love?

Your community needs you. There is an unending list of tasks that needs a task force. Don't wait to be asked—volunteer. Step right out there and say what you feel. Support the candidate of your choice. Circulate a petition for a stoplight at that busy intersection. Go to a school board meeting just once and see how your tax dollars are being spent. *Care* what goes on around you. It's your world, too.

8. *Spirituality.* I use the word spirituality more to connote what it does *not* mean than what it does. You will find more definitions of the word "spirit" and all it pertains to than there are religious sects in the entire world. For the moment let's say that spirituality is what you *are* that you can't name. It's neither your physical body nor your five senses. It is not your code of ethics or your material state, nor has it anything to do with your family, your job, your community—or even with your church.

Within each of us is a secret private something that is the essence of "I." We refer to it when we lament, "No one knows the real me!" That's quite true. We don't ever entirely know the real "me." But we know we're there. Why? Because this "me" is the core of our entire being. It makes itself felt in strange and marvelous ways; at other times it rears its head in an ugly manner, violent and hurtful. We talk of our "better side" and of "dark days."

What has this got to do with divorce, you might ask. A great deal, because a divorce forces or frees a woman to take the time to dig deep to find out about herself. Stripped of the predictable role of wife, often pleasant but always confining, the divorced woman can no longer react and live in a set way. She's on her own. How often have I heard a divorced woman say, "My God,

I didn't know I was so strong!" or "I've had to make friends with myself and I like what I've found." I've heard myself say that I was born at age thirty!

The divorced woman has a unique opportunity to begin to develop this "I" in any number of exciting, rewarding ways. It begins with a strong desire to conduct the quest. The ever present danger is that discouragements in daily living make "roles" look attractive again—especially the role of wife. "Sure it had its bad points," you might say, "but in marriage I at least had more financial security and somebody to share the load with." Don't let yourself be seduced by this kind of thinking!

Once you decide you are going to start your journey into "you," make a pact with yourself that you won't talk about what you are doing. You sincerely cannot explain it. I am having a very difficult time writing about it because it is something that you *feel* and *know*, not something you write or talk about. However, your quest should begin with reading what others have to say on the subject. I could supply you with my thirty-year reading list, but that would be unfair, because choosing what you read is part of the quest. You can start at the metaphysical shelf in a secondhand-book store. Buy one book and from it you will find reference to others that sound interesting. You can discover an old self-help book in a garage sale, or read an article in a science fiction magazine. It is all a great and marvelous adventure.

Meditation, or quiet times to think, plays a great part in your quest. Learning *how* to think for *answers* rather than just wishful daydreaming must be part of your plan. Tests of your power to *will* your senses should be included. Begin with simple little tests such as getting up fifteen minutes earlier to read, or by resisting dessert. This is called developing strength of character. You will be able to give yourself a positive, *constructive* order and expect it to be carried out.

You are *not* aiming at becoming a mystic or guru. You won't chant or put ashes on your forehead or don sackcloth. You absolutely must stay away from mind-expanding drugs or chemicals of any kind. I would suggest that you cut down on your drinking or quit it entirely. It is of no benefit to you. What you are striving for is the *development of your inner power*. You can depend on this power and you will learn to *trust your instincts*. You will not turn *outward* for answers; you will turn *inward*.

This is the secret to *enriched living*. This gives you the *confidence* to go after anything you sincerely desire. This is the center from which you emanate. This gives you an edge on the world and makes you a leader. This frees you from dependency on others. This . . . is your spirituality.

DEVELOPING THE OUTER YOU

You can now see why we started with the inner you. That's the most important part. You could be that woman on the cover of V*ogue*—you know, that woman with the flat stomach, the high, pointed breasts, the slim hips, and the bouncy hair—well, you could be that woman, but if you were a blank inside nobody would be at all interested in you. Of course we all want to look our best, and so we should, it goes without saying. A woman who doesn't "care" how she looks has psychological problems. She's indulging in a grand game of self-hate and defying anyone to pay attention to her.

Before we get into the night creams and face peels, let's talk about age. Age is meaningless—except to you. You are not the only person in the world who is growing older. Trust me—we all are. But that's *all* that's happening. We're not becoming less attractive, less efficient, less capable, less enthusiastic, or less desirable. We can continue to learn, to grow and to become. So stop looking in the mirror at those little lines around your eyes. Strike the words, "at my age," from your vocabulary. Refuse to categorize yourself as middle-aged or senior citizen or even swinging twenties. You are none of the above.

Probably the best commercial *ever* written has this theme: You're not getting older, you're getting better. It's true, you know. The only time we lament our age is when we feel insecure or threatened. We want to blame it on *something*, so we say, "I would have gotten the job if I were younger," or "He would have called again if I weren't in my forties," or "I'd do better in the class if I weren't ten years older than everyone else."

These are cop-outs, as the kids would say, or in better English, safe rationalizations, because age can be a factor in some jobs, some relationships and some learning situations. But not in all! Not even in the majority. I have shown this in other chapters, so in this one will stick to age and beauty.

The one thing you *never* want to be guilty of is *acting* your age. The youth movement changed all that. I don't mean that you should wear long hair and Levi's and hang around the discos pretending you're twenty-two. But you certainly can wear attractive slacks and a satin shirt and get out on the dance floor with your escort or your son. The difference is that you are being *you*, not a woman trying to be a kid. That's what I mean by *not* acting out an age, a charade.

The other extreme is to go to a disco in a polyester dress and sensible walking shoes and giggle and act embarrassed. Again you are acting out an age charade. Be comfortable where you are and get in the spirit of the event. This makes you an age*less* woman.

We've all seen, met or know a woman in her sixties, seventies or even eighties whose attitude toward life is an *active involvement*. Her eyes sparkle; her mind is alert; her conversation is stimulating. She is a pleasure to be around. When you are with her the last thing you are conscious of is how old she is. She is such a treat to be with that she becomes your contemporary. This is the type of woman *you* can become, now and later. That's the *last* time I want to hear about age! You are better *now* than you have ever been!

Sleep. A good night's uninterrupted sleep has to be the greatest cosmetic of them all. In fact, a plastic surgeon told me that a good face lift has the effect of making you look rested. So remember that unless what you are doing at night has merit, go to bed. Each of us functions at our maximum efficiency on different hours of sleep. If you know you are a bear unless you get a full eight hours, then be sure to get that full eight hours.

Ruth was a married woman living in Malibu. When her husband left her for another woman a good twenty years younger, Ruth was felled by the news. She literally took to her bed. She would crawl out to cook breakfast for her two children, then with a pot of coffee she would climb the stairs and sink back into bed. She ordered her groceries by phone, banked by mail, and seldom left her home.

It took two years of this molelike existence before Ruth got up out of bed and back into the world. She would probably have stayed in bed longer except that her ex-husband, a script writer, suddenly took a dive in salary. She had to get a job to make the mortgage payments.

This type of sleep is not therapeutic. It's an anesthesia. It is like a heavy drug that dulls your senses or a warm cocoon that envelops you in a false sense of security. Although sleep is beneficial for your looks, your temperament, your resiliency, your nerves, and your sexuality, too much sleep is *not* good for you or any of the above.

Diet. Weight is aging. There are just no two ways about it. You can have a pretty face, beautiful skin, healthy hair, and a beaming smile, but if you're thick through the middle you look "matronly." Any woman who is considerably overweight either has a physical disability or an inferiority complex. If you care about yourself, you care about how you look. When you overfeed your body you are feeding a complex. Or two or three.

Walk into any bookstore. There will be at least two or three diet books featured on a best seller table. Pick up any women's magazine and what do you see? The new ten-day diet, the peanut butter and brown rice diet, or the Oriental fast diet. Most restaurants feature the "diet plate" or the "calorie counter's special." Supermarket shelves stock water-packed fruit and sugarless desserts. We are a country of perpetual and perennial dieters!

You are what you eat, as some well-known nutritionist once said. I believe in good nutrition. I know about proteins and minerals and vitamins and yogurt and liver and kelp. So should you. You should know about the chemistry of your body *before* you embark on a diet. I firmly believe that if you *know* what you're eating and if you give a great deal of thought to it, you are on the best possible diet. Trying to follow a super fourteen-day wonder diet that requires combinations of certain foods; which requires weighing each portion; and which requires special trips to the market is not to your best advantage. Learning about food and planning your own diet *is* to your advantage.

Go to your local library and check out a couple of books on nutrition. Also look at the new beauty books on the best seller list. See what the experts have to say. Then *do* something about your weight! Come on, quit kidding yourself. You know (and I know and your kids know) that you're fat because you eat too much.

I do have some good ideas on how *not* to eat so much. About three years ago I decided I would never again eat anything that wasn't delicious merely to be friendly, polite, sociable, or just because it was there. I happen to be a very good cook and enjoy cooking. So why should I force down a mediocre restaurant meal or a heavy businessman's lunch or a creamy, gooey charity luncheon? Yes, you can sit there and just not eat. No one is going to take a fork and pry your mouth open.

Trick two is never to let another hors d'oeuvre pass your lips. I neither eat *nor* drink at a cocktail party. I make *no* issue at all of the fact. No one cares and no one pushes. When the waiter comes by with his tray to take your order, very quietly lean over and tell him to skip you the rest of the evening because you're not drinking. Do the same with the waiters passing the hors d'oeuvres. It works like magic. Don't try to fake it by toying with a drink or asking for ginger ale. You don't have to. It's your right to smile, have a good time, and leave the calories alone.

When you go out to dinner or to a dinner party, do the same thing. If a concerned hostess asks why you're not drinking or having an hors d'oeuvre, tell her you're saving yourself for dinner. If she has gone to a great deal of trouble over the menu she will be delighted because you will be one guest whose palate isn't dulled.

Trick three is always to leave something on your plate. Never take that very last bite. If you are serving yourself, take less, but if the food is being put in front of you, don't eat it all.

Trick four is no desserts. Ever. Not even that thirteen egg-white velvet chocolate delight. Sweets are a drug and can be addictive. It's almost impossible to take only one bite. So pretend you're a sugaraholic and kick the habit.

Other bugaboos are pastas and French bread. But for me life wouldn't be worth living without linguini and clam sauce, so trick five is, if you *know* you have to have a pasta fix, don't have anything else. Fast for the day if you can and try to eat early in the evening so you won't be going to bed with your full, full stomach.

You can regulate your intake of food any number of ways, so experiment. *Know* what you're eating and make what you eat count. It should be good for you *all over*.

Exercise. As you grow older you put on more weight even when your food intake remains the same. I don't know why. Perhaps it's body chemistry, less moving around, or a slowdown of digestion. Whatever it is doesn't matter. Doing something about it does.

Exercise, like diet, has to be a *part* of your life. It can't be something you make time to do—you won't do it, at least with the regularity that makes a real difference in how you look and feel. You absolutely *must* have some sort of physical action in your life.

1. *Walking.* Just walking around the house doesn't count. You have to get outside and vigorously *go* someplace. If you can walk to the store or walk to work, then do so. If not, plan a thirty-minute walk before breakfast or after dinner. Do it the same time every day and *know* that this is walk time, a time not to be rescheduled for another activity.

2. *Swimming.* I don't know a major city that doesn't have a YWCA with a swimming pool. Membership, swim cards, and lockers are certainly reasonable. Showers, hair dryers, and towels are available. Pool hours are arranged so you can swim before work, after work or on your lunch hour. I swim between four thirty and five thirty, and I wouldn't miss it for the world. Some cold, windy days I nearly freeze waiting on the corner for

the bus, but when my body hits that warm water, that more than makes up for it. Swimming is complete exercise and you will find you lose inches if you are faithful.

3. *Exercise Class.* Most YWCAs also conduct regular exercise classes. So do a great many park departments, dance workshops and church groups. Classes in beginning ballet, belly dancing and tap are really just exercise groups. They can be more fun than the traditional knee bends and leg lifts. There are also health clubs you can join to work out on their equipment. I would advise against the latter as they are often quite expensive, and you go by yourself. It's easy to put off that trip downtown when there is no group waiting.

4. *Other Forms of Exercise.* Cycling, jogging, and tennis are also good exercise. So are riding a horse, sailing a boat, and swinging a golf club, but these activities are hard to do every day or depend on a partner or cost a great deal of money. Walking and/or swimming are available, inexpensive, and effective.

Makeup. Good nutrition and faithful exercise will show not only in your body but in your face, skin, hair, and nails. Few women over sixteen, however, can leave their looks *as is*. We all look better with makeup and a proper hairstyle. If you can afford to go to a makeup artist at one of the well-known salons and learn how to do your face, by all means go. It will make all the difference in the world. Too much makeup is worse than not enough. An expert knows when enough is enough.

If you can't afford the salon, do what I do. When I feel in the need of a little new glamour in my life, I watch the newspapers for in-store demonstrations. Most major cosmetic houses send their representatives to the large department stores to demonstrate their products. They perform their demonstrations free on volunteers. You walk in and sign up. Pick a time you feel the store will not be too busy. I have found these representatives to be very talented and very polite. They depend on volunteers for the performance of their job so they are delighted when you ask to be the model.

Obviously the representatives are there to sell their wares. The theory is, of course, that once you see how glamorous you are in their makeup you'll buy all their products in sight. Naturally you can't afford it. You are there to learn, not to buy. I always thank the representatives profusely, then say I wished I could buy their marvelous products, but as a working woman, divorced, I simply can't afford them. I cannot tell you how many of the women representatives have said to me, "My, do I understand. I'm divorced myself." Don't ever be intimidated by salespeople. When the ad says "free demonstration" that's what you go in for and nothing more. Later you can go to the drugstore or the dime store and buy your cosmetics for one third the price.

Hair. Many department stores and private salons feature styling specials. Again, watch the ads and when Monsieur Georges can be had for half price, take yourself in for a new do. It's worth paying retail for a good haircut, so if you are looking very straggly don't wait for the price to drop. When your hair is properly cut and styled it is far easier for you to take care of.

Before you go to the stylist, thumb through fashion magazines until you see a picture of what you want. One picture is worth ten thousand waves of the hand. But keep an open mind. A first-rate stylist will have some good ideas, too. The important message to get across is that you are a working woman, divorced, on a budget, and you do your own hair. Therefore you need a style you can manage. It is worth your while to learn how to blow-dry your hair. It's a great freedom; no more rollers, no more pins, no more spray.

In taking care of your own hair, experiment with shampoos. Invest in a good conditioner and use it whenever you shampoo your hair. Let's talk color a minute. Gray, I think, is fine if you feel like a gray-haired women. Frankly, I don't think I ever shall. There are just too many terrific colors to choose from, and color is so easy to apply! The rule is, however, go lighter not darker, and never go black. Nothing brings out the lines and wrinkles in your face like that shoe-polish-black color! Leave the copper colors alone, too, unless you're a real pro. You don't want that carrot-top look.

Try streaking or frosting. Multi-color hair can be very effective. If you don't like the end result of your efforts, there is a product on the market that takes the color *out* of your hair. You can "erase" and start over. Ask someone whom you consider to be chic and well groomed what she thinks of your hair style and color. Often we think we look terrific when we look ten (or twenty) years behind the times.

Wardrobe. I used to find shopping for clothes a dreadful bore and a depressing experience. I never seemed to find what I was looking for until the fourth or fifth store. I hated the dressing room mirrors because I looked fat, while the new clothes made me want to throw out everything I had worn in. Who could find anything in those huge department stores with seven blouse departments and four shoe departments and six slacks departments. Coats on one, three, and seven; dresses on two, four, and five.

Then I discovered the joys of a boutique. Not any boutique, but one run by a man who loves everything I love. That's happiness. You see, the secret of shopping is to shop for a store— then stick with the store. They know you; you know them. Their sales are real because you *know* their merchandise. They call you when they have something new come in.

The second secret to shopping is to have a co-ordinated wardrobe. Everything in your closet should go with something else and have several uses. Separates are the working woman's best ally. Skirts, blouses, slacks, jackets and turtlenecks, marvelous turtlenecks!

I learned about a co-ordinated wardrobe from a man who travels the world constantly with one small-to-medium suitcase he carries with him. He wears gray slacks, shirt, tie, blue blazer, and a raincoat on the plane. If his first stop is Paris, he puts on dark blue slacks with the blue blazer, adds a blue-and-brown Tattersall vest, and you would swear it's a suit. His next stop is for dinner in Venice. He wears the gray slacks and blue blazer with a gray turtle-neck sweater. A conference in Cairo brings out khaki slacks and safari jacket. For luncheon in Nairobi he wears the khaki slacks and the blue blazer with an open-necked shirt. You see what I mean.

I've copied him with my black four-piece suit. On a ten-day business trip to London last October I wore the black skirt, black-and-white striped blouse and black jacket for luncheon. For the theater I wore the black slacks, a white satin shirt and the black jacket. A gray turtleneck with the skirt went for a conference, while the black slacks, a black sweater with a wide belt fitted an evening in a pub.

The best aspect of a co-ordinated wardrobe is that you need only *one* pair of shoes and *one* handbag. Naturally when you translate this into an everyday working wardrobe you'll need more than one pair of shoes. But keep the basic color scheme throughout your closet. Grays, blacks, beiges, whites, and reds can all use black shoes or boots. If you then fall in love with a pair of brown slacks you're stuck. Look instead for black-and-white check or hunter's green.

To co-ordinate your wardrobe, get a pencil and paper and write down what you own. Put your slacks on one line, then your skirts, blouses, jackets, etc., all on their own lines. I'm talking about the clothes you wear to work, those which should be the heart of your wardrobe. When you have it all written down, try to see what your basic theme is and how many different outfits you can put together. Just looking at your wardrobe on paper will enable you to come up with combinations you didn't realize you had.

My oldest daughter can go into my closet and borrow a pair of slacks, a shirt, a sweater, and a scarf and walk out looking like a model on a runway. She invariably chooses four items that I would *never* have put together. She has a terrific eye for color and a decided flair. I do not, so I get her to help me. This is what you should do next. Call over a friend whose clothes sense you admire and get her to look in your closet and go over your list. Ask her to suggest additions to your wardrobe. When you have saved enough money to buy something new, pick an item from her list.

The Duchess of Windsor once said, "A smart woman doesn't buy clothes, she collects them." When your wardrobe is coordinated, you are in fact collecting. You aren't going to be buying a new "outfit" which has no relationship to anything else in your closet. You are going to add a new piece which brings new life to what you already have.

This in a good many ways is an age of the costume. Although the little black dress flirts with a comeback now and again, it is still "anything goes" as far as party clothes are concerned. I've already described how I deal with the question of a nighttime wardrobe. If developing your own style doesn't appeal to you, then stick to long skirts and velvet or heavy satin slacks. You can work them right into your co-ordinated wardrobe, mixing them with turtlenecks and shirts. I've found a black jersey halter blouse to be an indispensable item of instant evening glamour.

For those once-a-year big evenings requiring a long dress, get a good black sheath with a flattering neckline. I've worn mine for eight years now and it's good for another eight. It is absolutely ridiculous to spend a great deal of money on an evening dress. If it is a lavender tulle with giant pink velvet roses at the hem, you will not want to wear it year in and year out. Not only will everyone remember it, but the roses will get flattened and the tulle wrinkled. You'll soon look like last year's Valentine.

Beware of jewelry. I think much harm is done to appearance by gaudy or poorly chosen costume jewelry. Jewelry doesn't have to be real to be effective, but it has to be right. When in doubt, leave it off. You can never be criticized for being too understated. *You* want to be featured, not what you put on your back.

What's underneath it are all the important elements: who *you* are; what *you* know; and what *you* have to offer. We telegraph to the world what we know about ourselves. Are we interesting or dull? Excellent or mediocre? A delight or a drag? It depends upon how much time we've spent *developing* ourselves. I've said it so often I'm like a broken record, but the great big truth of the matter is: Intelligence is the *ultimate* turn-on.

8

Men

and the Divorced Woman

I recently sent out a questionnaire through the newsletter of the National Association for Divorced Women. This newsletter goes to divorced women of all ages, interests, and varying geographical locations. One of the questions I asked was: *Do you have trouble meeting available men?* The answers which returned ran something like this:

"No. There are plenty of available men. They just happen to be married, that's all."

"What's an available man?"

"No, because there aren't any."

"Yes. I have trouble meeting men. All kinds."

"Yes, because I don't want a no-good drinking playboy."

"I ain't met one man yet. I live in a town of 17,000 married people with kids."

"An available man to me would have to be educated, interesting, sympathetic, and possess a fine sense of humor. Obviously I'm alone."

I could go on for pages. The man situation, as far as the divorcée is concerned, is quite something. The most recent statistics show that in this country today there are 23 million unmarried women and 16 million unmarried men. Those statistics don't begin to tell the story. There is another little factor called age. The fifty-year-old man can dip into the twenties and thirties for his women, as well as the forties and fifties; whereas the fifty-year-old woman must settle for fifty- and sixty-year-old men. This isn't fair, of course, but as long as men do the picking and choosing, that seems to be the way it is.

Can anything be done to help the divorced woman meet eligible men? You bet. It doesn't take numbers of men in your life to make it interesting. It takes a few, a couple, or just one. You'll notice I didn't say "available" men, because that puts a limit on your exposure to and enjoyment of men.

YOUR EX-HUSBAND

The man who appears in your life with the most regularity (at least for a while) is your ex-husband. Why? It's because of joint tax forms, business problems, relatives and the children, if you have children. He is not on the eligible list, but it would be to both of your advantages (and the children's) if you could have a working truce. Remember, you thought enough of this man to marry him. You may now shudder at the sight of him, but hardly anyone is 100 per cent bad.

An ex-husband could turn into a new friend. After the hurt and bitterness cools off, you might think about this. If you have children, it's extremely beneficial for the two of you to be able to sit down to discuss their problems. You are the two people who have their best interests at heart. You can accomplish more when your goals are the same, or, if not the same, at least compatible.

This doesn't mean that you become pals to the extent that he is back in your life, taking a beer out of the refrigerator at will and not sending the child support payments on time. Keep a certain formality and business posture. You can do this and still be friends.

If your ex-husband has remarried, it will be more difficult. New wives always seem to resent former wives. Your friendship should include her. After all, you'll be seated with her at your son's graduation and your daughter's wedding. If you are on speaking terms, friendly speaking terms, she will feel a greater disposition to do nice things for your children.

The point of all this is to show that the world is a difficult place. Why add to the difficulties when a friendly overture could smooth the way. You have enough real problems to face. You can eliminate the "hostile ex" syndrome by being smart. A friend is also far less dangerous than an enemy.

YOUR NEW SOCIAL LIFE

Your old social life, and in fact the bulk of *all* social life, is couple-oriented. We think by the twos in this country. When you split as a couple you will find yourself gradually eased out of the picture. A few old friends will still call you for dinner and once in a while you'll be invited to a cocktail party. Seldom will you receive an invitation to a dance.

I once said to a divorced male friend of mine that I thought this was quite unfair. Men seemed to perk right along, get invitations to dinners and receive bids to balls, while we women had to go to a movie with our kids. Not so, said my friend. He, too, had been dropped by the couple world. When he was first divorced it was a different story. He was most welcome to cry on the shoulders of his married friends, even to rest his head on an understanding wife's bosom. But as he began to adjust, take his laundry to Ling Lee by himself, move out of the hotel and into a charming pied-à-terre, and tell a clever joke at a dinner party, the invitations to friends' homes began to taper off. The wives, who do the inviting, didn't want their husbands to see what a high old time my friend was having as a divorced man. The absolute severing of the ties came, he said, when he took Miss Australia to a Christmas party in his old neighborhood.

Both the divorced man and the divorced woman have to build new social lives not dependent on their married friends. This is not all bad. In fact it's quite an intriguing idea. You are no longer the least bit restricted in choosing whom you invite into your life. You'll find the age limit expands both ways.

You'll be enjoying younger as well as older people. You'll become more inventive in your leisure time. You don't have the money to spend, so you'll discover free activities. When you do entertain, your menu will be simplified. You'll discover that no one minds sitting on the floor and eating on the coffee table.

Break the couple syndrome yourself. Invite *people* to your home, individual, interesting people whose company you enjoy. Mix and match. Have some friends from work, friends from night school and friends of your children. Forget even numbers and similar interests. You will be amazed at how soon word gets around that it's *fun* at your house.

WHERE TO MEET MEN

Having parties doesn't solve the problem of meeting single men whom you will want to relate to on a one-to-one basis. It's a way to spend pleasant evenings and enjoy people, but it does not take the place of a quiet dinner with an attractive man who only has eyes for you. Yes, attractive, available men are out there in the world. They happen to be just as anxious to meet attractive, available women as you are to meet attractive, available men.

1. *Through Married Friends.* This is not a contradiction. Your married friends may not invite you to all their parties, but your *close* married friends will want to help you. First you have to explain to them that you *need* their help. Often married people think divorced women are having the time of their lives. They hesitate to invite them to "ordinary family parties." Assure your friends that this is *not* the case.

Be specific in your wants. Ask your close friend if she *knows* any men to introduce you to and if she does ask her if she'll arrange a small dinner to do this. Volunteer to help. Bring the flowers or the wine. Come early and set the table. Let her know you *appreciate* what she's doing. A real favor you can do for your married friends is to offer to take their children for the weekend so they can go away.

One idea that has worked quite well with friends of mine is a share-the-wealth party. Each married couple invited is asked to bring two single people—a man and a woman. It is not necessary that the two people know each other or that they be the same age. One can be divorced and the other widowed. Both can be never-marrieds. You end up with a terrific mix of married couples and singles. You can ask two or three of your married friends to give these parties and meet thirty or forty new single men. Not all of them will be of interest to you, but what a nice number to consider.

2. *Through Work.* When you have a job and are out in the world, you can't help but meet people, including men who are going to be attractive to you. If you work in a downtown area, eat lunch at one of those sandwich restaurants where you have to share tables. Don't just take pot luck, look around before you alight. On a nice day bring a sandwich and walk to the nearest park or fountain. Sunshine has a way of breaking the ice.

If you are with a large company, see if they have a singles group. If they don't, start one. You will be amazed how many people are waiting for someone *else* to be the organizer. You can put up a notice on the bulletin board for those interested in starting a bowling league, or going to the opera, or studying Chinese cooking. Remember the cardinal rule: *Everyone you meet is a potential source for meeting someone else.*

3. *Through Classes.* Signing up for night school can be an interesting way to meet men as well as to learn something. If your prime motivation is to meet men, don't sign up for macrame. Look into woodworking, or stock-market analysis, or beginning navigation.

Dina is a divorced woman of Greek extraction in her forties. She had been saving money for three years to take a cruise of the Greek islands. In anticipation of her trip, she joined an adult education class to take lessons in the Greek language. At the end of the six weeks, the instructor invited a man from the Greek consulate to come to the class and give a brief lecture on the customs and culture of his country. After class Dina spoke to him about her trip. He suggested she drop by the consulate and pick up some pamphlets he had and a book she should read.

Dina made it a point to be at the man's office the next day. After she finished the book he'd lent her, she returned it and asked to borrow another. When she returned the second book, she said she was very grateful for his help and asked if he and his wife would like to come to her house for a Greek dinner that her aunt was going to prepare. The man was delighted and accepted gratefully. He then said he would be coming alone because he was a widower. Did they live happily ever after? I don't know, but they married and guess where they spent their honeymoon. Cruising the Greek islands.

4. *Through Travel.* We've already talked a good deal about travel and what a grand way it is to meet people. Let's talk just a minute about travel that would attract men. Contrary to what the ads would have us believe, I don't think most men go off on a trip with the express purpose of meeting women. They don't flock to Tahiti to ogle the beautiful natives or spend hours on the sands at Cannes checking the bikinis or absence of same. Certainly some men do, but those men you wouldn't be interested in anyway.

When a man puts out money for a trip he wants the same thing you do: value received. If he's on his way to Europe or South America he will do the same things you will. He will take a city tour, rush for a room on a train, or scout out a delightful small restaurant. Keep alert. The man next to you at the fountain may be alone. Ask to borrow his guidebook.

5. *Through Clubs.* There are as many types of clubs in this country as there are interests. There are cycling clubs, bridge clubs, square dance clubs, bird-watching clubs, swimming clubs, and great books clubs, not to mention the Young Republicans, the English Speaking Union, the Daughters of the Golden West and the Richard III Society. This barely scratches the surface. If you wanted to, you could join enough clubs or groups to keep you busy *every* night of the week and all day Sunday.

To indiscriminately join up with every group in town defeats your purpose. You are a motivated, productive woman who values her time. There is nothing wrong, however, in joining a club whose objectives genuinely interest you. Look in the society or family pages of your local newspaper. Most club activities are covered, and you can find out whom to call. The smaller the paper, the greater number of these items there will be, so check the neighborhood and the weekend throwaway papers.

One type of club which is becoming more and more prevalent is the local consciousness-raising group. Six or eight persons will meet in private homes to discuss issues of the day, community concerns, and personal problems. Often speakers are brought in from the government or business world. These groups are informal and often enjoyable. How beneficial they are would depend on the individual participants. You might consider starting such a group made up of divorced women. An exchange of information on jointly-shared problems can be a lifeline.

Political parties depend very heavily on their volunteer workers at *all* levels. You can *always* find someone running for office who needs you—and needs you desperately. If you want your volunteer work to be more meaningful, get a friend to run for the school board or planning commission and get behind her.

We all know that there is a rash of divorce in our nation's capital. Politicans can be very difficult husbands. It's not just the long hours, the days away from home, the hectic pace. It's also the ego problem, the dealing with worshipful precinct workers and the lure of power. Problems in a political marriage used to be suppressed for the sake of *his* career. It's not so any more. Political wives are saying, "What about *my* life, my feelings, my future?"

I only bring this up by way or warning. If you get bitten by the political bug, know what you are in for. Working for the "candidate of your choice" can be a heady experience and a rewarding undertaking. It can also be a mad monster that eats your time and keeps you away from *your* goals. It can also be trouble—romantic trouble you don't need. *Everyone* involved in the frenzy of a campaign is susceptible to a case of bad judgment.

6. *Through Your Church or Temple.* Slowly, slowly, slowly, the churches of the land are awakening to the fact that they should serve *all* the people, not just properly devout families. Single people need succor, too. Divorced people need direction, encouragement and, yes, forgiveness. They need to feel wanted and a part of the whole. They've suffered enough.

Properly run, a church or temple should be the center for activities designed especially for single people. What better place to meet, plan outings, and organize parties. The parish hall should be used, not kept as the private domain of the altar guide and the choirmaster. The meeting hall is as adaptable to a theater party as it is to a wedding reception. It's simply a matter of suggestion and direction.

Some churches have activities designed for singles. In addition to no-date dances, they will have picnics for divorced parents and their children, charter buses to ball games, and hold fairs in the parking lot.

On the serious side, a "full service" church should offer counseling to divorced persons and their children. Classes or informal discussion groups should be formed to deal with adjustment problems, religious questions, spiritual guidance. When all this is indeed happening, what better place to meet a man! If it isn't happening, find out why. After all, it's *your* church.

7. *Through Sports.* Milly was an airline stewardess, divorced, and extremely attractive, yet she had a difficult time meeting men. Bottom pinchers and joke crackers, yes, but men, no. Milly was from Montana and enjoyed the outdoors. She loved to fish, camp, and hunt. When I met her she was based in San Francisco and spent her free time doing city-type things. Get back outdoors, I suggested. Do what *you* like to do. Even if you *don't* meet a man, you'll be happier than you are barhopping.

The next time I saw Milly she was engaged. She indeed did meet a man. "Where?" I asked. "Fishing or camping?" "No," she answered. "Panning for gold. It's something I've *always* wanted to do. I bought the gold pan, bucket, shovel, and the other things I needed, and then read a book about it. The first time I went up to the Gold Country I spent all my time hiking and scouting for interesting sites. I found a terrific spot. The next time I went up I invited another girl to go with me and we took sleeping bags and cots. After working the stream all day we went to bed early.

"At midnight I woke up with this horrible light shining in my face! We were trespassing and this guy was mad as hell. After he calmed down he asked what kind of an air-head I was to be out in the country at night. Then he went back to his car, got a bottle of wine from a case he was taking to his house and built a fire. We started to talk and the three of us drank wine until sunrise. I knew I was in love! Crazy, isn't it?"

The moral of the story is, do what you *love* to do and if you do meet a man, fine. If not, *you've* had a terrific time anyway. If you enjoy the outdoors, go outdoors. If you enjoy sports cars, go to the rallies. If you enjoy shooting, find out where the nearest rifle range is. There will be any number of men at these locations who will enjoy you because you enjoy what *they* enjoy, too.

8. *In Bars.* It's my belief that you don't pick up anything but *trouble* in a bar. Just the fact that you are there sets the pace. I know that singles bars are now big business, considered "in" places and frequented by large numbers. I *still* don't think they're good places to meet men, but that's just my opinion. It's still a free country so if you feel this is where you stand the best chance of meeting men, that's your decision. I would, however, offer some words of advice.

A. Take enough money to cover the cost of your drinks and a cab home. It's foolhardy to drive, park, and walk around at night by yourself.

B. Don't buy drinks for anyone. That *really* labels you an easy mark. You are certanly not *that* desperate for company.

C. If you meet someone who asks you out, make the date for another night. If you leave with him now, *no one* will know where you are. Also, a future date gives you *both* time to think about it.

Before you succumb to the idea of flitting around a singles bar, I urge you to try some of my other suggestions. Who, really, wants to be known as "the girl he picked up in a bar"?

WHEN YOU DO THE ASKING

There are situations in which it is quite all right for you to take the initiative. When you are newly divorced and men don't know that you are available, it pays to do a little subliminal advertising. After all, you can't just wear a T-shirt that says CALL ME. Start by telling your close friends and a few select people at work. Don't make a general announcement at the water cooler. That *does* sound like a blanket invitation to all interested parties and you only want certain (eligible) interested parties.

1. *Two Tickets.* I heard one of my daughter's friends asking my oldest son if he would go to a school dance with her. After the girl left, I jokingly said to my son, "Ah, the old 'two-ticket' trick." He looked wide-eyed and asked me what I meant. I explained that this is an ancient custom devised by women to allow them to let a *certain* boy know they like him. What begins with a girl-sponsored dance in the gym moves on into the sophisticated world of charity balls, theater, opera, and that sure-fire winner—two tickets on the fifty-yard line.

If you have your eye on a certain man and all your hints have been to no avail, buy two tickets to an event and call him up.

"Hi John, this is Elizabeth from the office. I've run into a bit of good luck. A friend of mine on the newspaper gave me two tickets to the new play that's opening on Saturday and I was wondering if you would like to go?"

Okay, it's an out-and-out fabrication. If you can't stand blatant dishonesty, say you have two tickets and don't explain how you got them. If John can't go, you at least get full marks for trying. Ask one of your children instead, or take another friend. There's no need to miss a good show!

2. *Letters to Friends.* If you know single men in other locales

who would not be aware of your divorce, write them a nice, newsy letter and casually mention your marital status. After all, what are friends for? Write to your women friends also. They may know any number of attractive men and invite you for the weekend to meet them. Friends often have to be prodded to help. It's not that they don't care. They do. It's that they don't *think*.

TYPES OF MEN

It's always a danger to categorize people. As soon as you make your pontifical statement that thus and such is *always* true, up pops the perfect exception to the case. Nonetheless I am going to brave the criticism and lump great numbers of men into categories. After all, haven't they been doing it to us for years? Never trust a woman. All women love flattery. Redheads have fiery tempers. Big boobs are a sign of low intelligence. Really. What do *they* know! What follows is a carefully compiled list of the men available to the divorced woman—and everything I know about each group.

1. *Divorced Men.* Probably the greatest number of men you will date fall into this category. Divorce is epidemic, as we have said, and it's difficult to find a single man over thirty who hasn't at least one marriage under his belt.

Remember that a divorced man feels damaged, too. Women do not have the edge on suffering. No matter who started the proceedings, a divorce is a rejection. So when you are with a divorced man, be solicitous. Listen to his problems. Hold his hand. But don't voice your opinion of his problems. Most men are looking for approbation, not advice.

A divorced man is a good candidate for marriage. I did not say he would make a good husband. Getting to know him is the only way to determine that. A divorced man is vulnerable to marriage because he has been married. After struggling through marketing chores, making his own bed, and trolling for dates, most formerly married men develop a distaste for bachelorhood. They decide being married is preferable to being single. That isn't very flattering to the new spouse, but I feel it's pretty close to the truth. If you are dating a divorced man and are serious about him, just apply a little more pressure. You can probably have him if you want him.

2. *Younger Men.* There is an interesting trend just now of younger men preferring older women. I think this makes a great deal of sense if the age difference is not too great and provided the motives are pure. By pure motives I mean a relationship not based on monetary gains for the man, or a relationship based on a flaw of character. If a younger man is attracted to you because he is looking for a mother, or security, or as a punishment, then the relationship is in trouble. If, however, he simply is attracted to you because he finds you fascinating and enjoyable, then why not have the fun of such an attachment?

Marriage to a younger man, however, is a different story. My advice is to stick to a relationship and skip marriage. Vera is a divorced woman just turned fifty who is a well-known sculptor. She had a disastrous marriage to a man who was wrong for her in every category you could mention. It was a wonder how she could be creative, living under such circumstances. At the time of her divorce, she and her husband were living in Massachusetts. Vera hated the snow and cold weather but she was so worn down from the divorce that she didn't have the strength to move somewhere else.

Peter was a student at the university where Vera taught. He was her most promising student and was madly fond of her and had been a friendly comfort during the divorce. After her husband moved out, Peter began spending more and more time at Vera's home. The relationship, much to Vera's surprise, took a romantic turn and she found herself with a young, ardent lover on her hands. Aware of the criticism that would abound should her romance be discovered, Vera told Peter not to come to the house so often. She ignored him on campus and actually tried to hurt him by not answering his phone calls.

Vera was miserable because she enjoyed Peter's company tremendously. On one of the rare evenings when she allowed him to come over, she told him how much she hated the cold weather and dreamed of living in the desert. The next day Peter presented her with a plan. He proposed that the two of them take off for New Mexico and buy a small house where he would work making jewelry while she sculpted. Vera accepted. Without calling her married daughter in California, she sold her home and took off with Peter. They bought an old adobe and began a life of art in the sun.

Vera is not a shallow woman. She knows very well what she has done. But as she said, "I didn't take a baby picture with me and if anyone asks me if I have children I'll tell them I can't remember." She left her past in the past. For this moment she is timeless.

She knows the relationship is temporary, but she doesn't mind. Peter gave her the strength she needed to make a move she would probably not have made on her own. When he leaves, as he surely will, she'll miss him. She feels, however, that she is better for having known him.

The danger of a May-December liaison is that the older woman will lie to herself, delude herself, and go into a decline when it's over. If you can accept the current moment and not program the future (which is very difficult) you will be all right. It's when you hang in for dear life, visit the plastic surgeon, pump vitamins into your stomach and starve yourself into a beanpole that the relationship becomes harmful. If the younger man demands money, an inheritance, or any other form of payoff, you know you have made an error in judgment.

3. *Older Men.* A relationship with an older man makes far more sense, but it is not nearly as intriguing. It is, however, loaded with obvious benefits. An older man can be charming, solicitous, heedful of your desires, and a very satisfactory lover. Sometimes he's a *better* lover than a younger man. An older man has looked over the field, and if he's chosen you, you can almost bank on a monogamous relationship. He has outgrown the ridiculous habit of playing the field. If he's ready to settle down, he means it.

In dealing with men over fifty, remember the older the man, the more stereotyped male he is. Even the man in his forties isn't sure how he feels about women's lib. He was raised by a mother who "knew her place." He may feel threatened by a show of independence and of worldliness. An older man may also be sexually stifled and feel any "deviation" from the norm is perverted.

Another problem you may face with the older man is his children who could be close to your age—or even contemporaries. You could run the risk of having to continually be proving to them that you married their father because you love him, not for any monetary gains. Another problem you face are the wives of his friends, wives who could strongly resent a younger woman coming into their group. My advice in all these areas is to be yourself. Don't apologize or explain. After all, you know what you want, and it's your life—and his.

Karen was a very active divorcée in her middle forties when she met and married Harry, a widower in his early sixties. At sixty-four, Harry retired and truly enjoyed staying home and working in his garden. The only problem was, he wanted Karen to stay home, too. He liked her to serve them a picnic lunch in the garden and play gin rummy with him before dinner. He enjoyed taking off in the middle of the week for a trip to the mountains. Karen didn't. She was involved in hospital work and served on three boards. She hadn't stayed home in years! She tried giving up a certain amount of her activities but she became restless and resentful. The marriage limped along for another year and then Karen filed for divorce. *She* simply was not ready to retire.

If you are involved with a man of retirement age, consider what it would be like having him home all day. Is he amply provided for or will you be expected to work? How is his health? How does he plan to spend the rest of his life? What does he expect of you? These are the key questions that should be answered *before* you marry.

4. *Weaker Men.* Gail is an executive with an oil company. That is in itself remarkable. Since her divorce Gail has found that the stronger she becomes as a personality and the more her responsibility increases, the weaker the type of man she attracts. She does not want a man to dominate and direct her life, but

she does want a successful man who is dynamic and vital. These men, though, she claims, all want helpless women.

This is a problem. When a woman is a pillar of strength it's quite possible she will attract insecure men who are looking for a direction and a director. Unfortunately, another of our inherited stereotypes is to believe we need a strong man. Maybe the last thing in the world a strong woman needs is a strong man. In many ways a man who appreciates and applauds a strong woman is himself strong, not weak.

A weak man, however, is a very bad marriage risk. What constitutes a weak man? I feel the macho character who pounds his chest and shouts that "no woman of mine will work" is not strong but weak. By keeping the little woman in the kitchen he can never be threatened by her success. A man who constantly belittles your accomplishments, is meager in his praise and negative about your abilities, is a weak man. He needs to put you down to build himself up. A man who is soft and gentle, a whiz in the kitchen and unenthusiastic about sports is not necessarily a weak man. But a man who rules you by guilt, panders to your fears, and fills false appetites most certainly is.

A weak man can tyrannize because he has inherited custom on his side. "Man is strong. Man must lead. Man must be the head of the household." You've heard these admonitions all your life. This is the conditioning that softened us up to the point we believe a man is strong simply *because* he is a man. A man who takes advantage of this conditioning is most certainly weak.

It is difficult to determine in the beginning of a friendship or romance what psychological problems may be a part of a man's character. He may have lived with his emotional handicap for so long that he is quite adept at hiding it. A man with an unhealthy reliance on his mother may not reveal this trait until the two of you clash and he takes her side even when she is obviously in error. A man who lies about his job, puts up a false front, and exaggerates his abilities may take a while to unmask his true self. You want to *believe* a man is successful and competent. The fact that he must play-act is a good indication that he is a weak man with serious problems.

I caution you to avoid weak men because you don't need any more problems in your life. You don't need to add the burden of bolstering up or straightening out a grown man who has been unable to do it on his own.

5. *Successful Men.* A successful man must not only achieve, but he must sustain that success, and do it daily. This creates a fear of failure which surrounds him. Daily. The woman in the life of a successful man is the hardest hit; the late dinners, the missed trains, the extensive absences, the withdrawal into self. Most women who say they want a successful man don't realize all these things. When they do, they often take them as a personal affront, and with hurt feelings and teary eyes demand to be treated better. The truth could well be that the man is doing all he can, giving all he can give. The bulk of his energy, emotion, time and yes, his love, goes to *being* successful.

If you find yourself in a relationship with this type of man, be honest in your judgments. He's not doing anything *against* you. He's doing it *for* himself. A man with a driving urge to succeed, whether it's in business, politics or research is so dedicated to the battleground of success that he finds little else in life as attractive. "It isn't the money," as a very success-oriented man told me, "because money is just a means of keeping score. It's the supreme challenge of setting goals—and getting there!"

There is an excitement to a successful man that I find very intriguing. There is also a one-dimensional quality that can become quite boring. Success-seeking men are not good bets to spend hours in art galleries or discussing new psychological theories or lingering over a bottle of wine on a mountain top. But as I said they radiate an excitement and create an aura of vibrancy. You can only be happy with such a man if *he* is the center of your life. Enjoy the perks of his success. Be there when he needs you. Offer understanding and compassion. Arrange your life to his unpredictable schedule. Or find another man.

6. *Bachelors.* A bachelor is a never-married man. If he's in his thirties he really hasn't earned the title yet. He's considered

unmarried—which alludes to the fact that he probably *will* marry. An unmarried man in his mid-forties, fifties, or sixties is a bachelor, and the older he is, the deeper his confirmation. When you know this about a man you plan accordingly.

I love bachelors. Two of my closest friends in this world are bachelors. This wasn't always so. I once made a long and heartbreaking assault on a bachelor which left me shaken but wiser. Now I enjoy them for exactly what they are and hope to heaven I have outgrown the notion that they will ever be anything but bachelors. If you're smart you'll do the same. Go to dinner with them, ask their advice, cry on their shoulders, but don't fall in love with them. Trust me, it's heartbreak alley.

Many bachelors will tell you they are only "waiting for the right woman." Of course this could be true, but more often than not it's all part of the allure, the bait. Bachelors *know* they are an attractive item and they seldom miss an angle. What woman wouldn't rise to the challenge of seeing if she is that certain special someone.

I know an attractive bachelor who takes great delight in thinking up fantastic schemes to impress women, then, just as fast, drops them and moves on. I watched him pick up a woman at a cocktail party in Los Angeles and invite her to dinner. When they got into his car he asked her if she liked Mexican food and when she said yes he drove to the airport and they flew to Mazatlán. Once there he bought her a bathing suit, and a couple of caftans, and they spent the weekend. After they flew back to Los Angeles he never called her again. She finally called me because she knew I was a friend of the man, and asked me what she should do. "Nothing," I said. "This is the stupid, shallow life he leads. What you miss is the excitement and the good times—not the man. Be thankful to be out of his life. He is a man going nowhere."

Many divorced women reach a plateau in their lives when they say they will never marry again. A woman who has made this statement then feels it's fine to establish a long-term relationship with a bachelor or a gay man. Again, I feel this is not going to work to your advantage. What woman can absolutely guarantee that she will never marry again? Even if you think you might not, why limit the possibilities by entering a relationship that keeps you in circulation on one hand, but blots out your options on the other.

7. *Rich Men*. How often have you heard a divorced woman say, "This time I'm marrying for money. No more of this love nonsense." Maybe you have even said it. It can get very depressing being a divorced woman living on limited funds. You can get very bitter thinking how you gave the best years of your life to *him*, and look what you've got to show for it. Nothing. Well, in theory a rich man sounds attractive, but are you willing to pay the price?

Rich men are usually selfish, self-centered, impatient, opinionated, thoughtless, and spoiled. Why? Because they don't have to be unselfish, concerned, patient, broadminded, thoughtful, or polite. They abide by their Golden Rule: He who has the gold makes the rules. Certainly not all rich men possess these faults, but enough do to make it worth your while to beware.

My grandfather always said a man who married a rich woman works hard for his money. So does a woman who marries a rich man. Your life must revolve around him, unless of course *you* have money, also. There are luxurious compensations to be sure, but you have the responsibility of his happiness twenty-four hours a day. After all, he married you to be happy, and if he isn't whose fault is it? Not his, he'll say. It's yours.

There are several categories of rich men. The man who has made his money himself wants the world to know about it. One way of showing his wealth is by the woman he marries. The extreme example which pops into my mind is the Greek ship owner and the American widow. This type of man wants the best (or the best known) and the most expensive.

A man who has made his money early and gone through a couple of splashy divorces may want to settle for a woman who will bring him genuine warmth and companionship. He still, however, will be demanding and self-centered. You are definitely coming into *his* life, not he into yours. A wealthy man in Denver married a woman who was his nurse in the hospital. She is still his nurse in many ways. Granted she has a lovely home and surroundings, but as she says she's "on call" twenty-four hours a day.

A man who is from a wealthy family and has inherited money has yet other demands. He has always been a participant in the "good life" and his preference in women runs to those in his same "station." He probably has a position in a bank or brokerage house, but he knows why he's there. Since he wants to hang onto his money and not *really* work for a living, he usually marries (or merges with) a woman of private means. Why take chances?

The reason I mention all this is as a guideline. You certainly don't want to be the lively divorcée in the life of a rich man who is enjoying your company but who will eventually *marry* someone else! If, however, you meet a rich man and genuinely fall in love, I am not suggesting that you turn him down, quoting me, and miss an opportunity to live what could quite possibly be a storybook life. I just say to beware of the power of money. Know that it has the ability to create good and evil alike. It also has the power to shape—or misshape—men and women.

8. *Foreign Men.* The world seems to be shrinking in size. Inexpensive travel has made it possible for hundreds of thousands of Americans to take off for Europe, South America, Mexico, the Orient. The same seems to be true for travelers from other countries. How often have you stood on a street corner waiting for the light to change and heard the camera-laden people behind you speaking in Japanese or German or Italian. Because of this, it is quite possible that you will meet men from other lands, here or in their countries.

I adore foreign men. I've had marvelous times in Mexico City and Rome and Beirut. I find foreign men have an appreciation of women often lacking in our American men. I know, however, that when you involve yourself with a foreigner, you involve yourself with his culture, his traditions, and his family. This can cause any number of problems. Enjoy their company, would be my advice, but recognize the relationship will change drastically if you marry.

The son of one of my Arab friends married an American girl

he met in college in Texas. When he returned to Arabia he brought her to the tiny village in which he lived. The women of his family absolutely refused to receive her. The young couple settled in a large town nearby and shortly thereafter the wife had her first child. Her family were unable to make the long, expensive trip to Arabia and the girl felt quite alone. Her father-in-law often comes to see her, his son, and his grandchild —but not the women. And it is certainly the company—and love—of the women that she needs.

The cultural differences between races living in the same country are not so oppressive. But the differences do exist. They can be as simple as dietary requirements, holidays, and customs of child rearing. Because these differences do exist, it doesn't mean they are impossible to overcome. Love *can* conquer all. Still, winning a man's family can be a hard task—even for love.

9. *Married Men.* This category of men seems to be in abundant supply. They are the "misunderstood" group who want you to believe it's just a matter of minutes until they file for divorce. A married man can be a tempting companion for a divorced woman. When you're lonely, unsure of your own attractiveness, starving for a little affection, you simply aren't too choosy from which direction it comes. As a divorced woman I urge you to make this rule: *Avoid married men.* Have absolutely nothing to do with them. When you become involved with a man with a wife you are setting up a situation loaded with disaster potential. Here are the well-known traps.

A. *The Obviously Married Man.* Some men are very upfront about their married status. "I'm married, you know. I have three swell kids I think the world of. I can't get divorced, but that doesn't mean we won't be good for each other." This man is honest. He isn't promising anything. He suggests a relationship in which he fills your voids and you fill his. On the surface it appears ideal. Except for one thing: the relationship works *entirely* to his advantage. When you get lured into this trap you take yourself out of circulation. Instead of building a social life of your own, based on friends of your choosing, you wait around for him to call.

A relationship with a married man is tempting because he gets you out of the house, he takes you to dinner or a movie. A married man will be physically attentive, pleasant to be around. He will even tell you he loves you and if he weren't stuck in this marriage, he would marry you in a minute.

The woman in this situation lies to herself. She says she can handle the quasi-relationship. She says she's aware of the situation and she won't get involved. She says she's using him. How many women can truly mean that? Underneath, this woman is usually saying she can get him to leave his wife. It's just a matter of time. So she stays with him and it isn't until four years and five scenes later that she realizes he meant what he said. He is *not* going to get a divorce.

Nancy is a secretary in a New York brokerage firm. She is not very turned on by her job. She has had trouble meeting men since her divorce. Then along comes Charlie, married Charlie. She is a sitting duck. Within a month he's seeing her two nights a week. As his wife and kids live in the country, he just calls home and says he's got a late meeting so he's staying over in town. Charlie stocks Nancy's bar and kitchen. She's so flattered, she doesn't realize that the money he's spending is less than a hotel room would cost . . . not to mention additional female companionship. The relationship perks along.

Nancy falls in love with Charlie and tells him so. Charlie says that's fine but to remember that he's married. Nancy makes a small scene and Charlie says he'll "think about a divorce." That's enough to shut her up for another six months. I don't need to go on with the story because you know the ending. Nancy, sitting alone on New Year's Eve, drinking a bottle of champagne, finally admits to herself that *this* is her future with Charlie. She calls him the next day at home and tells him. Charlie, pretending to his wife that it's a business call, hangs up quickly. He's relieved. She *was* pushing too hard. Time he moved on.

B. *The Separated Man.* When a man tells you he's separated, he's not telling you anything. It could mean that he's filed for divorce, or moved out of the house, or that his wife is at the hairdresser. Before you become involved with this man, find out his exact definition of the word "separated." We *all* know that in most states either party may begin a divorce action. We also *all* know that in most states either party can get a divorce without the consent of the other. We also *all* know that a "legal separation" doesn't mean anything except that the husband generally still supports his wife, does not live with her, and is *not* free to remarry. We *all* know that the only separated man is the one who is about to be *finally* divorced.

Bea was thirty-six when she met Warren. He was a wealthy builder from Indiana on convention in Los Angeles. Bea worked for one of the manufacturers exhibiting at the trade show. Each evening she joined a jolly group to go on to dinner. Warren was a member of one group. They went out alone the next night and the night following. Warren had the contract to build a giant shopping center and housing project in Arizona. He talked Bea into giving up her job and moving to Phoenix. He rented her an apartment, furnished it, joined a tennis club for her, and spent at least two weeks a month in Arizona. Bea enjoyed Warren and her new freedom tremendously.

When Warren was not in town, Bea swam at the club, played tennis, and joined a backgammon group. When Warren was in town, he joined her group of new friends for dinner, for parties, for tennis. As she explained to her friends, Warren was "separated" from his wife. When I met Bea she was a dumpy little woman with the splotchy skin of an alcoholic.

"Look at me!" she cried. "I'm fat and fifty, fat and fifty! My life has been ruined. He wouldn't let me work. Now I hardly see him anymore, maybe three times a year. Sure he sends me money, but what if he stops? Then what can I do!"

What could she do? She had no claim on Warren, and

it frightened her. She tried to go after him legally, claiming "common law wife," but her lawyer told her she didn't have a case. She finally threatened to sue him for breach of contract, so he gave her a condominium and a small lump sum of money just to keep her quiet. There was no more tennis club and no more parties. The last I heard she was a cocktail waitress in Flagstaff, having sold her condominium to support herself.

C. *A Friend's Husband.* There are those married men who consider all divorced women fair game. Some of these men are married to your friends. It can often come as a shock that the first caller after your divorce is the man married to your best friend. He says he's always liked you and wants to know if you'd like to have lunch. Or he might not be so obvious. He might call to say how sorry he is to hear the news and if there is *anything* he can do please let him know. When he happens to be in the neighborhood and drops by to see how you're doing, you're moved by his thoughtfulness. Just don't be moved into the bedroom.

To avoid all problems with friends' husbands, don't phone them for advice about your homeowner's insurance policy or how to work the electric lawn mower or when to put up storm windows. Get your help from your cousin or the divorced man you're dating or the Yellow Pages. Leave husbands alone.

You need your married girl friends and if word gets out that you have your eye on someone's husband, the ranks will close. With a bang. The married women of the world control almost all of the social calendar. They say who comes to dinner, who's invited to the art show, who serves on the committee. They can make your life very pleasant —or miserable. They can be quite mean and ease you out of the car pool, keep your child out of dancing school, and steer all single men to their divorced friends whom they can trust.

Beth and Barbara had been friends since childhood.

When they married they bought houses three blocks apart. Beth and her husband divorced, which only intensified the friendship between Beth and Barbara. Vance, Barbara's husband, said jokingly that he now had two wives. Beth was included in all their parties, was over at their home for dinner at least two nights a week, and was invited to go skiing with them for a week at Vail.

During the ski trip, Beth and Vance found themselves alone for lunch one day. Barbara was too tired from the previous day's skiing and went back to the lodge to sleep. Vance and Beth decided to have an alpine picnic. They filled their boda bags with white wine, bought some cheese, bread, salami and two oranges, then took the lift to the top of the mountain. There they found a sunny spot to have their lunch under the bright Colorado sky.

It was almost innocent fun with the funny jokes Vance told, with Beth making a crazy "snowperson," Vance tossing the first snowball, and Beth pushing him down in the soft powder. When he pulled her down beside him and kissed her, it was the most natural thing in the world. The next kiss wasn't. The last kiss was a frantic, impassioned embrace that sent them down the mountain and into Beth's room at the lodge.

Their affair lasted three months before mutual "friends" took Barbara aside and told her what they suspected. Barbara faced the two and gave them an ultimatum. Vance, tired of the intrigue, took Barbara in his arms that night, begged her forgiveness, and promised *never* to see Beth again. He didn't. Neither did Barbara. Neither did the other friends. It was all Beth's fault for leading him on like that, they said. Vance didn't disagree. A smart man, he kept his mouth shut, thankful that it had worked out the way it did.

You can say that it *wasn't* Beth's fault. You can say Vance is a bastard and should have stood up for Beth. You can *say* anything you want. That doesn't change the situation, does it? Beth is still the loser because she has cut herself off from people who could quite possibly have been the source of much pleasure, and a good source through which to meet others.

Let's go back to the statistics. Twenty-three million unmarried women, 16 million unmarried men. A divorce rate of epidemic proportion. A woman with a good man can well be concerned. All the players in the game of life are not good sports playing by the rules. A great many single and divorced women do figure that any man is fair game. This is a sadness because these women are letting themselves in for trouble. A man who cheats on his wife will cheat on you. A man who leaves his wife will leave you. No, *your* married boy friend is *not* different. He's further proof of the problem.

WHAT DO YOU WANT IN A MAN?

As a writer friend of mine said to me, "A divorced woman should learn from her first marriage; it's a shame to waste all that original research." It's quite true. Women don't spend enough time analyzing men to find what it is they do and do not like; do and do not need; do and do not find attractive. Too many women are just so happy to have a man that they'll settle for all his faults.

I feel that it is far better to know yourself and to set standards for what you are looking for in a man. Begin with your ex-husband and list all his faults on one side of a page and his virtues down the other. Look at each "fault" and try to figure out *why* this was annoying to you. Let's say you've put down that he never complimented you. Was that because he thought you were unattractive and inefficient or was it because he just never gave compliments to anybody for anything? Was this, then, a realistic fault?

It could be that your ex-husband gambled and lost money you could ill afford. That's a genuine fault. If he refused help with this problem and you feared for the welfare of the family, then you were right to take a stand. You know that next time you do *not* want a man who gambles.

Was your ex-husband a boat freak who wanted to spend all weekend down working on his rigging and brass work? Did he insist that *every* vacation be spent on the ocean with you barely able to stand upright in the galley? Did he spend more money on sonar equipment than it would have cost to add a family room to the house? You obviously should look for a man whose hobby is not an obsession, who has a realistic idea of sharing, and who believes with you that boats should *all* belong to other people.

After you have spent considerable time analyzing your ex-husband, design what you would consider the perfect man. In doing research for *What Every Formerly Married Woman Should Know*, I sent out a questionnaire that asked women to rate (by number) what they were looking for in a man. How would *you* rate the following in importance in your life?

_____FINANCIAL SECURITY
_____SEXUAL COMPATIBILITY
_____MUTUAL INTEREST (SPORTS/HOBBIES)
_____RELIGIOUS COMPATIBILITY
_____GOOD STEPFATHER FOR CHILDREN
_____GOOD-LOOKING
_____WELL EDUCATED
_____INTELLIGENCE
_____OFFERED EXCITING LIFE
_____WELL MANNERED
_____COMPANIONSHIP
_____PERSONAL NEATNESS
_____OTHER_____

Go down the list before you make out your rating and write down what each entry means to you. Financial Security might mean a man with a good job, or a retired man with a set pension, or a wealthy man who owns apartment houses. We each have different sets of values. Mutual Interest could mean to you a man who likes to travel, or play dominoes, or go to sport-car rallies. Companionship could mean a man who likes discussing his work and problems with you, or a man who likes to help in the garden, or a man who comes home for lunch.

What you are doing is setting up "ideal conditions." You are also forcing yourself to think about what indeed you do like about certain men. Now you do your rating. If you are among the majority of the women who answered my questionnaire, Financial Security is among your top four priorities. This tells you that you should not fall in love with an unpublished poet. Sexual Compatability and Companionship were usually in the top four. Religion was near the top or the bottom of the list, depending upon the woman's convictions. Good Looks hardly mattered at all.

An ideal man is as difficult to find as is an ideal woman. When you create that ideal man in your mind, however, you are more likely to come closer to your goal than will the woman who has no idea what she wants. You will discover there are certain qualities in a man which absolutely turn you off. When you *know* that a loud man who tells lewd jokes bores you to death, why spend embarrassing evenings with such a man just "to get out of the house."

You can develop a satisfying social life that does not depend upon a man "freeing" you from the house. I hope we've all outgrown the notion that men have the only keys to the Fun House. I look at today's young college students who go out in groups or "gangs" as they call themselves. My daughter took me to her favorite hangout when I was in New York. She said she comes into the city with a couple of chums. They all buy their own drinks and they all enjoy each other's company. There is no frantic pairing off or embarrassment if there seem to be more guys than girls.

Get together a group of your own to go to the places you want to go. Save single dates for men close to your ideal. This way you don't run the risk of a disappointing relationship, or even a disastrous second marriage. You owe it to yourself to be discriminating. It's when you'll "settle for anything" that *anything* comes into your life.

WHAT DOES A MAN WANT IN A WOMAN?

Remember, men are also setting standards and ideals. A good, reliable man doesn't want to "settle" for what's readily available. He has some ideas of what he's looking for in a woman. Women tend to forget this. They will lump all men together and figure they're all after the same thing. They are not. Most men I've interviewed on the subject, however, agree that these six basic characteristics make a woman quite desirable:

1. *Womanliness.* The reason most men like women is *because* they are women. A smart woman *knows* this and accentuates the differences. In today's world of threatening women, one secret to handling a man is to make him feel more like a man. I don't mean to fall into the helpless female role. That's unattractive. I'm talking about all those little nuances that mark you as feminine—a lady—a gentleperson. Bad manners are unfeminine. (They are also unmasculine.) I think foul language and coarseness are unfeminine. A disdain of how you look; how you dress; how you walk; and how you smell is unfeminine.

2. *Comfort.* One of my most cherished remarks is from a man who told me that what made me attractive was that I was comfortable to be with. I asked him to explain this. He just said it was like coming in out of a cold night; finding a warm fire; sinking into a deep chair; and heaving a sigh of relief. He knew he could absolutely relax and be himself with me.

Men get tired of being performers, just as women do. It's hard to be constantly on your guard, smiling, talking in banal informalities, trying to figure out *how* to please the other person. Sometimes a man wants to talk while sometimes he absolutely does *not* want to talk. Sometimes a man wants to go to a fine, expensive restaurant, but sometimes he wants to open a can of chili and heat it up himself. Sometimes a man feels romantic and wants to loll in bed with you all day Sunday. Sometimes that man will want to go off for a week's hunting without you.

If a woman is always demanding that a man behave in a certain way at certain times she is *not* comfortable to be with. If a woman is always questioning and complaining she is not comfortable to be with. If a woman thinks only of herself and her wants, she is not comfortable to be with.

3. *Understanding.* How things look, sound, or appear is not necessarily the way they *are*. If a man is late picking you up for dinner, it doesn't have to mean he was with another woman. He could have been detained in a meeting, caught in traffic, or simply forgetful. If you see the man in your life in a restaurant with another woman, it doesn't necessarily mean he's found someone else. She could be his cousin, a client or a friend with a problem.

Jumping to conclusions is the most hazardous jump in the world. It is usually an indication that something *else* is wrong in our lives. Give a man every opportunity to explain, apologize or state his case before you jump all over him.

A part of understanding is realizing that men are searching, too. Look at the shelves of self-help books in the library. They are decidedly *not* all for women. Men have problems. Men have identity crises. Men have fears and doubts. The national quest seems to be a frantic search for self. Happiness is finding out who you are.

Realize this uncertainty in men and respect it. They are not always the pillar of strength or the Rock of Gibraltar. Be lavish in your praise; long in understanding; and miserly with your criticism.

4. *Fairness.* Whenever I think of fairness, I think of that song, "Why Can't a Woman Be More Like a Man?" I think about it because of the frustration it implies on the part of the man. Yet when it *comes* to fairness, I think women are often the silent losers. Men, simply because they *are* men, don't need to be as fair as women. Still they scream the loudest, "You are not being fair!"

What is fairness, anyway? It's the ability to share the limelight. It's keeping quiet when it's his turn to talk. It's going to a baseball game *once* in a while. It's believing in him when he *swears* it will be different this time.

Fairness also means being fair to yourself. He should cook while you finish an important report. He should go with you to a lecture on Balinese art. He should be willing to leave a good party early when you have to get up at 6 A.M.

Fairness also means being fair to your children. When your son has an important Little League game, you should give up your date and attend—or invite your date to come along. When you've promised to meet your daughter on your lunch hour to buy her a new pair of boots, you should decline that sudden invitation to lunch. You know in your heart what fair is. Fair is fair.

5. *Intelligence.* I can truthfully say that I've never known a man to say he wanted a dumb woman. In fact, most of the men I've interviewed have said that what they look for above all else in a woman is brains. I'm going to say it again: *intelligence* is the ultimate turn-on. You don't have to be born with 190 I.Q. to be intelligent.

Intelligent women have a purpose and a system of values. An intelligent woman is aiming toward a goal and her life is success-oriented. She attracts people because she knows where she's going. Gloria is a young divorcée in her twenties. She had always wanted to live in California, so she came to San Francisco to look for a job. She was told that women with Ph.D.s were waiting table. Jobs were *that* hard to get. Gloria smiled and said she wasn't worried, because she had a good basic understanding of the stock market and she felt there was a place there for her. Within two days she had a job as an assistant to an investment counselor, an apartment on Nob Hill, and two new friends. As a friend of mine said, "She'll *always* do fine. She's a winner."

What makes some women winners? I think it is a *faith* in their own ability and intelligence. Gloria started out on a par with a great many other girls, but somewhere along the line she learned that absolutely invaluable lesson: She bet on herself. So many of us defer to others' judgments; seek auxilliary opinions; and solicit outside help—while all the time *we* are the source of the best information. We are just the last to believe it! Treat yourself with a little more respect! Spend more time learning. Develop new talents. Your body is an incredible machine that when properly used will be a never-ending source of joy to you.

6. *Attractiveness.* A certain element of physical attraction is necessary in any relationship. Two people have to *look* good to each other. I didn't say that he had to be Adonis and you Venus; still, a certain chemistry has to be present as a spark or a turn-on. This is something you can't manufacture, but you can certainly help it along.

The first step is to beat the cupcake syndrome. *All* men are not looking for a shapely twenty-three-year-old blond with long legs. Some men are, but forget them. Most men are looking for a woman with the virtues we just described. To beat the cupcake syndrome, quit worrying about how young you're not.

A friend of mine, a divorced man in his fifties, sent me a chart called Rating Used Ladies. This chart is based (loosely) on the Blue Book that lists the market value of used cars. I was about to put it on the back of my desk (it's six pages long!) when the first line caught my eye: "A U.L. (Used Lady) is one who has been divorced at least once. These ladies are generally attractive, amiable, and smart. They are far less demanding and much more satisfying than New Ladies and most of them are lively as June Bugs."

After that I had to read on. The note from my friend, a big backer of U.L.'s, said the chart expressed his feelings exactly. The U.L. (us) is a very desirable commodity—especially after thirty-five! I have said it and said it but until *you* over thirty-five's and forty-five's and fifty-five's believe it, you are going to continue to feel that you are undesirable, over-the-hill and decidedly *used*. But don't take my word for it. Listen to some more of what the author of this formidable document has to say.

"ON PHYSICAL APPEARANCE: The U.L., when it comes to being feminine, is desperately professional. She bathes and lotions herself constantly and her hair and underwear are always spanking clean. She smells good whereas the younger New Lady often gives off the aroma of linseed oil, her breath smells like a health food store and her long and stringy hair looks like it's never met a hairbrush.

"ON PERSONALITY: The U.L. is a source of strength and security. She will treat you as you always expected to be treated by your first wife.

"ON INTELLIGENCE: The U.L. who is in there pitching has gone back to school, or gotten a real estate license or opened a boutique. She often has interesting or influential friends, entertains with style and speaks in a manner that is classy—and understandable.

"ON SEX: The U.L. has a civilized, pleasant attitude toward the whole thing, does her part, is never 'too tired' or conversely, too ambitious. It means she does not try to take charge and insist on creative monkey business when you have to get up early the next day. It means she won't try to fake you out with phony yelling and biting and scratching. It means she doesn't lie there like a slice of smoked salmon. She's good for a long run performance—not a one-shot spectacular."

So there you have it, from the horse's mouth, as it were. When it comes down to the nitty-gritty, a real man of thirty or forty or fifty or sixty wants a *real* woman. A great woman is truly ageless, so forget the cupcakes. They are not your competition. They could *never* hope to have what you have to offer.

Françoise Sagan, writing in *Vogue* several years ago, said that the reason some men prefer younger women is that they are not on to them. Speaking of the older woman, she says, ". . . men will find it very much harder to make us suffer and this is not unimportant and they know it." Hasn't it in fact been part of the stereotyped roles we are all out to break? Transcending the bugaboo of age will be a freedom to men as well as to women. They will no longer have to suffer the infuriating giggles of a mindless nymph in order to impress the old crowd.

Years are your friend, not your enemy. A smooth skin is the compensation for youth, for frivolity, for confusion. Listen once again to the words of Françoise Sagan. ". . . this slight wrinkle in the corner of the mouth that annoys us in front of our mirror, men know that it is the scar of another love, a great love, and that it will prevent us from throwing ourselves out the window for them or for following them blindly in their whims."

An astrologer friend of mine loves her wrinkles because, she says, she had such a good time earning them. But if that wrinkle is truly annoying you or your chin line is not as firm as it was, you can indulge in the surgeon's scalpel. Cosmetic surgery is readily available. You can do anything you wish to create illusion and foster fantasies. I find nothing wrong in it at all. But cosmetic surgery is *all* it is. You still have to supply the substance, the elements that make you *attractive*.

HOW YOU LIVE

The kind of man who will be attracted to you is determined by a great many factors. One of the determiners is how you live. Whether you know it or not, your physical surroundings and your attitude toward them, telegraph a message to the world.

1. *Your Area.* Where you live, as we have discussed, influences your life. City, country, suburbs—they all have their pluses and their minuses as far as children, jobs, and accessibility are concerned. Where you live also regulates the type of man you meet. It's unlikely that you'll meet a rancher living in the heart of Manhattan. It's also unlikely that you'll meet a dynamite corporation lawyer in Minot, North Dakota. A man who loves sailing doesn't hang around in Bartelsville, Oklahoma, nor does a forest ranger work in Kansas. Check your chart to see if you are in the right geographical location to meet the man of your dreams.

2. *Your Style.* How you live within your walls is also a determining factor. Do you give formal dinners or call out for pizza? Is your furniture Italian Renaissance or is it early Louis B. Mayer? Is your home spotlessly clean or a study in disarray? Believe it or not, this can influence a man. If you are dating a C.P.A. who likes traditional maple furniture smelling of lemon oil, chintz drapes, and a wood-burning fireplace and he walks into your garage studio apartment with pillow furniture and

macrame curtains, he may decide you're just too far out for him!

I'm absolutely not suggesting you change your style. That's *you* and I applaud it. Just don't make the mistake of trying to fit a square man into your round life. Imagine you are a famous set designer. The producer of the show has just handed you your very own list of what *you* want in a man and says, "Here, design a setting for him." If the man you described wouldn't fit in your life-style, then you have the wrong man or an invented atmosphere, because both should mesh somewhere along the line.

The friends you have determine the type of man you'll meet. They will be introducing you to their crowd. If you see a lot of the crowd who work at the local state college, you will be meeting other teachers, professors, and administrators. All of us tend to judge people by the company they keep. If you have flaky friends who have a habit of showing up at mealtime, a man will assume you are not discriminating and are pretty desperate for company. If, on the other hand, he meets interesting, stimulating people at your dinner table, he will look forward to being included.

Every possession you own tells its own story. The car you drive. The books on your shelves. The records you play. The wine you serve. The handbag you carry. The spices in your kitchen. The rugs on your floor. They're *all* you.

3. *Your Job.* Where you work, the job you have, and the salary you receive all determine to some degree the men you will meet. Working in a hospital is a good way to meet doctors. Working in a brokerage house isn't. When you are saving every extra dollar to go to architectural school, you aren't going to have the funds to travel to meet men. To compensate, slant your after work hours to activities where men will be present. At the moment, your goal to get into architectural school is the A Priority in your life. Think of the interesting people you'll meet once you're there!

It could develop that you would want to take a lesser-paying job that is more interesting and where you would meet a greater variety of men. Consider such a move only if it fits in with your long range plans. You don't find men planning their work life around meeting women. Remember too, that when you have a challenging, dynamic job you intrigue men because of your position. A successful woman is as attractive as a successful man!

4. *Your Achievements.* In this country we love winners, from football heroes to corporation presidents. Our politicians run the gamut from stars to villains depending on our support and adulation. When you are promoted in your job; made an officer of a company; sell an article; close a deal; win a match, you are an achiever. You attract. If you are a major achiever, you will attract the syncophant along with the genuine admirer. It behooves you to know the difference.

A successful woman can attract the less successful men—the man looking to improve his position through her. A woman who has influence is often importuned to use it. A woman of means is constantly in demand. It's amazing how the world opens up when you are an achiever. You are not born with success; you *make* it happen. You can break through into this exciting world by setting goals and going after them. We *still* live in a land of opportunity.

5. *Your Hobbies and Interests.* What you do in your spare time determines the men you meet. If your hobby is needlepoint you won't meet nearly the number of men you would if your hobby were fly casting. Joanne was a military history buff. She could draw freehand maps of every battle of the Civil War. She belonged to the military book club and spent days researching the name of a certain general. She loved her hobby, but it was a solitary one.

Last summer she read of a showing of war relics to be displayed in New York. On her vacation, Joanne drove from her home in Virginia to New York and stayed a week. She had planned to spend three days. The show comprised collectors from all over the country, who put up booths to display, sell and trade their treasures. In one day Joanne met more people who shared her interest than she had met in a lifetime of study. She exchanged cards and addresses; next summer she plans to take a trip across the country to visit their shops.

If you have an interest or hobby which is confining, see if you can't figure a way to broaden your base, or at least get together with others whose interests are similar.

An enterprising young man in San Francisco who liked to jog decided to invent a way to make it more interesting and attractive. He designed a course with sixteen "stations" along the way. Each station is a calisthenic exercise with the flat-board, bar, or pole necessary to perform that specific exercise. The course goes around the Marina Green, behind the St. Francis Yacht Club, down the beach to Fort Point and back.

Two weeks ago I walked to the area to see it. The place was jammed with Sunday joggers having a terrific time. People were talking to each other at all the stations, giving hints on how to improve their chin-ups or leg lifts. A TV crew from a local channel was filming part of the activity. It's absolute proof that you can create—or participate—in life. There are *still* new ideas to be carried out. You can find more activities in which to participate than you have hours in your day.

6. *Your Children.* Rejoice that you have children. Never say, even in a fit of depression, that your life would be better without them. It couldn't possibly be. A good mother who is having fun with her children is an attractive sight. I have met many fascinating people *because* of my children. My life has been enriched because of my children. I once broke an engagement to a man, who was completely devastated, *not* because he was losing me, but because, he said, he would miss my kids!

Most of the divorced men you date will have children. When it is the father's day to have them, invite him to bring the children to your house to be with your children. When a man sees that you enjoy children—his as well as yours—you can't help but take a leap in his estimation.

MEN AS FRIENDS

It's quite possible to meet men through your men friends. Not all the men you meet will be potential companions or husbands, but some will become good friends. There's nothing like a good male friend to give you advice on how to deal with the other men in your life. There is also nothing like a good male friend who enjoys you for your company.

One good side effect coming from the breaking down of the male-female stereotypes is that new ways of friendships are developing. A man and a woman in an office situation can enjoy and respect each other's ability. He will not be pinching her bottom. She will not apply fresh lipstick before she goes into his office. They are people doing a job, accomplishing tasks— and enjoying the fact that they find each other pleasant to be with.

I grew up in a family with no brothers or close male cousins and I absolutely did not know how to enjoy men for themselves. It was a popularity contest. I worried if every boy I met didn't like me. When I didn't have a date, it was a devastating put-down. When I entered business for the first time I was controlled by emotions. I needed to be praised and to be liked. If someone complained about my work I took it as a personal complaint against me. It was a pretty miserable time.

You can love men without being in love. You can have many loving friends whom you enjoy enormously, but who relate to others for their physical love. It's necessary to have love in your life, to be a loving person. Because you are unmarried doesn't mean you are unloved. There is a great difference between unloved and unchosen. Open your heart to those around you and let the love roll in. It doesn't always have to come from an attractive, available man. It's still love, and that's the sunshine of life.

9

Sex

and the Divorced Woman

In today's crazy moral mix-up, I hesitate to venture yet *another* opinion on the subject of sex. It's all been said as many times as there are ways to do it. Not only has it all been said, but it is now being acted out at your accommodating neighborhood movie house by people whose names are household words. Yes indeed, sex is big business.

As a divorced woman, you will find that sex is one more problem you have to juggle in your crowded and active life. Somewhere between trips to the supermarket, going to work, paying the bills and changing the sheets, you are supposed to put a dab of Estée Lauder behind your ear, slip into something lethal, and snuggle up in what's-his-name's arms. But before you turn out the lights, let's discuss a few things, m'dear.

Many of us grew up under such pronouncements as "You don't kiss a boy until the third date." A girl who "went all the way" was as good as finished as far as the "nice boys" were concerned. You flirted and kissed and danced cheek-to-cheek, but you kept your knees locked. If you began to weaken in the back seat of his car, you cried and said please don't. Or you jumped out and made a mad dash back to the safe virginity of the dorm.

You may have guessed that it's all different now. Today's young people seem to be making up their own rules. The divorced woman has to make hers up, too. No one, to my knowledge, has written a Behavior Code for the Divorced Woman. It is entirely up to you how you act in any given situation. With the exception of rape, it is still the woman who says yea or nay. Don't wait until the last moment before you decide. Spend a little time formulating your code of behavior.

YOUR CODE

Before you make any moral pronouncements to yourself, let me pass on this newsy note. Everyone *isn't* doing it. If you believe the propaganda to the contrary, you will be joining the ranks of the ridiculous. There is absolutely no truth to the rumor that you have to be a willing and at-random sex partner in order to be modern, popular, or where it's at. In fact, I would say the opposite is true.

Keith is an attractive divorced man in his late thirties who works for an import-export company. I've watched him parade a string of models, secretaries, stewardesses, art directors, and one concert pianist through my home. Each time he comes to dinner, it's with a new Sharon or Tammy or Evelyn. One night he arrived late, alone and with a terrible scowl on his face. After dinner I asked him what happened.

"You'll never believe it. This dumb broad wanted to go to bed *before* we came to your party. Sometimes I swear to God I'm going to marry the first girl who *won't* go to bed with me on the first date."

Perhaps Keith is an extreme case or perhaps this is a pose on his part. Some would say that these women have a right to sleep with whomever they want whenever they want. Certainly it is their "right," but I think they are being very unfair to themselves. How can you possibly know someone in so short a time? Good sex, great sex has to be mental as well as physical.

Remember too, that the man involved has *his* behavior code. He was raised by a mother who loaded him down with a lot of the same maxims we carry around. He has *his* idea of what an intelligent woman will and will not do. The older the man, the squarer the maxims. Some men will "test" you and be secretly relieved when you say no.

There are no set number of times you should see a man before you sleep with him. The determining factor is how much you care about each other—when you want to say with your body what you feel in your heart. Only you can determine this. You can tell when a man genuinely wants you. You feel loved, adored—never used or cheated.

In forming your behavior code, I would have a clause in there which disposes of the tit-for-tat men who use this sort of approach:

"What do you mean no sex? I paid for dinner!" or:

"If I'd have known *that*, I wouldn't have brought you," or:

"Come on, we've had a good time. Nobody says 'No' any more. You women are liberated, remember?"

You do *not* have to give your body to pay for a dinner, a theater seat, or a day at the races. If you are going to do *that*, make it worth your while, for, say, a Mercedes or a ten-unit apartment building. I overheard a man talking to a woman in a small Italian restaurant. The man said, "I'm looking for a gal who wants to go out occasionally for a simple meal and a little uninvolved sex." I so wanted the girl to say, "Listen. I can cook my *own* simple meals and to me sex is very involved." Honestly, some men you could just kick in the shins.

The main plank of your behavior code should be: What will the act do to me? Absolutely never "go along" with it, then spend the next day agonizing over what you did. Don't sleep with someone if you feel that will intensify a relationship that is detrimental to your best interests. This *can* happen. Monica has spent three years in a relationship with a man who treats her very badly indeed, except in bed. Monica had no sexual experiences before her marriage and the marriage ended because her husband was impotent. Along came Harry, who opened up all the sexual wonders of the world for her. She absolutely cannot believe what she has missed. Yet Harry has a drinking problem, can't keep a job, disappears for weeks at a time, and only returns to Monica when he needs money. Monica feels "hooked."

There is no valid reason for Monica—or any woman—to think good sex is only available with one certain man. There are other men in the world—thousands of men. Some are good lovers; some are great lovers; some are lousy lovers; and most are average lovers. A man's sexual achievements should *never* be the sole basis for a relationship. You *can* find someone else. How do you know you won't find someone *better*?

ALL THINGS CONSIDERED

In addition to your behvaior code—and the man in your life— a great sexual experience depends upon many factors. If any part of either of your lives is out of whack, it is going to affect the performance. To enjoy a healthy sexual relationship, consider the following factors.

1. *The Norm.* There are all manner of sex experts and quasi-experts telling the populace how to make love. They have put "freedom of orgasm" right up there with freedom of speech as one of our national birthrights. If you don't have one, lady, you're un-American.

Who knows what an "orgasm" is? As one woman told me, "For years I thought I was having wonderful orgasms. Then I got divorced, met this man and *really* had one." Who knows how many women have been born, spent fifty wonderful years with a loving husband, and died never having had a biologically perfect orgasm?

My advice is to forget the experts and forget the norms. Do what you enjoy and enjoy what you're doing. Don't keep that sex manual on the bedside table open to page 83 and wait for *that* to happen. What if it doesn't? Is your life ruined? And how do you know that what you're doing isn't better anyway?

Another "norm" that is way off base, is the notion that our male population is made up entirely of "cocksmen." There are a great many perfectly normal men who *don't* want to do it all the time. To go one step further, there are a great many men who would not put sex at the top of the list of their favorite activities. I have a dear friend, a painter, who said that if I would explain that to women I would be doing men a tremendous favor.

When a man is reading, poring over his stamp collection, or in his studio painting, he is not necessarily thinking about sex. In fact, it's a good bet he isn't. In walks the woman in his life, out for a little action. When he doesn't respond with ardor she thinks there's something the matter with him—or with her. There is nothing *wrong* with either of them. The man cares for her and adores making love to her—*but not right now*. He is happy and very *turned on* by what he's presently doing.

This brings us to the frequency norm. It is impossible for anyone to decide arbitrarily how many acts of intercourse should take place within a given time in order for a relationship to be "normal." It is equally absurd to base your table of action on habits of friends; an interview with Richard Burton; or the performance of your ex-husband. Sometimes you are going to feel like it and sometimes you are not. When you feel like it: that's your frequency norm.

2. *Initiating the Action.* In a good sexual relationship, both partners should be initiators. No longer does the woman have to lie there and wait to be tapped on the shoulder. That's another of those norms which says the man is the aggressor. That's fine in the early stages of a relationship, but when she is deeply involved, the woman should let her desires be known. Most men, I think, want to be wanted.

3. *The Time, the Place.* This is sometimes the most difficult part of a relationship. As a divorced woman and working mother, your life can be filled to the brim. Going out to dinner, back to his apartment, then home at two in the morning—it takes a great deal of advance planning. You can be absolutely exhausted by the time you wash your hair, pick up the sitter, feed the kids, and put on your face. When you finally make it to his apartment all you can think about is that alarm clock at six-thirty tomorrow morning.

One way to show the man in your life how much you care is to arrange a totally free weekend together. The next weekend that the children visit their father plan a leisurely schedule around just the two of you. It could be a long walk Saturday to poke around bookstores; his favorite dinner in front of the fireplace; eggs benedict and champagne for Sunday breakfast; and a ball game on TV with beer and pizza. (You don't have to watch. You can sleep or do your nails or read one of the books you bought the day before.)

Hurried, frantic, tired sex is never as satisfying as leisurely, carefree, rested sex. It's almost better to have one sensational sensual weekend than a month of improvised encounters. When you are worried about getting home on time or when he is exhausted from a difficult client meeting, you can jeopardize your future with a disappointing experience.

4. *His Mental State.* A man brings a great many things to the bedroom besides his manhood. For one thing he brings all his past experiences. If he has always had satisfying sexual encounters, he looks forward to the evening with excited anticipation. If he has been through a devastating divorce in which his wife accused him of being less than a man he is going to need tender help and understanding. We are all a sum total of what has gone before.

A man also brings with him his definition of how a woman should be treated. Martha and Ben had been dating for three months before they had a sexual encounter, and it happened quite by accident. Ben had a small farm outside of town and on the weekends they would take their mutual children, load up Martha's station wagon, and head for the country. Between them they had seven children and it always worked out that they had at least three in residence every weekend. Suddenly one Friday night Ben showed up at Martha's with no children. As it turned out, Martha's three were also gone. Ben seemed a bit upset, as if he weren't quite sure what to do.

Martha was delighted with the turn of events. She grabbed her coat and suitcase and said, "Let's go!" When they arrived at the farm, Ben unloaded the car and took what seemed *hours* to Martha to light the stove, start a fire, bring in extra logs, and make their drinks. When he finally settled down in the big chair by the hearth, Martha asked him what in the world was the matter. He answered that it was nothing, he guessed he missed the kids.

After dinner with a brandy by the fire, Ben seemed more relaxed. He picked Martha up and carried her to the large four-poster in his bedroom. Once he was under the covers with her, his uneasiness returned. As he held her in his arms for the first time, his movements were shy and awkward. Martha was almost aggressive in her movements toward Ben. Then it happened. His ardor disappeared. "Ben," said Martha, "I wish you'd tell me what it is."

"Nothing, it's nothing. It's just that you're Allen and Andrew and Becky's mother, and, hell, I don't know! I just can't see making love to a mother!"

It took several hours of quiet talking, gentle probing, and loving movements to make everything all right in Ben's head. Martha was a mother. He loved her and looked forward to the weekends in her company, but he could never quite bring himself to treat her as he would a woman without children. Martha's motherhood put her above other women. When she had natural normal reactions he was undone. She was wrong. The love-making was wrong.

It took them several weekends alone before Ben was able to enjoy Martha and enjoy the weekend. He had to rearrange his notions of women and motherhood. He had to accept the fact that it was *all right* for Martha to feel the way she did and to do the things they both enjoyed. Had Martha been less understanding, the relationship could have been irreparably damaged.

When dealing with the man in your life, try to get him to talk about women, about his mother and about his ex-wife. When you know these things about a man, you can treat him accordingly. A little forethought can turn a good relationship into a great one.

A man also brings his work to bed with him. If he has had a successful day he feels like a joyous romp. If he has had serious reversals or difficult personnel problems he may feel more like getting drunk than making love. If he is silent, it could be that he is hesitant to discuss his problems or worries with you because you are not his wife. He knows that you have problems of your own, and he doesn't want to add to your burden. It's sometimes impossible for a man to leave his office—when he leaves his office.

When a man has deep-seated psychological problems, one of the places they may show up is in his sex life. Norman's wife left him for his best friend, and he was distraught. He kept up a good front by laughing and joking about how he had "traded one forty-year-old wife for two twenties." He appeared at all the parties, always with some young thing on his arm.

Four years after his divorce he met Ann. She was not twenty. Nor thirty. She was forty-two, stunning, and a very successful landscape architect. Norman was captivated. He dated Ann for six weeks, calling her daily and sending flowers and clever gifts. Then he suddenly stopped his attention. He absolutely dropped her. Ann was mystified. She thought back in their relationship and tried to think of something she could have done to hurt his feelings or to make him think she didn't care about him. She truly couldn't remember an incident that would warrant the severing of the relationship.

Ann agonized over what to do. She cared about Norman and she hated to see it all end like this. One evening she dropped by his office just as he was leaving. She said she wanted him to take her around the corner and buy her a drink for "old times' sake." Norman agreed. He was obviously moved at the sight of her, but he remained aloof. After the first drink, Ann ordered another and a double for Norman, and then another. When it appeared that the alcohol had begun to take effect, Ann said it was time to go. She maneuvered Norman out of the bar, into her car, and through the front door of her apartment, where he collapsed on her couch.

In the morning over coffee Ann asked him what in the world had happened to them. She didn't hint or hedge, she asked him point blank why he had ceased to call her. Norman, sitting on the edge of the couch, put his head in his hands.

"Okay, Ann. You want to know what's the matter. Just this. I can't get it up. Plain fact. After my wife left I tried and it's just gone. I knew if we kept seeing each other, you'd find out and think I was queer or something." He didn't look at her. He was too shaken by his admission. Ann, in a moment of rare insight, started to giggle. "What's so goddamn funny!" he roared.

"What is so funny, my dear, is that last night you performed like a bull elephant!"

Norman, of course, had done nothing but pass out on the couch. That marvelous fabrication, however, was all he needed to hear. Roaring like a bull elephant, he swept Ann up out of her chair and into the bedroom, where he did indeed end a four-year celibacy.

5. *His Physical State.* A tired man does not make a good lover. That doesn't mean he has lost his sex drive. A man can have low blood sugar, a thyroid condition, or just be plain pooped. If the man in your life is perpetually tired, suggest that he have a physical check-up. A man living alone often neglects his health. He doesn't eat right. He forgets to take vitamins. He may drink or smoke too much. All these factors detract from his performance as a lover.

Show compassion for the man in your life. Ask him to take better care of himself. Suggest healthful activities such as swimming or riding a bike. Get him out in the country. It somehow is always easier to complain about a man than to help him out constructively. When you show concern for the whole man— mental and physical—you will have just that—a *whole* man.

6. *Comparisons.* We all compare. We compare how we look as opposed to how our roommate looked when we saw her at the class reunion, or how well our child does in school as compared to our neighbor's child, or how green our grass is as compared to that of the house next door, or how thin we are as compared to the other women at work. What good does it do? It may motivate us to lose five pounds, fertilize the grass, or help our kids with their homework. So it isn't really a *bad* thing.

If, however, we bring comparisons into the bedroom, we can cause trouble. "Well, Jack wasn't the world's greatest lover, but he at least cared what happened to me!" If you're talking to the new man in your life and Jack is your ex-husband, then you are being not only cruel, but stupid. What you and Jack did is of absolutely no concern to your new man. If you have a complaint about the love-making, gently and kindly state your case. "Darling, if you would just kiss me a little longer, I'd be a new woman."

Equally destructive is the overstatement. "You're great! Absolutely the best bed partner I've ever had!" Think what *this* does to his imagination. "I wonder how wide a survey she's taken. What's she conducting, the Bedsprings Olympics?" You are way ahead to just enjoy what's happening and say so. You don't have to make comparisons, draw conclusions or give progress reports.

7. *True Confessions.* The man in your life knows you're not the Village Virgin, but he doesn't need to be reminded. The prone position turns some women into mechanical mouths and they talk and talk and talk. They go through the romances in their lives, quoting chapter and verse, as if they were Sheherezade. No one, my dear, gives a damn. You are not going to impress the pants off Oscar by telling him what a foxy devil you've been. In fact, that's a sure way to get him back in his pants and out the front door.

Leave a little mystery in your life. What has been, has been. You've learned from your experiences, so leave it at that. I can absolutely guarantee you that a man will find you more attractive when you leave a little to the imagination. If a man is boorish enough to demand to know about the other men in your life, say it was so long ago that you've forgotten. If he continues to probe, tell him that you've tucked them away in your memory album, because you so enjoy being alone with him. This may sound like a soap opera, but that's all his inquisitiveness deserves.

BIRTH CONTROL

It is *still* up to the woman to take the "precautions." Abortion may be legal, but it is a drastic remedy and one to be avoided, not just for the humanitarian consequences, which are heartbreaking to say the very least, but because an abortion is not without danger, both physically and mentally, to the woman. It is not a procedure you want lightly to inflict upon your body and your soul.

The Pill, which is the most common form of birth control, has played more than a minor role in changing the moral code. Fear of pregnancy kept a lot more of us remaining "nice girls" than did any threat of "loss of reputation" or fear of God. The Pill has created carefree love-making and uninhibited sex, and freedom, baby, freedom. It has also been known to cause blood clots, blindness, loss of hair, and any number of other ailments. If you are on the Pill, you know this already. If you are not on the Pill, you probably know more.

On the technical side, I will now quote from my desk reference book . . . And the Pursuit of Happiness.[1]

"Birth control pills are composed of estrogen and progesterone (hormones which simulate pregnancy and inhibit ovulation.) In addition, progesterone causes a thicker cervical mucus (which acts as a barrier to sperm) and modifies the uterine lining enough to prevent implantation. Possible minor side effects include nausea, breakthrough bleeding, breast tenderness, weight gain, and skin discoloration. Physical problems which can be aggravated by the pill include high blood pressure, migraine headaches, asthma, varicose veins, diabetes, cancer, kidney disease, hepatitis, and epilepsy. The most serious possible side effect is blood clotting; the symptoms are dizziness, change in vision, severe headaches, severe chest pains, pain and swelling in the legs. Any of these symptoms should be reported to a doctor immediately. The usual incidence of blood clotting is three women per 100,000; the incidence for women on the pill is twice that; the incidence for pregnant women is 22 women per 100,000. There is no evidence that the pill causes cancer. However, if cancer already exists, the pill will cause it to grow faster; for this reason it is particularly important to have regular examinations and PAP smears. Periods are generally shorter and lighter when a woman is on the pill. When going off, some

[1] By Shirley L. Radl and Carol A. Chetkovich, Metamorphosis Press, Palo Alto, California, 1976

women ovulate normally, whereas others experience temporary infertility. It make take a few months for the menstrual cycle to adjust. If one pill is missed in the middle of the cycle, it is highly unlikely that pregnancy will occur, but if two or more pills are missed, a back-up method (foam or condoms) should be used. Overall effectiveness is about 99 per cent."

Recently the IUD (intrauterine device) has come on the market to mixed reviews. It has done unfriendly acts such as growing into the body. This device (isn't that a wonderful term) is still "in work" so I would check around before I rushed down to my neighborhood GYN to have it installed! Here is what . . . *And the Pursuit of Happiness* has to say about the IUD.

"This is a small piece of plastic which is inserted into the uterus by a doctor; plastic strings attached to the device extend into the vagina. The way the IUD works is not known; one theory is that it prevents implantation of the fertilized egg by irritation of the uterine lining; another is that it speeds up the passage of the egg through the tubes, so that the egg arrives in the uterus before the uterine wall is ready for implantation. Insertion is done during the menstrual period because the cervix is more open at that time. The device may be expelled; this occurs most commonly in the first three months after insertion; expulsion rate is higher in women who have not had children. IUD strings should be checked weekly to make sure the device is still in place. Possible side effects include longer, heavier periods, bleeding between periods, more intense or prolonged menstrual cramps. More serious possible effects include perforation of the uterus and infection. The effectiveness of this device is 90 to 98 per cent."

In addition to the pill and the IUD, there is the old faithful diaphragm, better known as, "Wait just a minute, dear, I'll be right back." The diaphragm doesn't hurt you, but unfortunately it doesn't always help you. It slips, it slides, it rarely fits. But, as I said, it doesn't hurt you. Once again, let's hear from the experts.

"This (diaphragm) is a soft latex cup with a spring rim, which covers the cervix. The main purpose is to hold spermicidal jelly or cream in place (the jelly or cream must be applied inside the rim of the diaphragm.) It may be inserted six hours prior to intercourse, but if it is in for more than two hours, or if intercourse is repeated, additional applications of cream should be used *without* removing the diaphragm. Insert the cream as you would the foam, with an applicator. Do not douche or remove the diaphragm for six to eight hours after intercourse; no harm is done if it is left in longer. The diaphragm should be refitted after a pregnancy or if there is a gain or loss of ten pounds or more. Effectiveness is about 90 per cent."

In addition to this collection of apparatus, you can find any number of foams and jellies, which are guaranteed not at all, but they don't hurt you, either. You may think from this irreverent treatment that I am against birth control. This is absolutely not true. I am very well aware of the dangers of overpopulation, the tragedy of the unwanted child and the hardships of a large family. I favor birth control. What I am angry about is the Great God Science hasn't come up with something kinder to women. I am also angry that the onus is put on us!

Yes, there is a birth control device for men, the condom, or rubber, as it is known in slang circles. It is about as reliable as a diaphragm and twice as inconvenient. Briefly, you could describe it as a thin balloon which the man in question fits over his erect penis before intercourse. The experts say that if you are having relations with a man who uses a condom, you should add to your safety by using a cream or jelly.

Then there is the ancient rite of "withdrawal" in which the man (technically) pulls out before any sperm is released. This method wouldn't get a one on *my* scale of ten. I'm not going to mention the rhythm method because someone tried to explain it to me once and it sounded highly complicated and unreliable. It has to do with days that you are fertile and days that you are not. You have to know your cycles. Who could possibly figure *all* that out!

So what's one to do? That's up to you, your doctor, your drugstore, and your lover. You'll have to work it out because it is a personal and private problem. It could be that before too long there will be a pill for men. Then the only problem will be whether or not he remembered to put the disc in his shaving case!

. . . MORE SEX

Because of our sudden national preoccupation with sex, I think
it's highly possible to find a book, a pamphlet, a device, a center, a
group, a program for any sex problem that may be troubling you.
If you think you want to delve into all this, you're on your own. I
think I would start with your gynecologist followed by a trip to
the library. If all else fails, your neighborhood porn shop has a
neverending array of pamphlets and devices. It will blow your
mind, if you know what I mean.

Which brings us to kinky sex. What's kinky? I guess crotchless
bikini pants and chains and whips—and all that comes in between. I would certainly not want to hazard a guess as to what is
normal and what is perverted. The generally accepted rule seems
to be that no sex act between two willing adult participants
should be labeled perverted. If one partner halfheartedly goes
along with the action, but doesn't really approve of what's happening, then that person is practicing perversion.

You don't have to do anything you don't want to do. What's
more, you shouldn't. If you feel revulsion at certain practices, how
can you enjoy yourself at them? Sex, above all else, *has* to be enjoyable or why bother? If you continue in a sexual practice that
revolts you, you run the risk of losing interest in all sex. You have
absolutely as much right as the man in your life to direct the love-
making.

It is not a perversion, however, to want to experiment. A
healthy interest in adding new delights to a relationship is to be
desired. It can be quite exciting to buy one of the better sex man-
uals, curl up in bed together, and spend a couple of hours poring
over the possibilities. Some will work and others will send you
into gales of laughter. That's good, too. It's a loosening up, a
shared closeness.

A problem that few books seem to stress is a woman's opinion
of her body. When a divorced woman in her forties, fifties, or sixties begins seeing men, she may hesitate to have sexual intercourse
because she doesn't want to get undressed. She may have stretch

marks from pregnancy, less-than-firm breasts, an abdominal scar, or she may be ten or fifteen pounds overweight. It is extremely difficult for this woman to have the carefree abandon of a twenty-two-year-old cupcake with a smooth stomach, slim hips and high, pointed breasts. I'd cavort naked with the best of them if I looked like that. But I don't, and neither do most divorced women.

That is not to say, however, that when the lights are out we cannot earn rave notices in the boudoir. What holds some women back is sheer embarrassment over their physical condition. A man can think a woman is cold or even frigid when fear of the spotlight is all it is. If this describes you, then learn to get around it by buying the most flattering nightgown you can afford. Always be freshly bathed and smelling of luxurious body lotion. When questioned about the gown, tell him he may remove it in bed after the lights are out.

I realize that some women reading this will think they have mistakenly picked up a novel from the twenties. Others will know exactly what I mean. When my novel, *The Sand Castles*, went to my editor, he called a few days later to tell me my sex scenes had "a whiff of the fifties." What I replied to him was, "John, dear, *my* sex life has a whiff of the fifties!" If your sex life has a whiff of the forties or fifties, that's all right. Remember, your lover came from the same era. You may evoke to him delicious memories of Myrna Loy, Gene Tierney, or Lana Turner. You never saw those gorgeous ladies in the "altogether."

Probably the greatest perversion of them all is to engage in isolated acts of intercourse with a variety of men as part of an evening's entertainment. If this describes you, ask yourself why you do it. Is it an insecurity on your part that says a man won't like you if you don't? Are you trying to be liberated? Whatever reason you've given yourself, it's not good enough. You are risking your chances of having a great sexual experience by cheapening the act. You are practicing self-hate.

As a final yardstick, do not listen to what others say is bizarre, unnatural, or perverted. You and the man in your life are the sole judges, and your opinion is the only one that matters. Other values, other morals and other opinions don't belong in your bedroom. *Others*, after all, aren't doing it. If *you* like it, then enjoy it!

STAYING OVER

When you are steadily seeing one man, the question of his "staying over" at your place will have to be faced. Whether or not you should allow this depends upon where and how you live.

  1. *The Divorced Woman Living Alone.* On the surface, it would seem to be perfectly natural for the man in your life to stay overnight with you in your home or apartment. What may be natural may not necessarily be what's best for you. Let's look at the drawbacks.

  A. *Gossip.* No woman is an island, to change a phrase. You do have family, friends and neighbors. If you live in a home in a neighborhood, *his* car in your driveway overnight could cause speculation. It isn't just that people might talk about you, but that the gossip would get to your parents or someone else who might be upset terribly. It's fine to wave your hand and say you don't care, but you should. You truly don't want to inflict sadness in someone's life.

  If you live in an impersonal apartment house and he were to come over by cab, that's a little different. If it's a small, folksy building you risk the problem of meeting the lady next door in the elevator at seven in the morning. I'm not a remnant from the dark ages. This advice is *for your benefit.* I firmly believe that you should only agree to his staying over if it can't possibly harm you. *You* are the only one in this relationship I am concerned about.

  B. *Habit.* What starts out as an occasional "overnight" could well turn into a semi-boarder situation. This, frankly, constricts your social and personal life. You have things to do. You may give up a night school class because he's there. You may give it up so many nights that you have to drop the course—a course that could be important to your career. You find your life suddenly revolving around *his* needs instead of yours.

  Marion had a very nice cottage on the grounds of a large

estate. As an editor of children's books, she found the quiet conducive to her work. She had been dating Sheldon for about two months when he stayed over on a Saturday night. He stayed the next Saturday, too, and the following weekend arrived Friday and left early Sunday morning. Marion, who needed her weekends to read manuscripts, didn't accomplish a thing while he was there. She was forced to work late two nights during the following week.

Sheldon came over one night during the week and brought some "shirts and tennis gear" for the weekend, which he began at noon on Friday. When he left Monday, he left a pile of dirty clothes which he suggested that Marion "send out with her things." When Marion finally balked at his cavalier attitude he seemed shocked. Wasn't she having a good time, too, he asked? No, said Marion. She was too worried about her job to be having a good time. She wanted her privacy—and her life—back.

C. *Other Men.* When you let a man stay over you run the risk that another man in your life will find out. You can't speak freely on the telephone and you can't accept a friend's offer to "stop by." What happens if you have a surprise caller at your door? Certainly it's your life and you can do as you please. When someone else is there it ceases to be just you. When confronted by another man you can explain or you can decline to explain, but you can't do anything about what he thinks.

D. *Cost.* It costs money to house a man. It's not only the food and the liquor. It's extra laundry, the sheets and the towels. It's extra electricity as the stereo plays on hour after hour. It's bathroom supplies and broken glasses and telephone calls. It all adds up. Some men will bring a couple of steaks and a bottle of wine, but what about all your herbs, spices, olive oil, butter, and coffee that he just takes for granted?

The most advanced case of sponging I ever heard was of a man who ordered the Sunday paper delivered to his favorite date's home (and *charged* to her) because he liked to read it in bed Sunday morning. Watch out that your nice, cozy apartment doesn't become the attraction in a man's life. When you stay at *his* place you know you're first in his life.

2. *The Divorced Woman with Children.* If your children are living with you, make it an unbreakable rule that no man stays overnight in your home. In some states you could lose custody of your children on this point. You would be branded an unfit mother, and whether or not it's *fair* would have nothing to do with it.

You have the responsibility for your children and it is up to you to make their years with you as rewarding and happy as possible. Your children have gone through a divorce. They are confused. They have lost their live-in father. For you to add to their confusion by letting men stay overnight in your home is unfair and uncaring.

Your children are still forming their values. Can you tell your sixteen-year-old daughter that her boy friend cannot stay over— but *your* boy friend can? Don't you think a fourteen-year-old boy *knows* what is going on in the bedroom when your friend is there? This could cause your son all manner of problems later in life.

A man who asks to stay over at your home when he knows your children are there is showing a great insensitivity toward you and your life with your children. He is putting his wishes above all else. Who wants *that* kind of man in her life? Whatever reason or excuse he offers is simply *not* reason enough.

You may feel that it is acceptable for a man to stay over when your children are not there. This is certainly preferable, but you still don't know what can happen.

Sandy, a divorcée with two children, lives in Newport Beach in a very nice home with a swimming pool. One weekend, when her children went to stay with their father, she said her current male friend could spend Saturday with her.

On Sunday morning, after a leisurely breakfast, she and her friend decided to take a dip in the pool. Nude. After they frolicked in the water, they began to make love sitting on the second step. At absolutely the wrong moment, who should come racing around the house and into the back garden but her two daughters and their father! They had stopped by to see if she wanted to go sailing with them. When they rang the doorbell and she didn't answer, they decided she must be in the garden taking a sun bath!

As carefully as you *think* you plan, incidents and accidents will happen. That's why it's *so* important *not* to take chances. Whatever moments of happiness you gain in such a situation are not worth the risk to your children's mental health. If the children are away in camp, on a skiing trip or staying on their grandparent's farm, you can be reasonably assured of privacy. If they are at a friend's, at the movies, or at their father's apartment, you can't.

Nothing grows faster than children. Soon they will be gone and you'll marvel where the time went. You'll be alone—and still young. No, forty is *not* old. Neither is fifty. You'll have plenty of time for nude swimming, breakfast in bed, candlelight dinners. What's more, you will enjoy yourself as you never thought possible.

LIVING TOGETHER

There is a phenomenon in our country today, gaining any number of followers, called the *living together arrangement*. Men and women are entering into loose alliances in which they live in the same house or apartment, share expenses, cohabitate freely, and act almost like married people. Except they aren't married. They live in this way only until it doesn't "work" any more, or one partner gets bored or finds someone else, or they decide to get married.

Any self-respecting divorced woman who cares about herself and her future is stupid to get into one of these arrangements. To me they are loaded in favor of the man, while the woman, time and time again, loses her toehold on the future. Let's look at the arguments against the LTA.

1. *Your Children.* If you have children living at home, and you enter into a LTA, you can lose custody of your children. If you are getting spousal support, you can lose that, too. I don't feel that children would gain anything by living with a man who is not their stepfather. It is an added confusion and embarrassment in

their lives. Because the man is not their stepfather, he feels no responsibility toward them, nor do the children feel compelled to acknowledge his authority. Children are conformists. It is hard for them to accept a living pattern that none of their friends share. It's hard enough for them to have divorced parents, but they usually know other children in the same situation.

When the LTA splits up, the child or children must make yet another adjustment. If they liked the man in question, they have suffered another loss. You are setting a precedent for the child or children that could keep them from ever having a normal family life.

2. *Your Social Life.* When you live with a man without the benefit of marriage, you take yourself out of "circulation." You are restricting your social life and preventing yourself from meeting a man you would *like* to marry. Those in favor of the LTA say that it is a good way to *test* marriage. How can it be? It is a relationship without commitment—which is the basis of marriage.

3. *Role Playing.* I don't care how modern you say you are and how much you believe you can live with a man on an equal footing, it just seems to me this is impossible. You will find yourself slipping into all the traditional roles. You'll cook because you do it better. You'll clean because you understand the routine and can do it faster. You'll shop because you know your way around the supermarket. You'll take his shirts to the laundry because it's nearer to your office.

This by itself is not all that distressing. What should disturb you is that it takes *extra* time that belongs to you. Your career should be as important to you as his is to him. You'll find when you give in on the little points you begin to give in on the big ones. You may end up quitting your French lessons because he hates listening to your tapes. You may give up a promotion because it means moving to another town.

What happens is that the man gets all the conveniences of having a wife, and you're paying for the privilege! When you split the costs, he is relieved of any of the husbandly responsibility. No wonder men think this is a terrific arrangement. Why get married and lose half your income!

4. *Emotional Instability.* The lack of commitment, which

devotees of the LTA find so attractive, is the factor which poses one of the biggest problems. It encourages jealousy. When he's late for dinner or she gets a mysterious phone call, each one wonders what the other is up to. You aren't married. Technically you can do as you darn please, yet you have this unstable dependency upon each other.

If you deeply love the man you're living with, you live under the constant threat of his leaving. You baby him; you give in to him; you cater to his wants. You can become so stifling that you create the very disaster you are trying to prevent. You can cause him to leave!

5. *No Financial Responsibility.* As a responsible divorced woman, you should be building toward your future: saving money, buying furniture and investing in a piece of property. If you are living with someone your goals get clouded. The entire relationship smacks of impermanence, so you put all your energy and money into today.

If you co-mingle your funds you are going to have a hard time proving what is yours. When the relationship ends, your ex-roommate can walk out the door with the stereo you helped pay for, the waterbed, the butcher-block table, and all the plants. If you want them back you have to go to court with *proof* that you paid. The time and hassle will cost more than the goods! In marriage these problems are handled under "property settlement" and you at least get *some* protection.

When you openly live together without being married, the laws covering "family law" *do not* apply to you. You can sue on breach of contract and recover funds *if* you had a written or verbal agreement. You are not entitled to division of property or any form of "spousal support." If you have a child together (perish the thought) the father must pay child support—if you can find him!

If the house or apartment in which you live is in your name and he leaves you with unpaid rent, utilities, and phone, those are *your* bills. The landlady, utility company, and Ma Bell are not the least bit interested or concerned with your love life. When service is discontinued for non-payment, there goes your credit rating!

6. *Set a Pattern.* When you agree to live with a man without

benefit of marriage you lose all your leverage for ever marrying him. That's not telling you to be dishonest. It's your *right* to prefer marriage, and if he doesn't like it that's his problem. Don't be duped into this "Let's try it and see if it works."

When Angie first met Danny he was just divorced and said he couldn't handle a legal commitment, so why didn't they live together for a "couple of months." Then when things were "back to normal" they would get married. That was eight years ago! Whenever Angie brings up the subject of marriage, Danny says what they have is terrific. How could marriage be any better! Angie hates to mention finances because that sounds unromantic and grasping, but she is concerned about her future.

Danny is an executive with a paper company. He earns very good money, but has not given anything of permanent value to Angie. He pays all the bills, buys some of her clothes, and pays their travel expenses, but that's it. He has turned down her idea to buy a condominium, saying he likes to rent. He owns a cabin at a lake, but he has put it in his children's name. Angie has a part-time job that she loves, but she couldn't possibly support herself on it. As she says, she has everything—and nothing.

When you live with a man without being married, you set yourself up for a senseless, nomadic existence. Suppose Angie and Danny break up. When Angie meets another man, what is going to prevent him from saying, "Look, you've lived with one guy for eight years. Why not live with me? Why talk marriage? What's the matter, did you love him more than you love me?" With no substantial livelihood on the horizon, Angie is tempted again. After all, he'll pay the bills. But when they split, then what?

A woman has to set the pace. A man will abide by her standards—if she sticks to them. Angie made her mistake by moving in with Danny. If she had said:

"I understand about your not wanting a commitment and I agree with you. But I want you to understand my feelings, too. I love you, but I don't believe two people should live together unless they are married, so let's continue to see each other until the time comes."

Let's suppose that in three months Danny was so in love with Angie that he married her. Then let's suppose that at the end of eight years they got divorced. Angie would be entitled to some sort of property settlement and spousal support. "Splitting," after living with him for eight years entitles her to nothing.

7. *Unfair to Family.* A great many parents of the women who are entering into LTAs are quite distressed about it. Relatives are concerned. To some parents it's a horrible blow and to others it's an embarrassment. No one would knowingly want to hurt a loved one. Still, when you quite openly go against your parents' values, you are wounding them. They have a right to their standards, too.

You can say that your parents should accept your life-style because it's your choice. It is not easy for someone to turn off a long-held conviction. If you are going to demand your freedom of choice, remember that they have theirs, too. You could be causing a break with your family that would be extremely hard to mend.

8. *The Family.* The LTA is one more assault on the family, which is still the backbone of this country. It may sound strange to be talking about "family" to divorced women, but I think you'll agree that it is desirable to be married, in general. Your last marriage didn't work, but maybe your next one will. If you agree to an "alternate life-style" you'll never know.

Marriage laws were developed for the protection of women and children. To cast aside this institution for a temporary alliance having questionable merit for the woman seems wrong indeed. Remember that what seems sophisticated and fun at twenty or even thirty is downright foolhardy at forty or fifty. I am interested in *your* welfare. You should be, too.

10

Marriage

and the Divorced Woman

"Being a woman," said Joseph Conrad, "is a terribly difficult trade since it consists principally of dealings with men." Certainly this is true in marriage. Having done it once (or more) the divorced woman is well aware of the myriad problems involved in *any* relationship with a man, particularly marriage.

The statistics report that a divorced woman has a better chance of marriage than a never-married woman. Perhaps this is because of the divorced woman's firsthand experience. Whatever the reason, for those of you who would like to marry again, that's good news.

We have all been influenced by the women's movement, some of us more than others. Today's motivated, successful, independent woman has many options, *among* them marriage. It is certainly not wrong for a woman to *want* to get married. Without this commitment no marriage can work. A woman who wants to marry can take constructive action in her life to help her find the right man with which to share her life. The advice I am about to offer is for the woman who wants to get married again.

YOUR ATTITUDE

The first prerequisite to getting married again is making the decision that you *want* to get married. Once you say that to yourself, your outlook changes. You shift a few priorities in your life. You should, however, keep your lifetime goals clearly in view. Your life should still be *you-centered* and your career should not be sublimated. Do not compromise. Marriage should be an addition to your life, not your life.

Your attitude toward marriage will be reflected in your attitude toward yourself. Take an interest—a big interest—in how you look, how you dress and how appealing your home is. After all, every man who comes through the front door will be making silent judgments. Let's look at your attitudes one by one.

1. *Toward Yourself.* Before someone else can care about you, you have to care about yourself. You show in the way you handle your life whether you like yourself, have faith in yourself and trust yourself. Never talk yourself down by saying I'm not this, I'm not that. This is a very unfortunate habit, guaranteed to discourage men.

Why would a man want you unless you have something to offer? Don't hide your accomplishments. No one likes a braggart, but no one is interested in a dull person either. The age of wanting a simple good woman who doesn't excel at anything is long past. You're proud of what you've done because you're proud of you.

2. *Toward Your Body.* Big is *not* beautiful. How you treat yourself physically is just as important as how you treat yourself mentally. Eat properly. Exercise. At all times look your absolute very best. A man is proud to be seen with an attractive woman, just as a woman is proud to be seen with an attractive man. I didn't say young, or beautiful, or rich. I said attractive.

I am in favor of cosmetic surgery only if you have kept the other parts of your body in good shape. What good is a face lift if you're forty pounds overweight? When you have a regard for yourself it shows. It shows, and it speaks well of you.

Cleanliness is a rarely discussed subject except on TV commercials. I have seldom read a beauty hint book that said—bathe. Bathe at least once a day. Brush your teeth, use a deodorant, shave your legs, cream your body, and use a *good* perfume. Women living alone often get sloppy. Don't let this happen to you.

3. *Toward Your Career.* I have yet to meet a man who was not

impressed—and attracted by—a woman who knows where she's going. There is something quite sexy about a successful woman. I can't tell you how many dinner parties I've attended when I have been seated next to a man who was also next to a gorgeous young woman on his other side. I've gotten so I almost make a game out of it. At first the man will barely nod to me, then turn his eyes on the luscious lovely. I forget him during the first course and even the entree.

By the time salad arrives if the man has any brains at all he will casually turn to me and make a few polite inquiries as to who I am and what I do. Within ten minutes it is almost a sure bet that he's mine for the rest of the evening. Why? Because I happen to lead about as interesting a life as you could possibly dream up. I can truthfully say that I wouldn't exchange places with anyone. I am certainly not young *or* luscious, but I have something to say. I created my life out of the ashes of great defeats and it wasn't easy. So when I say *you* can, I know what I'm talking about.

You don't have to be Chairman of the Board to be fascinating. All you need is a healthy, creative interest in *what* you are doing. That makes it interesting to others. To say, "Oh, you wouldn't care about what I do," is a certain way to guarantee that he won't. I once heard a woman who was security guard in a department store describe her job. She made it sound as if she were J. Edgar Hoover, James Bond, and Sherlock Holmes all wrapped into one. Why was that? It was because she absolutely loved what she was doing and she was *good* at it.

4. *Toward Your Home.*   Your home is one of your greatest assets! It can be a simple two-room apartment or a seventeen-room villa. It truthfully doesn't matter. What does matter is your attitude toward it. What men living alone usually miss the most is a homey atmosphere, that special warmth that only a woman can create. That is not a sexist remark. Men can create pleasant atmospheres, too. But a man cannot create the *same* atmosphere a woman can, so capitalize on it.

Some divorced women tend to become sloppy housekeepers because no husband is around to complain. They have had *enough* housework to last them a lifetime and they'll be darned if they'll clean house. It's your home now. When you neglect it, you show a disrespect for yourself. You are saying you don't care *how* you live. This is a mistake, for you and your children as well as for the man in your life.

Keep your home picked up and surface clean. I would certainly *never* win the Good Housekeeping Seal of Approval, but my home is pleasant to enter. The secret is to create an atmosphere in which your guests feel like staying, talking and enjoying themselves. When the man in your life is coming over, give special attention to the bathroom. Wash the handbowl, put out a new bar of soap. It's truly the small things that matter.

Nothing does more for a house than the aroma of good food. Cook for him at home as often as you can. The secret to being a whiz in the kitchen is to master ten dishes. That is all. You don't need to be a French chef, but you definitely should know your way around the stove. When you know ten sure-fire dishes you can have the ingredients handy or be able to assemble a simple market list for a quick trip there. When you know ten sure-fire dishes you can always dash out to the kitchen and whip up something. When I say sure-fire, I mean ten dishes that you can cook from memory and which you know are simply delicious.

Here are ten sure-fire dishes that come to mind:

1. Cheese soufflé
2. Spinach quiche (any quiche)
3. Spaghetti al pesto
4. Broiled chicken
5. Sensational green salad
6. Lamb curry
7. Linguine and clams
8. Minestrone
9. Steak Diane
10. Boeuf bourguignonne

That may not sound impressive, but that isn't the point. Only two dishes on that list take over an hour to prepare. What is impressive to a man is your ability to joyfully go into the kitchen and come up with a dish that is good to look at and delicious to eat. Anyone can open a can of tamales. You be the woman who can *cook*.

5. *Toward Your Children.* How you treat your children in

front of your beaux is very important. I'm not suggesting that you have two separate behavior patterns, but there are certain things which by avoidance will make your time together more pleasant.

For one thing, discipline your children in private. Not only is it unfair to embarrass them in front of company, but it also embarrasses the company. When you speak to them harshly or critically in front of a man, they automatically resent that man.

A woman enjoying her children is an attractive sight. A woman unhappy with her children is a very unattractive sight. Your face becomes distorted and your voice shrill. Wherever you are with your children and the man in your life, make it as pleasant as possible.

Although you should not hide the children in a closet, you should arrange things for them to do so they are not underfoot. Don't wait until the last minute to do this, think ahead. Get the toys out of the living room, the bikes out of the front hall and keep the radio on an adult station. Loud teen-age music is, to many men, an instant turn-off.

When you pay attention to these categories you create a pleasant, inviting atmosphere for a man. You also create a pleasant, inviting atmosphere for anyone who comes through the front door, including yourself. This isn't a façade; it's the way things ought to be. It takes very little extra effort to raise your life from chaotic to well run. It's a matter of consistency. When you regularly care, it becomes a habit.

MEN . . . AS HUSBANDS

Now that we have your life in order, let's talk about men. If you want to marry again, the first rule is to limit your socializing to *eligible* men. Cut out the chair-warmers. We have already discussed those eligible, but here they are again:
1. Never-married men
2. Divorced men
3. Men whose divorces are *in* the process
4. Widowers

The chair-warmers are:

1. Married men
2. Confirmed bachelors
3. Suspiciously separated men
4. Gay men
5. Half-husbands

THE INELIGIBLES

To help you determine if a man is decidedly a chair-warmer and not a possible marriage mate, let's look at each category and how they can fool you. (Men think *all* women want to be married and they use that knowledge well.)

The Married Man. First, he'll lie. Not all married men lie, of course, but a large enough percentage to put you on your guard. He will assure you that he is absolutely free as a bird. You can watch for these signs that will tell you differently.

1. He's never told you where he lives.
2. He lives in another town or city.
3. He can never see you on a holiday.
4. He takes you to quaint "out-of-the-way" places.
5. He's never given you his phone number.
6. He's never said, "Drop by my office on your way home and we'll go out for a drink."
7. You have never met his married friends.
8. You have never met any of his family.
9. He never takes your hand on the street.
10. He looks guilty.

If you suspect that a man is *not* telling the truth, find out. *Demand* to know where he lives. *Insist* on a phone number. Drop by his office. Ask him to take you to the most popular restaurant in town. It could happen that he complies in all these requests, but you *still* have this nagging feeling. You can check with his secretary, or hire a detective or follow him home. These are not the actions of a neurotic woman. You have a right to know if you are being treated honestly and fairly.

If a man tells you he is married but not happily, say how sorry you are, then walk away. Do not get involved in this potentially heartbreaking situation. Tell him to call you when his divorce is final. If a man tells you he's married, but he and his wife have "this understanding," congratulate him, then walk away. What kind of understanding could be of possible interest to you? You're interested in a relationship that could end in marriage.

Confirmed Bachelors. It's always difficult to say who is confirmed and who is not. It is safe to assume that a never-married man over forty is not going to be easy to lead to the altar. He has lived exactly as he pleased for enough years to be set in his ways. Certainly it is not impossible to marry such a man. The danger is that you will invest three or five or eight years of your life in a relationship that isn't going to end in marriage. You feel when you've gone *this* far, it's a shame to give up. You can have a marvelous time in such a relationship as long as you recognize it for what it is. If marriage is your goal, put a time limit on your relationship with a bachelor, then give him an ultimatum.

Suspiciously Separated Men. As we discussed in chapter 8, a man who tells you he's separated isn't telling you anything. Pin him down. Exactly what *is* the status of his marriage? Has either he or his wife filed? If he says those papers are in the process, ask a lawyer to look it up. *All* filed papers can be verified.

Lucy had been dating a charming older man for months and months. The man was separated from his wife and promised to marry Lucy the minute his divorce was final. The man supported his wife quite comfortably, as he did himself, and he contributed generously to Lucy's expenses.

One day Lucy had lunch with an old friend who was a lawyer. She told him she was going to get married when her friend's divorce was final. The lawyer suggested they take a little trip to the courthouse to check on the progress of the divorce. Guess what they found out?

The wife had filed and indeed there were papers on record. They had been filed two years previously. Lucy asked the lawyer what that meant. It meant, he said, that it was up to her husband to answer and since he did not appear to be in any hurry the matter would not move ahead at all. In fact, he said, it would soon be dropped.

Lucy confronted her friend. In many angry words he told her what she had done was disloyal and dishonest! They broke up. The last time Lucy saw him, he had another younger woman on his arm. I leave it to you to decide who was disloyal and dishonest.

Gay Men. An obvious homosexual is not going to present himself as a prospective husband. A man who is a "closet gay" may, for a number of reasons. Some gays, for business or other reasons, want to present themselves to the world as straight. They take women on dates, to parties, and to the theater. If the man is atractive, successful, and attentive, it is hard to say no.

The danger of spending too much time with this sort of man is that you may fall in love with him. Then what do you do? Some women think that they can sway any man into the heterosexual world. This is an illusion. When you spend considerable time with a suspected closet gay, you are keeping yourself out of circulation. If you can go out with this man to places where you will meet other men (hopefully heterosexual), a few dates present no major investment of your time. Don't, however, become "window dressing" for a man with other preferences.

Half-Husbands. There are certan men who like to be in a home atmosphere without taking any responsibility. These men will be darling to your children, fix the sprinkler heads in the backyard, and carve the Sunday chicken. Then they go home. It's very difficult to know when you have a half-husband who has *no* intention of ever marrying—or a genuine potential husband. Here you have to decide on a time limit and give a subtle ultimatum.

THE MOST ELIGIBLE MEN

It is generally dangerous to say a certain man is the *most* anything, but I feel there is a definite pattern that is worth mentioning. Here is my definition of the man most likely to marry.

1. He is recently *divorced* (must be under two years—preferably one year).

2. He has children and misses them.
3. He doesn't like to cook, clean, or take his shirts to the laundry.
4. He has a good job which he enjoys.
5. He does not enjoy having a different date every night.
6. He is not very good at organizing his social life.

It doesn't matter *why* he got divorced unless it was because he is an alcoholic, has severe mental problems, or beat his wife. You can determine these things by spending time together and by questioning a wife of one of his friends. This is not devious and underhanded. Your future is at stake.

The reason he must be recently divorced is because this type of man usually marries within eighteen months of his divorce. If he stays single past the two-year mark, it often means that he is *enjoying* his bachelorhood thus he will not be so marriage-conscious. That doesn't mean he isn't a likely prospect. He is, but under two years he's a *very likely* prospect.

WHERE ARE THE ELIGIBLE MEN?

Eligible men are everywhere. If they were clustered together in one spot, I'd be the first to tell you where it is, but fortunately they are just about every place one can mention. You can meet them at work, at school, while traveling and in crossing the street. As we discussed early, the best place to meet them is through your married friends.

There are certain places where you are *not* likely to meet eligible men. One of them is engaging in strictly female activities: PTA; women's clubs; fashion shows; charity groups, garden clubs —you know the activities I mean. As a career-oriented woman, you don't have time for these activities anyway.

There are certain cities where the odds are so unfavorable that they should probably not be chosen as your new home: Washington, D.C., San Francisco, and New York. It seems incredible that these big cities should not be teeming with eligible men, but this is what my spies report.

Certain small towns are just as bad. When everyone *knows* everyone else in a town, you can predict the history of all the men. When someone new *does* venture into town, chances are that he's married. Medium-to-large cities seem to be the best meeting ground.

Whether or not you *move* should be determined by your job, your life, and your needs, not by the availability of men. If your career plans do include a move, pick an area where you will be able to make friends easily. Remember, *other* people are still your best source.

There are also certain *places* where you probably will not find eligible men, such as the YWCA, tearooms, and beauty salons. Instead of heading to a restaurant known for its finger sandwiches and cottage cheese, have lunch at John's Bar & Grill. If you want to join an exercise class, see what the local men's club has to offer. Instead of browsing in the lingerie section of your local department store, stroll through the men's department.

Although we've said you can meet men literally anywhere, certain types of men do frequent predictable places.

You meet doctors in hospitals and their offices. You meet lawyers in courtrooms and county offices. You meet merchants in stores and shops. You meet chiefs at police stations, firehouses, or on reservations. You meet them other places, of course, but at these places certainly.

If you have a legal problem, why not do a bit of snooping and see if you can find a lawyer who is eligible? You can ask among your friends if any of them know an unmarried lawyer. If they don't, look in the Yellow Pages under Attorneys and find a name. Then look up the name in the white pages. If his home address is in a neighborhood of homes, you can bet he's married. If his address is a downtown apartment he could be single. To double-check, you could call his home number during the day to see if a woman answers.

I can just hear you saying, "How devious." I don't agree. It would only be devious if you made a practice of such detective work. You need to go to a lawyer with an honest problem, so there is no harm in investing an hour in discovery techniques.

Certainly you don't want to spend every waking hour poring over the phone book. That would keep you from your pursuits and your career. You will meet *more* men through your pursuits and your career than you will from the phone book.

HOW TO MARRY A RICH MAN

Some women feel that the most eligible men in the world are rich men. Now, how do you find them? Since I have known more than one woman who has made a career of marrying rich men, I decided to research the subject. I had thought one day to do an article on women who marry rich men, but I got involved in more-important projects and forgot the whole idea. When I began this book, I discovered my notes, which I pass along to you just for fun.

1. *Money/Power/Sex.* Rich men are rich because they love money and power. After that they love sex. Before you can possibly hope to interest a rich man you have to understand that. If you do become involved with a rich man, you are still going to be number three in his life. When I say that rich men love money, I don't mean the physical dollars as much as what the dollars represent. Money, they will tell you, is just a way of keeping score.

Power is what the money can buy. From a headwaiter to a senator, it's what keeps their attention. Power is never having to stand in a line. Ever. Power is the ability to pick up the phone in your office and make it happen around the world, without leaving your office. Power is heady stuff. I don't believe I can think of a single rich man who would trade it for a woman.

Most rich men are married. The highest percentage are still married to their first wife. Rich men work extremely hard and keep long hours. Why? It's because they love it.

2. *You Need Money Too.* In order to try to marry a rich man you will need mobility and some money. It's almost impossible to compete in this arena without cash in your jeans. The days of his finding his "million dollar baby in a five and ten cent store" are over. This happens only on the Late Show.

3. *Your Friend in Camp.* In order to meet rich men you have

to go where they are. Their encampments are hard to penetrate unless you have a friend in camp. The women I studied who married rich men had a sister married to an important man, or a friend in the entertainment business, or a brother who was a yacht broker—someone who could introduce them nicely. You are not going to meet a rich man on a bar stool unless it's in someone's villa in Acapulco.

It is the job of your friend in camp to engineer the introduction. One woman met her husband at the race track. She had a school chum who had a box next to his. Another met hers on safari, while another met her rich husband skiing at Jackson Hole. Another purpose the friend in camp serves is to verify *who* is rich. A man with a big bankroll, a flashy car, or even a good-sized yacht is not necessarily a rich man. He can have a certain amount of money, but when I say rich, I mean *rich*. Wealthy, on the other hand, is a word reserved for gentlemen of old family with old money. That's a different ball game altogether. For purposes of this discussion our "rich men" made it themselves.

If you don't have a sister married to a banker or a brother who runs a private jet charter service or a best friend who operates a small, chic hotel in Cannes, then you have to look for a contact before you look for the rich man.

Women's Wear Daily, Vogue, Town and Country, Holiday— any of these publications faithfully chronicle the goings on of the very rich. A careful reading of these publications will tell you where the rich eat, buy their clothes, keep their boats, go to the barber, and board their children. These places are where you should begin your search for an ally.

4. *Your Wardrobe.* No Eliza Doolittle outfits will do in this crowd, dear. You have to know what to wear. If the group at Gstaad is skiing in Jeans and Chinese peasant jackets and you show up in white stretch pants and a fur parka, you are out. Your outfit could have cost $740 while theirs cost only $39.95, but that doesn't make any difference. You look gauche, and that's the cardinal sin.

If you aren't sure what people are wearing to a certain area, underplay it. That will always get you by. But if an event is formal you will need a designer gown or an *awfully* good copy. Whites are worn on the tennis courts and canvas shoes on boats. Status goods covered with initials (much as I *hate* to say it) are a good idea. They show that you quite possibly belong there.

5. *Your Background.* You absolutely do not need to be from a prominent or wealthy family or be college-educated. What you need are street smarts. You must be able to do a quick study, think on your feet, and anticipate what's coming next. You can make up what you lack in formal education by studying. Read the *Wall Street Journal* and the latest best sellers. Read any privately issued newsletters you can find as well as journals on finance, oil and gas, and international corporations.

Don't invent a family, but be mysterious about the one you have. When you finally meet Mr. Wonderful, he won't care where you came from if he wants you, but his friends will. Don't answer their questions. Be polite but evasive and they'll soon tire of their probing. Don't be a name dropper. I mean, nobody who's *anybody* does that. Even if you know someone enormously famous, keep it to yourself—until you can mention him or her in a way to serve your purpose.

6. *Be a Good Sport.* One thing you absolutely must be is a good sport. Rich men seem to spend a great deal of time outdoors, so if you're worried about your hair or the prevalence of bugs or how rough the water is, he will not consider you a good companion. The best way to get along is *never complain.* That doesn't mean you won't be miserable some of the time. You will; just keep still about it.

7. *Develop Skills.* Rich men are attracted to women who can ride, shoot, hunt, fish, play tennis, water ski, speak French, play bridge—practically any skill you can name. But the catch is—they must do it well. Like making money, it represents a challenge, so when you take on a project be prepared to *work* at it.

Because of the lives they lead, rich men will love you if you are a good cook. He never knows when the chef on his yacht is going to quit. If you can take over in the galley for a day or two, you're a heroine. If you're up in the mountains trout fishing, he will be eternally yours if you can decently fry a fish. When he tosses a brace of pheasants on the table, know what to do with them. Most of the time you're with him, you'll never see the inside of a kitchen, but if you do, don't recoil in horror.

8. *Why Does a Rich Man Want a Wife?* Rich men want and need wives to make their lives fun. They spend most of their time and energy making money. They don't have time to plan social activities. Rich men want well-run households. I don't care how many servants they may hire, no one takes the special interest that a wife does. Rich men know this. They also need someone to spend their money, and wives are very good at this. Only by spending can they justify having all that money.

Wives are a status symbol. Remember that you have to have something to offer. Looks are important, but not as important as a sense of humor, a good disposition, and well-developed skills. A rich man wants to be proud of his wife. Looks fade but talent doesn't. Rich men want wives to enrich their lives. They want a woman to do everything for them that they can't do for themselves.

A rich man doesn't care how much money his wife spends as long as his life runs smoothly. When he comes home, it is to a haven of luxurious tranquility. His drink, his dressing gown, his favorite music, his dogs—whatever he wants—are available. That includes his wife. Rich men's wives are always *there* at night. They may spend all day at the spa, but they come home in time to dress beautifully and see that *everything* is in order.

Rich men are selfish, and a rich man's wife knows this. She *earns* her money. As far as sex is concerned, she is never too tired. As long as a rich man's wife does all that is expected of her, he will treat her extremely well, will seldom cheat, and will stay married for a long time. The only danger is if he gets bored.

Do you still want to marry a rich man?

THE DANGERS OF BEING MARRIAGE-ORIENTED

When a man or a woman sets out "to get married," they often become so attached to the idea that the act of marriage becomes more important than the person. Psychologists say that men and women marry when they are the most vulnerable. As a divorced woman, working and trying to get your life in order, you are definitely vulnerable. You are, in fact, a prime candidate for marriage.

1. *Settling.* The greatest danger of being vulnerable to marriage is that you will settle for *a* man, not *the* man. We all know there is no truth in the saying that there is only one man for you. That's nonsense. There are any number of men who could be right for you. There are also any number of men who are wrong for you.

You don't *have* to get married. Remember that when you are tempted by a man who doesn't come up to your expectations. He is *never* going to be better than he is at this moment. You don't marry a man to change him, reform him or promote him. You marry him because right now you love him and *everything* about him.

You can *always* get married. Yes, you can. You don't have to marry this man. If you can find one man who wants to marry you, that means you can find another, and another. Changing your mind, waiting awhile, this is healthy. If the relationship is good, this will prove it. If it is bad, waiting will end it. It's better to find out *now*.

2. *Trying Too Hard.* A recent article in the International *Herald Tribune* quoted from a book published by two psychologists in which they said that men prefer women whom others find hard to get. Remember our mothers' telling us the same thing? Isn't it amusing that a modern psychological study would still be advising us to play hard to get?

I believe it to this extent. It's very unflattering to be desired by someone who desires everyone in sight. We all want to be considered special. A woman set on getting married often does try too hard, causing the man to lose interest. If you are too eager and too readily available, the man wonders why.

3. *Greener Pastures.* The opposite of settling for less is not to settle at all. Some women are so afraid they'll miss Mr. Right that they won't spend enough time with any one man. They are on to the next before the last one has had half a chance. You want to play the field to a certain extent, but not as if you were running for office. When you meet someone with potential, give the relationship time to grow.

HOW TO CLOSE

As we said earlier, there comes a spot in a relationship when it's time to fish or cut bait—marry or move on. It is usually the woman who presses the issue, although technically it is the man who does the asking.

1. *That Gut Feeling.* If you have been seeing a man for several months, he likes your children, he says he loves you and you feel you love him, then you probably have the gut feeling that this is it. Only he hasn't mentioned marriage. You had a glorious weekend in the country, walked in the woods, had dinner at a wayside inn and he said he couldn't remember when he'd been happier . . . but he didn't mention marriage.

2. *Listen.* When you get the gut feeling that this is it and no marriage proposal is forthcoming, it's time to be still. A man will tell you *all* about himself if you'll just shut up and listen. When you do *listen* to what he's saying, he gives you clues to his feelings, his emotions, his fears and his anxieties. When you know these things about a man, you can figure out *why* he hasn't asked you to marry him.

Willa is a divorced woman in her very early sixties who had dated a widower for four years. Willa lives in the country and every Friday night her friend arrives to spend the weekend. Willa thought how marvelous it would be if they could marry so he would be with her all the time. She decided to solicit the help of her married sister and her husband. She invited them to join her the next week and before her friend arrived she told them her problem.

The weekend went wonderfully well. On Sunday night, after her friend left, Willa asked her sister what she thought. Her sister had a great deal of advice and lectured Willa for thirty minutes. When she finished, Willa asked her brother-in-law what he thought. He simply had this to say, "Talk less and walk slower."

It worked like a charm. The very next weekend on their usual long hike, her friend proposed.

When you listen, you may discover that a man is having problems at work. When a man has problems at work, it is not conducive to his taking on a wife. The man may tell you that his last physical upset him. That news doesn't make you want to rush to the altar. He may have a son about to enter college, a daughter who wants a big church wedding, and an ailing mother. When a man faces increased financial burdens, the last thing he thinks about is taking on a wife and another two kids.

3. *Make It All Right.* When you know these things about a man you can act accordingly. Your job is to let him know that marrying you would be the best thing in the world that ever happened to him! Convince him that marrying you will *solve* or *ease* his problems, not create new ones. You are concerned about him and you want to help.

Too many women think only in terms of what they need and what they want. The secret to dealing successfully with men is to figure out what they want and offer it. Learn what he is missing in his life. I'm not suggesting that you falsify emotions. If you love this man, it will be a pleasure to comfort him.

4. *Timing.* It may be that the proposal is *still* not forthcoming. If you feel you have spent as much time with this man as you care to unless you marry him, then it's time to ask him! You must be absolutely ready in your mind to walk if he says no, or it won't work.

The first thing to do is to set the stage. You certainly don't want to ask him on the way to a movie. Pick a night when you can have a long, uninterrupted evening. Suggest dinner in a quiet restaurant. You don't want to cook because that would disrupt your presentation.

Wait until you are seated in the restaurant and he has his drink in his hand. Begin the conversation with how much you care about him. Be specific. Tick off all his good points, then bring up some happy memories the two of you have shared. Gradually lead into the idea of marriage. Give him one last chance to pop the question. If he doesn't, then you simply say you want very much to marry him and you hope he feels the same way.

5. *Tie It Up.* Once you have put your question on the table, don't issue ultimatums. Don't explain, justify or magnify. You

love him and you want to get married. Now it's time to shut up and listen. If he says yes, then tie up *all* the loose ends. Say that you think a week from Saturday would be a good time for the engagement party, and why not a wedding two months later?

If he says he's surprised by your feeling and doesn't know what to say, ask him to explain how he feels. If he says he just doesn't know, he'll have to think about it, answer, fine, you'll come back here for dinner in a week. If he says he doesn't think that's enough time, you say you're sorry, but you think it is. You've been going together for eight months and you feel you both know a great deal about each other, and it's time to come to some conclusions.

Now, he may agree to coming to a conclusion in a week or he may not. If he agrees to the week, you know where you stand. If he says a week just isn't long enough, then you ask him to set the time limit. Don't settle for anything over a month. When the specified night arrives, he will say either yes or no. If he says yes, set the date.

6. *If He Says No.* That's it. If you vacillate you lose. After he has said why he doesn't want to get married, say you are so terribly sorry, you understand, and you hope *he* understands. Tell him that this is the end of the relationship and you won't be seeing him any more. You *must* mean it.

If, in a few days he calls, do *not* see him. If he says he thought about things and he feels that you should try again, set a definite time limit. If you like, tell him you'll see him for two weeks, no longer. You *have* to be specific. If you aren't, this relationship will drag on, never getting anywhere, keeping you from meeting others. All you will be getting is older! If you want to get married again, don't give away years of your life!

Be prepared to hear all manner of argument when you give a man a time limit or an ultimatum. He will argue that you have ruined the romance. He will say that no one can love on a deadline. He will try to give you half an answer, a semi-no, a promise. He may even stalk away without giving any answer. You must be prepared to lose him completely when you give your final word. You must *not* give in. A man has an ingenious way of knowing when you're bluffing.

7. *Have Backup Activity*. Before you give your ultimatum, have plans for the next weekend and for a couple of nights during the week. Invite six people for dinner Saturday night. Make a midweek movie date with a girl from the office. If he says yes, you are engaged, you can change or rearrange your plans. If he says no, you won't have as much time to feel sorry for yourself.

GETTING MARRIED

If he says yes, set the date. Then begin the wedding plans. If either or both of you have children, tell them and plan to include them in the ceremony. Tell your family and close friends. Some of them may want to plan parties that will add to the excitement. What you plan for the actual ceremony should be simple and in good taste.

I frankly feel that second-married people should avoid a big church wedding. I think it is in bad taste. If you are religious and want a small service in a chapel, that's between you and your fiancé. It is my feeling that home or garden weddings are the best. The children can invite some of their friends and it becomes a happy family affair.

If your children are grown, you may not want a wedding. You can marry in a judge's chambers. You should do something to mark the occasion. Perhaps you want to go to Las Vegas, or be married on an ocean liner or in a chapel in Greece. Whatever you do, it should be special and personal and mutually agreeable. To force an unwanted ceremony on your bridegroom is not a good way to begin a marriage.

STAYING MARRIED

Remember how you acted *before* you were married? Well, that's the secret to staying married. A good, sound marriage is based on understanding, the ability to adapt, shared interests, defined boundaries, honesty, and newness.

1. *Understanding.* When two people are engaged in a relationship of any kind, each will react *differently* to problems depending upon inherited values, habits, wants, temperaments and needs. Each sees the problem in his or her *own* way. One of the greatest virtues in life is to be able to see someone else's *point of view.*

When your mate's reaction to a situation differs from yours, try to remember that his position is simply. . . . his position. He is not trying to be cruel or malicious, underhanded or hardhearted. He sees through his eyes; you see through yours. Before you speak out in anger, ask yourself, "How *does* this problem look to him?" When you know that, you are being understanding.

2. *Adaptability.* When the honeymoon is over, the process of settling-in begins. He may leave the cap off the toothpaste while you don't wash the dinner dishes until morning. That cap off the toothpaste is extremely annoying to you. He hates to have his morning coffee in a dirty kitchen. Okay, now what? Are you going to let minor annoyances and inconveniences grow into major crises, or are you going to adapt?

If the cap off the toothpaste bothers you so much, buy your own tube. If he is surly in the midst of the dirty dishes, do them the night before or give him his coffee in the living room. The chances are that he is *not* going to learn to recap the toothpaste just as the chances are that you are going to continue to leave the dishes in the sink. So adapt!

3. *Shared Interests.* Whatever you did together that you enjoyed before marriage, continue to do. If you both like to play tennis, don't stop now because you've got other things to do. That's not fair. You may not be able to play every time he asks you, but try to. If you won't, he'll get another partner and some of your companionship has gone.

If you don't retain shared interests from before the marriage, work on developing some. If he likes to read boating magazines, you might try to develop an interest. Ask him to take you to the harbor on a Sunday to explain the different parts of a boat. If you are taking a night-school class in child psychology, ask him to come along. Whenever your interests overlap you are building bonds.

4. *Defined Boundaries.* There are certain areas in which you do not want an overlap. No man wants his wife telling him how to run his business. No woman feels she needs a family conference in order to buy new living room drapes. If he asks for your opinion, or if you want to know his color preference, fine, but meddling is out.

There may be times when you want to visit your family by yourself or he wants to go camping alone with his son. Honor these independent actions. Too much togetherness is as damaging as not enough.

5. *Honesty.* Be absolutely honest in your life with your new husband. Try not to give him reasons to doubt you. That doesn't mean you sit down and give him the whole story of your past. Leave the past *in* the past. There's only the present and the future to be concerned about. If you are going to lunch with an old friend, *you* be the one to tell your husband. If you feel you would like to spend a Sunday without his children or your children, a Sunday on which the two of you go off by yourselves, tell him. Be honest.

Bringing things out in the open keeps your life in perspective. It's when you tell half truths, harbor hurts, and feel neglected that the marriage gets into trouble. You *cannot* be everything to each other. This is impossible. You can, however, make certain that what you *are* to each other is real—and honest.

6. *Newness.* Every marriage needs sparks of newness to keep it alive. When boredom sets in, the partners may look for activity elsewhere. I recommend that a woman, for many reasons, keep active in her career after marriage. Getting up early, putting on your false eyelashes and good pantsuit, rushing off to an exciting job keeps *you* vital and interesting. You keep your marriage vital and interesting. If you give up your job, work part time at something. Take courses or find stimulating volunteer work. Don't just stop in your tracks and devote full time to the house. No house is worth it!

If you have children, that's a different story. It is a great luxury to be a full-time mother. You should, however, plan your time to include career-oriented activity. Now might be a good time to go back to school. Your children will grow up. When they begin to leave home you will find it less of an emotional tug if you are involved in work you enjoy.

It seems to be up to the wife to take on the job of social chairman in a marriage. Knowing this, plan a small dinner party each month. Reserve theater tickets ahead of time. Arrange a picnic with all the kids on Sunday. Give some thought to vacations before they are upon you. Plan family get-togethers that include his relatives.

Another way to bring newness into a marriage is to take up a hobby or sport together. Learn to scuba dive. Get two other couples and a teacher and hold a weekly Spanish class. Begin a collection, such as old bottles or antique clocks. The activity itself doesn't matter as much as the fact that you're doing it together.

7. *Build Him Up.* All men know their shortcomings. They don't need you to remind them. No one is perfect, in case you hadn't heard. No husband (or wife) is perfect. You can improve your mate by concentrating on his good points and by encouraging him. You can build him up to heights *neither* of you had dreamed possible. Men thrive in an atmosphere of love and respect. All men want to be heroes in their homes.

Most men are battered all day in their jobs. They want to come home to a sanctuary and be appreciated for daily facing the fray. It isn't any easier being a man than it is being a woman. Anything you can do to smooth the way for both of you strengthens the marriage. People grow and change in a marriage, not because they are married but because they are people. Your actions toward your husband can influence his growth. When you have faith in him he is encouraged to try his very hardest.

8. *On Love.* Love does not come *from* marriage; it is brought *to* marriage. Your attitude about love sets the pace. Remember that problems in a marriage cannot destroy real love because love belongs to the partners, not the marriage. Face each problem by first restating your love for each other. Then *together* tackle the problem.

A FEW HARD FACTS

The country is in a divorce cycle. By following the divorce statistics to their expected conclusions, it can be assumed that marriages *now* being formed are more likely than *not* to end in divorce. When you know this, it's foolish not to make a few plans before you marry again.

Keep Your Job. Now that you have found employment that you like and at which you can earn money, why give it up when you marry? You've managed so far; you can manage marriage, too. Discuss this with your fiancé *before* you marry. Most men no longer object to their wife's working. In some circles it is almost a status symbol. Most couples need two salaries to keep ahead of inflation.

Keeping your job is your security. Should you divorce, face fierce financial losses, or become a widow, you know that you can take care of yourself. Keeping your job allows you to help your children with their education. Keeping your job gives you an independence that makes you more attractive to everyone around— particularly your husband.

Go to School. If you have a job that you don't like or which has very little future, see if you and your new husband can get by on his salary so that you can go to school. With proper training you can obtain a better position. Perhaps you want to get a law degree, learn accounting or become an interior designer. Now is the time. The time and money you invest now will pay dividends later. It used to be common for wives to work to help their husbands through school. Why shouldn't a husband work to help his wife through school?

The better your job, the more secure your future. Men are proud of their wives' accomplishments. After you finish your education perhaps your husband would like to retrain for a job he would prefer to his present one. When a couple work together, there is very little they can't accomplish.

Keep Your Property Separate. Whatever you owned before your marriage is separate property. Keep it that way. If you own your own home, do not change the deed. Nora had a lovely home which she received in a property settlement from her first husband. When she married again she put the house in both her name and her new husband's. They were married for three years. When her second husband sued her for divorce, he claimed half the house. He said she had given it to him. It was impossible to prove otherwise because there was his name on the deed!

When a woman remarries, she hates to say to her new husband that she is not going to share with him. The sharing is all right as long as she keeps *all* property separate. Keep deeds in your name as well as stock certificates, bonds and bank accounts. Do not commingle the funds. If you want to share with your husband, give him some of the money you earn in dividends, rents, or interest. The minute you change property to his name, you may be bestowing it upon him as a gift!

Keep Your Own Name. This is a very ticklish situation because men find it extremely difficult to understand *why* a woman won't change her name. "If you love, me, want to marry me, and live with me, why won't you take my name?" What you have to explain is that your own name is your identity and your link with the past. Explain that your divorce put you through an identity crisis that you simply could not face again.

Since you have been employed under your own name, changing it would require a great deal of confusion. In addition to all the employment forms, it would mean new stationery, new cards and a new phone. You have established a continuity which you do not wish to break. If you have achieved great success under your own name you hate to give up that identity. It's not as if this were your first marriage and you want to be Mrs. Smith so you can do grown-up things like open a charge account, buy monogrammed towels, and wear a wedding band.

You and your new husband are adults. Part of being adult is to realize—and accept—decisions made by other adults. When you tell a man that you want to keep your own name you are not saying that you don't *like* his. You are not doing something *against* him, you are doing something *for* yourself. Not all women want to keep their own names. Perhaps you are dying to change your name. That's fine because that's your decision. Just be certain, though, that it *is* your decision.

. . . ONE LAST WORD

A very good friend of mine called me the other day and in a breathless voice tinged with excitement, she said, "Guess what, I'm happy! I'm really, really happy!" Before I could stop myself I just blurted out, "Well, it's about time. You've been a real pain in the neck!" There was a silence on her end of the line, and then a giggle. "I have, haven't I?"

My friend had been an exasperation to me because of all the divorced women I've talked to, she perhaps has the most to be grateful for—and happy about. An extremely talented woman with an exciting, well-paying job, my friend owns a fabulous home, possesses a beautiful face, slim body, a fine mind, and is surrounded by loving, admiring friends. It was not *fair* for her to be unhappy.

"Okay," I said, "tell me about it."

"I don't need to be married to be happy! I just don't *need* to be married. Today I bought a ticket to Athens and booked myself into a hotel and I'm going. Alone, as you said. But that's not why I'm so happy. I was sitting in my kitchen having a cup of coffee this morning, feeling so alone and lonely, and all of a sudden this tiny ray of sunlight shone on my hand, it hit me just where my wedding ring used to be. It was a straight, almost pointed beam, and I looked up to see where it went and this thought just came to me—I am wedded to life. This sunbeam and I belong to the same world. Does this sound crazy? I hope not, because I mean it. We all share the same sunlight and we don't need someone else to turn it on for us. You know, I don't think I'll ever again give anyone the power of standing between me—and the sunlight!"

Life, our life, is such a gift. It's also a rare adventure. Grab it and ride with it and just see where it takes you. That, too, is your birthright. When unhappy moments try to make you a prisoner of gloom, look up. You and the sun are sisters. If she can shine—all by herself!—so can you.

So there you have it. I've tried to cover all the main living areas of the divorced woman. If you have a particular problem that I haven't covered, write to me. If I don't have the answer, I'll help you find someone who does.

Index